# The Coup and the Palm Trees

**GEOGRAPHIES OF JUSTICE AND SOCIAL TRANSFORMATION**

SERIES EDITORS

Mathew Coleman, *Ohio State University*
Ishan Ashutosh, *Indiana University Bloomington*

FOUNDING EDITOR

Nik Heynen, *University of Georgia*

ADVISORY BOARD

Deborah Cowen, *University of Toronto*
Zeynep Gambetti, *Boğaziçi University*
Geoff Mann, *Simon Fraser University*
James McCarthy, *Clark University*
Beverley Mullings, *Queen's University*
Harvey Neo, *Singapore University of Technology and Design*
Geraldine Pratt, *University of British Columbia*
Ananya Roy, *University of California, Los Angeles*
Michael Watts, *University of California, Berkeley*
Ruth Wilson Gilmore, *CUNY Graduate Center*
Jamie Winders, *Syracuse University*
Melissa W. Wright, *Pennsylvania State University*
Brenda S. A. Yeoh, *National University of Singapore*

# The Coup and the Palm Trees

AGRARIAN CONFLICT AND
POLITICAL POWER IN HONDURAS

**ANDRÉS LEÓN ARAYA**

The University of Georgia Press
*Athens*

© 2023 by the University of Georgia Press
Athens, Georgia 30602
www.ugapress.org
All rights reserved
Set in 10.25/13.5 Minion 3 by Rebecca A. Norton

Most University of Georgia Press titles are
available from popular e-book vendors.

Printed digitally

Library of Congress Cataloging-in-Publication Data

Names: León Araya, Andrés (León A.), author.
Title: The coup and the palm trees : agrarian conflict
 and political power in Honduras / Andrés León Araya.
Description: Athens : University of Georgia Press, 2023. |
 Series: Geographies of justice and social transformation series |
 Includes bibliographical references and index.
Identifiers: LCCN 2023020927 (print) | LCCN 2023020928 (ebook) |
 ISBN 9780820365367 (hardback) | ISBN 9780820365374 (paperback) |
 ISBN 9780820365398 (pdf) | ISBN 9780820365381 (epub)
Subjects: LCSH: Honduras—Politics and government—1982–
 | Zelaya, Manuel, 1952– | Palm oil industry—Honduras—Aguán
 River Valley. | Land reform—Honduras—Aguán River Valley. |
 Honduras—Politics and government—1933–1982. | Neoliberalism—Honduras.
Classification: LCC F1508.3 .L466 2023 (print) | LCC F1508.3 (ebook) |
 DDC 972.8305/2—dc23/eng/20230524
LC record available at https://lccn.loc.gov/2023020927
LC ebook record available at https://lccn.loc.gov/2023020928

| "Ode to the African Palm" | "Oda a la palma africana" |
|---|---|
| You came when we least needed you | Viniste cuando menos te necesitábamos |
| and remained longer than we expected. | Y te quedaste más de lo que esperábamos. |
| | |
| You displaced the ancestral kapok tree that used to rise upon my fields | Vos desplazaste al ancestral Ceiba que se erguía sobre mis suelos |
| and shook off the maize that filled my plains... | Y sacudiste el maíz que llenaba mis praderas... |
| | |
| Oh, African palm! | ¡Oh, palma africana! |
| neither white, nor black... | Ni blanca ni negra... |
| red and bloodied. | Roja y ensangrentada. |
| You are not from the Aguán | No sos del Aguán |
| neither of the peasants | Ni de los campesinos |
| nor from Honduras or Central America. | Ni de Honduras, ni de Centroamérica. |
| You are of the looters that ruin us, | Sos de los saqueadores que nos arruinan, |
| of Facussé and his killers. | De Facussé y sus asesinos. |

Chaco de la Pitoreta (2012, 67) "Versos para leer desde la trinchera"

To Neil Smith, may you find him wandering these pages.

*A Gilberto Ríos padre, que la tierra te sea leve.*

*A Lastenia, Marta, Irma, y Consuelo, que guiaron mis pasos por tierras catrachas.*

# CONTENTS

Introduction  1

**PART I. The Prehistory of Neoliberalism**

CHAPTER 1. Dictatorship and Reform: From Carías to Military Reformism  23

CHAPTER 2. Disciplining Peasants, Disciplining the Land: The Political Economy of the Honduran Agrarian Reform in the Bajo Aguán (1962–1980)  44

CHAPTER 3. The Hidden Abode of Primitive Accumulation: Agrarian Counterreform, Gender, and Neoliberalism  74

**PART II. The Assault on Power and the Coup**

CHAPTER 4. Democracy as Disaster Capitalism: Land and Neoliberalism in the Aftermath of Destruction  103

CHAPTER 5. The Failed Assault on State Power  125

CHAPTER 6. Militarization, Rent Capture, and the State-Narco Relations  148

CHAPTER 7. Honduras, the Neoliberal Workshop or the End of a Cycle?  167

Conclusion  179

Acknowledgments  195

Notes  199

Bibliography  211

Index  231

# The Coup and the Palm Trees

A road crosses endless rows of oil palms, Bajo Aguán region, 2013. Photo by the author.

# INTRODUCTION

On June 28, 2009, between 5 and 6 a.m., Lieutenant Colonel René Antonio Hepburn Bueso, accompanied by a special detachment of the Honduran army, proceeded to execute a search warrant on President Manuel Zelaya's house. Once at the property, Hepburn Bueso encountered a group of "armed personnel in uniform," identified as members of the president's security team, who sought to prevent him from carrying out the warrant and dismissed the validity of the order. After disarming and subduing the guards, the soldiers entered the premises and proceeded to capture Zelaya. Sometime later, he would be taken to the Soto Cano Airbase, commonly known as the Palmerola Airbase and home of the U.S. military Joint Task Force-Bravo, and placed on a military airplane bound for Costa Rica, cutting his term short less than six months before the next elections. Soon the news would spread all over the world: "In the first military coup in Central America since the end of the cold war, soldiers stormed the presidential palace in the capital, Tegucigalpa, early in the morning, disarming the presidential guard, waking Mr. Zelaya and putting him on a plane to Costa Rica" (Malkin 2009).

Internationally, the coup was received with outrage and condemned by almost everyone, ranging from U.S. president Barack Obama—who called it a "terrible precedent" (Cooper and Lacey 2009)—to Venezuelan president Hugo Chávez, who asserted that "behind these soldiers are the Honduran bourgeoisie, the rich who converted Honduras into a Banana Republic, into a political and military base for North American imperialism" (Kozloff 2009).

Depending on where you stood on the ideological spectrum, the ousting of Zelaya was the result of Venezuelan meddling or U.S. imperialism; of Zelaya's populism and alleged attempts at remaining in office beyond the upcoming elections; or the Honduran elites' rapaciousness and antidemocratic spirit. What almost everyone seemed to agree on was that what was at stake was the survival of democracy itself, and that the coup was the result of Central America's "bad democracies" (Torres-Rivas 2010) and the regional political culture of impunity, corruption, and state capture by the elites (Ruhl 2010; Chayes 2017).

In this book I would like to offer a different perspective on the military ousting of Zelaya, one that goes beyond the national narrative of "failed" democracies and focuses on the historical process of state formation in Honduras that created the conditions of possibility for the coup to take place. To do so, I focus on the Bajo Aguán region on the Honduran north coast. This is a region that, while historically understood as a "lawless frontier" beyond the control of the state, has served as the stage for a set of political projects with a deep influence on how the Honduran state has evolved.

### Enter the Bajo Aguán

The lower section of the Aguán River basin, the Bajo Aguán, is a valley of fertile alluvial lands that extends for over two hundred thousand hectares (Jones 1985, 140) (see map 1). During the 1920s and '30s, extensive sections of land were given in concession to the Truxillo Railroad Company—a subsidiary of the United Fruit Company (UFCO)—for the creation of banana plantations, in exchange for the construction of a railway that would connect the port of Trujillo with Juticalpa, Olancho. By the late 1940s, as a result of the spread of Panama disease, a banana blight, the company abandoned the region (Soluri 2009), leaving behind scattered settlements of the former railroad and plantation workers, as well as Salvadoran immigrants and Garifuna communities (Casolo 2009; Castro 1994). During the 1970s the state sought to carry out the Bajo Aguán Project (BAP) in the region; the project was a colonization scheme and the centerpiece of the Honduran agrarian reform (Posas 1981), which included the organization of over 150 peasant cooperatives that became the nucleus of the most robust peasant movement in Central America (Edelman 1998; Kay 1998). Later, in the 1990s, the region was transformed into the country's "capital of the agrarian counterreform" (Macías 2001), as most of the land distributed within the BAP was concentrated, by hook or by crook, by a handful of large landowners. Soon after, in the aftermath of Hurricane Mitch in 1998, a new cycle of agrarian conflict emerged in the region, pitting peasant communities against state and private security forces and claiming the lives of more than one hundred peasant organizers in the process (Boyer 2010; Ríos 2014; Bird 2013; Kerssen 2013; OPDHA 2014). In the run up to the 2009 coup, the peasant organizations of the Aguán were among the more active political actors in the country, both supporting Zelaya's plan for a constituent assembly

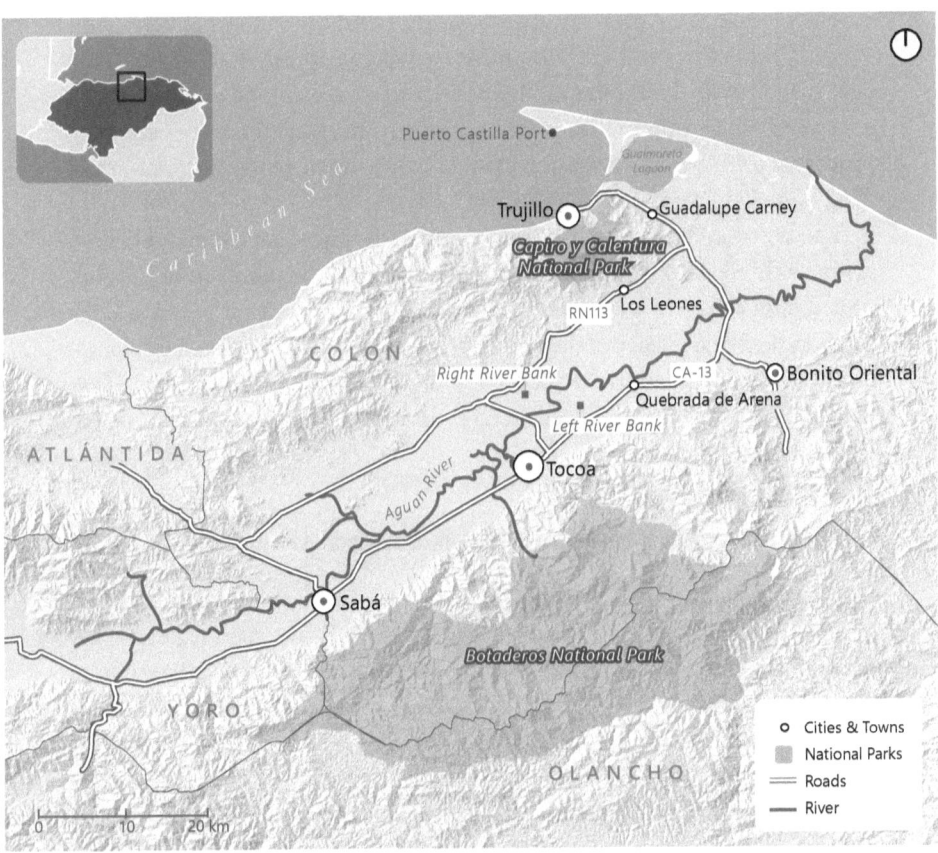

The Bajo Aguán Region, (Paulo Luna, 2023)

and pressuring his government to provide them with access to land. Later, in the aftermath of the coup, these peasant groups continued their political activity, first as important members of the National Front of Popular Resistance (FNRP), the broad alliances of sectors organized against the military coup, and then by continuing their struggle for land in the form of a set of massive land occupation in the Aguán.

Finally, in 2015, the Rivera Maradiaga brothers, leaders of Los Cachiros, an important drug trafficking cartel that operated in the Departments of Colón and Olancho, turned themselves in to U.S. authorities. Their subsequent testimonies began exposing a web of criminal activities that included money laundering, drug money political donations, corruption, and bribery that rose all the way up the country's political and economic hierarchy (Dudley 2016; Chayes 2017; Barahona 2018).

Thus, while the Aguán tends to be understood as a marginal place, as a frontier almost beyond the Honduran state's control, its history has been deeply intertwined with that of the process of state formation: from banana enclave to centerpiece of the agrarian reform; from epicenter of the neoliberal process of primitive accumulation of the 1990s; to home of the most important drug trafficking cartel in recent history.

The fact that this history has been dominated by agrarian conflicts between actors with very different political projects in mind also points us to the continued importance that land has when thinking about political power and the state. As such, the history of the Aguán presents us with a privileged viewpoint of the process that led to the 2009 coup d'état and its consequences, a viewpoint that can be better followed along the thread of land, how it has been understood, governed, and struggled over.

## The Aguán, Zelaya, and the Sons and Daughters of the Agrarian Reform

On June 17, 2009, a little more than a week before his ousting by the military, Manuel Zelaya visited Tocoa, the largest city in the Bajo Aguán region, to negotiate with the leadership of the Unified Peasant Movement of the Aguán (MUCA) a solution to the weeklong occupation of the Exportadora del Atlántico palm oil extracting mill. Owned by Miguel Facussé, one of the richest men in Honduras and into whose story we will delve further on, this extraction mill was one of the clearest representations in the landscape of the material and symbolic power of the palm oil plantation economy in the region. By transforming the fruit of the oil palms into palm oil, the extraction mills show clearly who controls—directly and indirectly—both the thousands upon thousands of hectares covered by palm trees and the labor army that toils in both the fields and the mills. Furthermore, the mill sits on lands that MUCA contended had been illegally taken from agrarian reform cooperatives during the 1990s.

This was not the first time that MUCA had appealed to direct action to try and force the hand of Zelaya's government. More than three years before, on February 7, 2006, in what came to be known as *"la marcha de los 5000 machetes"* (the March of the 5000 Machetes), members of the peasant movement had occupied the bridge above the Aguán River near Tocoa, the principal road connecting the region with the rest of the country, to protest the dispossession of their lands. At that time, an agreement had been reached between the government and peasant organizers that would have given the twenty-eight peasant groups organized into MUCA access to land and technical and financial support, as well as starting an investigation into the alleged illegality of the land sales of the 1990s. However, as it has usually been the case in the history of the relationship between the peasant movement and the Honduran state, once the former lifted their protest, the latter made as if it had never happened. Yet again, much had happened between 2006 and 2009.

For MUCA, their current predicament, mainly the lack of land to work, was connected to the agrarian reform period of the 1970s and 1980s, as well as the agrarian counterreform of the 1990s, that led to the sale, and concentration in very few hands, of seven of every ten hectares distributed during the agrarian reform period. In fact, informed by their "memories of dispossession" (Hart 2006), they presented themselves as the "sons and daughters" of those who lost the lands. More immediately, the occupation of the bridge and the extracting mill was part of an escalating cycle of peasant struggle that began roughly in the late 1990s, in the aftermath of Hurricane Mitch (1998), and that eventually saw organizations such as MUCA become the unlikely allies of Manuel Zelaya and his government.

As the protests of both 2006 and 2009 show, this was not a smooth process. When Mel, as Manuel Zelaya is popularly known, first arrived in office in 2006, there was not much to differentiate him from his predecessors. In fact, his father was well known, infamous really, for his involvement in the Los Horcones Massacre of 1975, in which fifteen peasants, religious workers, and students who were taking part in a "hunger march" toward the capital demanding land for the landless were found dead in a winch well located on an estate owned by the Zelaya family in the Department of Olancho. Paradoxically, as we will see in chapter 5, it was in part as a result of the mobilization of organizations such as MUCA that roughly after two years in power Mel took a "turn to the Left" and intertwined his fate with that of a broad alliance of subaltern organizations, including MUCA, that had been pushing back against the imposition of the neoliberal project in the country since the early 2000s.

We find a good example of the intertwining between MUCA and Zelaya's government in the attack against Fabio Evelio Ochoa, an important figure of the leftist Democratic Unification Party (UD) in the Aguán region and candidate for mayor of Tocoa in the elections of November 2009. On June 23, less than a week before the coup, Ochoa was returning home in the afternoon, after speaking on a local radio show, when he was intercepted by a group of gunmen who opened fire upon the Ford pickup truck he was traveling in. He received one bullet to the head, another one to the back and two more to his left arm, and although miraculously he survived, he was left with severe brain damage.

Ochoa had spoken on the radio show in favor of the nonbinding vote that

Zelaya was calling for on the twenty-eighth to decide whether an extra ballot box should be included in the upcoming November elections. The extra ballot was to determine whether a constituent assembly should be convened by the next government to rewrite and reform the 1982 constitution. Popularly known as the "Fourth Ballot Box" (*la Cuarta Urna*), this vote was the most visible detonator of the ousting of Zelaya by the military. On the one hand, it triggered fears that Zelaya was attempting to change the constitution and remain in power beyond his one term, following the example of his friend and ally, the Venezuelan president Hugo Chávez. On the other hand, for organizations such as MUCA or the UD it represented an assault upon the political structures that enshrined and protected the rule of the political and economic elites, in tandem with U.S. imperialism.

For example, Marielos, a fortysomething mother of four and member of MUCA, to whose story we will return in chapter 4, writes in a diary that she began in 2013 to reflect upon, and keep an account of, her life and the history of MUCA:

> The coup d´état, if I'm not mistaken, was ordered by the *terrateniente* (large landowner) Miguel Facussé, after the peasant organization MUCA had made a massive occupation and roadblock in front of his Exportadora del Atlántico [palm oil] extracting mill. This occupation began on June 6, 2009, at 1:00 a.m. . . . [and] took place after we researched how it was that he came into legal possession of agrarian reform lands. . . We discovered that he had acquired some of his lands illegally through trickery from former cooperative members . . . We continued to resist in the occupation for ten days. On Tuesday 16 of June, Mel Zelaya came to Tocoa and met with the peasants of MUCA; and in that meeting, Manuel Zelaya Rosales promised that the agrarian reform lands in the Bajo Aguán would be returned to the peasants. This was the vile sin that Mel committed, wanting to help the impoverished people of his country [and why he was toppled in the coup].

Following Doreen Massey (1999; 2013), Gillian Hart (2002; 2014) proposes that we think about places not as bounded enclosures, nested in a hierarchal relation to other scales such as the "global," but rather in terms of their interdependence with processes taking place on other scales within a larger whole. For Hart (2002), this definition of place brings to the fore Stuart Hall's (1996) ideas on articulation as both connection between different elements, and enunciation, or the production of meaning through language, where what is connected tends to be contradictory and in need of constant renovation and reenactment.

Through accounts like Marielos's, we can explore the articulation—the connection and enunciation—between the general geopolitical and national dynamics of the coup, focusing on the particular experience of the Aguán. For her, and many others to whom I spoke to and met in the Aguán, there was a straightforward relationship between the ousting of Zelaya and the political action of peasant organizations such as MUCA: their actions had led to an agreement that would "help the impoverished people of his country," which, in kind, triggered the reaction of the elites and the military.

This book proposes to take this argument seriously and delve into the convulsive history of the Aguán as a way of exploring a sort of a double history. The first is the history of the production of the Aguán, through a process of agrarian reform and counterreform that created a set of subjects and landscapes; this history explains the region's position by the time of the coup, as an epicenter of the palm oil industry and the drug trade. The second is the history of the process of formation of the Honduran state between 1963, when the military consolidated their rise to political power with a coup, and the 2009 ousting of Zelaya. This implies thinking about the production of oil palm-covered landscapes in the Aguán, in relation to attempts by different actors (local cattle ranching elites, landless peasants, developmentalist generals, transnational companies, and U.S. counterinsurgent experts, among others) to influence and control the logics of domination and state formation in Honduras, and how they created the conditions of possibility for the military coup to take place.

Finally, most existing analyses focus on the process of the coup "from above." That is, they focus on Zelaya's alleged attempts to remain in power beyond his term, his conflict with the country's traditional elites, and his "left turn" in terms of the negotiations that led to Honduras's entry into Venezuelan-led projects of Petrocaribe and the Bolivarian Alternative (ALBA). Much less attention has been placed on Zelaya's left turn "from below," understood in terms of the relationships his government cultivated with subaltern organizations. By using the Aguán as the focal point of this analysis, we can see how the "national" drama of the coup was related to historical and regional patterns of subaltern political organization.

**The Narrative of the Transition to Democracy**

Most of the recent literature on political change in Central America focuses on the supposed "transition to democracy" that began in the 1990s after more than twenty years of armed conflicts. As a result, topics such as institutional design, political culture, elite capture, and democratic governance have replaced discussions of the unequal distribution of resources (particularly land), class struggle, and U.S. imperialism that dominated the debates regarding the "backwardness" or lack of development of the region in the previous decades.

There was nothing innocent about this shift, which must be read within the context of the rise of a new geopolitical discourse based on the supposed supremacy of Western liberal democracy and the "end of history" (Fukuyama 1989; Huntington 1993). Within this discourse, as Neil Smith (2000) pointed out, class as an explanatory concept disappeared at the same time that it should have become more central in explaining the transformations that different parts of the globe were experiencing under the imposition of the neoliberal project and what came to be known as the Washington Consensus.

For the Central American region specifically and Latin America in general, these factors led to the emergence of the discourse of the "transition to democracy," which claimed that in the aftermath of the Cold War and the region's armed conflicts, the path toward "progress" and "development" would come through the dual creation of democratic political regimes and free markets (O'Donnell, Schmitter, and Whitehead 1986; Robinson 1996; Figueroa Ibarra 1993; Rovira Mas 2002).

As a result, the history of the region stopped being told by many as a political problem, in terms of the unequal relations of power between different actors, and became a moral one: elites are corrupt, civil society is disempowered, political parties are dominated by bossism, and transnational companies, if not reined in by proper institutional design, tend to be rapacious. The result is what Doreen Massey (1999) dubbed convening space in temporal terms, where the conjunctures of different societies are placed on a single timeline and where difference is explained through words such as "advanced," "backward," "developing," or "modern" (Ferguson 1990; Edelman and Haugerud 2005; Li 2007; Escobar 2011). For Massey, the main implication is that societies are understood not as being different but rather as being ahead of or behind in the same story.

According to William Robinson (1996), "transitology," as the study of democratic transitions is also known, was an important part of the U.S. foreign policy goal of maintaining that country's dominant position in the aftermath of the Cold War. With the demise of the communist "red menace," sustaining authoritarian regimes that followed the national security doctrine became more expensive both in terms of political legitimacy and economic and military aid. The result was the promotion of a highly ideologized definition of "freedom" as procedural democracy and free markets, which declared the end of the war—be it cold or hot, as in the case of the regional armed conflicts—and its causes almost by decree.

According to the Venezuelan anthropologist Fernando Coronil (2019), this emerging framework of the transitions to democracy in Latin America must be understood within a historical context characterized by five main features: first, the devastating effects of the military dictatorships of the 1960s and 1970s; second, the disenchantment of much of the Left with Cuban socialism in the 1980s and 1990s; third, the Chilean military coup in 1973; fourth, the breakdown of the socialist regimes in Eastern Europe; and fifth, a change in the intellectual climate due to the impact of poststructuralism, the crisis of Marxism, and the appeal of the individualistic perspective of rational choice theory. As a result, Coronil tells us, the scholarship on transitions to democracy in Latin America was characterized by a sense of the urgent need to achieve democratization within the existing capitalist system, even among scholars who still cleaved to socialist values.

In other words, a watered-down version of democracy became the dominant way of thinking about the political, with less attention being paid to the structural dynamics of capital accumulation that defined the field that was supposed to be democratized in the first place. Further, in this procedural definition of democracy, these mechanical procedures have become values in and of themselves: their presence is equated with the existence of democracy itself (Gallardo 2007).

### From Transitology to the Trajectories of Spatiotemporal Change

With transitology comes the separation between the political (formal democracy) and the economic (liberalization), which has led different analysts to imagine two transitions: an incomplete political one, with some advances in terms of individual rights; and a failed economic one, in terms of inequality and collective rights (Martí i Puig and Sánchez-Ancochea 2014). There are, however, many instances or "transitions" in which this separation between the political and economic is simply not sustainable analytically, for example, the regional transition from agro-exporting countries that produced most of their food to exporting countries that import most of what they eat. In the case of the North Triangle (El Salvador, Guatemala and Honduras), we might also mention the transition toward what are popularly known as "narco-states."

Regarding the former case, while the economic insertion of Central America into the global market has always been dependent on exporting raw material and tropical foodstuffs such as coffee, sugar, and bananas, in the aftermath of World War II and up to the 1980s, there was a concerted effort by the different governments to produce a domestic space of capital accumulation in the shape of national markets, as well as a regional common market. This was a result of a set of policies, ranging from agrarian reforms to industrial promotion laws, that sought to include, in order to pacify, the various subaltern groups created by this process of modernization: a growing and unruly landless peasantry and a combatant, albeit incipient, labor movement. However unequal and limited in their success, by the decade of the 1970s these policies allowed the different countries to cover domestically most of their demand for staple crops (rice, beans, and maize), and to a lesser extent for meat and dairy products.

Thirty years later, in the 2000s, all the countries in the region, except for Nicaragua, were significantly dependent on food imports to cover their national demands (Baumeister 2013).[1] While in part related to the accelerated pace of urbanization and the increasing importance of the *maquila* (light assembly manufacturing) and service sectors in the region, this transition has largely been the result of an agrarian devolution characterized by the concentration of the best and more fertile lands in very few hands, the expansion of monoculture plantations, and an accelerated process of the expansion of the agrarian frontier. Once again, the state has had a very active role in this process. During the 1980s and 1990s the different governments in the region, with the support and pressure of various international financial institutions (IFIs), embarked on processes of "structural adjustment" oriented toward the liberalization of the economy and giving free range to market and corporations to rearrange how resources and surpluses should be used and distributed.

In the agrarian sector, in a process that can easily be described as one of "organized abandonment" (Gilmore 2007), economic and institutional support was withdrawn from those producing for the domestic market and reoriented toward the exporting sector. The result was the creation of a set of surpluses— of land, capital, and labor—that help explain both the current regional "success" in terms of agro-exports and the region's atrocious levels of poverty, inequality, and the massive migrant exodus toward the United States.

Furthermore, the incessant search by capital for new spaces of accumulation, as well as the despair of many households in search of a piece of land to secure their survival, has led to the expansion of the agrarian frontier into protected areas and spaces with less-than-ideal ecological conditions. The result has been an accelerated process of deforestation and erosion with adverse effects in terms of climate change, destruction of biodiversity, and encroachment into Indigenous and peasant lands.

At the same time, these dynamics intersect with different forms of organized crime, particularly drug trafficking. For example, a recent study, using data on both deforestation and drug trade in Central America, has proposed that around 30 percent of the recent loss of forest cover in the region is related to narco activity (Sesnie et al. 2017, 16). According to this and other studies, part of the money made by the Central American traffickers is laundered by buying or dispossessing lands that are then used to extract wood and create cattle ranches and monoculture plantations (McSweeney et al. 2018; Devine et al. 2020; McSweeney and Pearson 2013; Grandia 2013).

The end product has been the convergence between an export-oriented extractive economy, based on the expansion of monocultures, and an extremely violent form of capital accumulation based on drug trafficking. Both activities, as well as the legal commerce of commodities, are predicated upon the production of similar types of spaces to succeed. This includes, for example, the construction of good infrastructure, territorial control, the protection of private property, and the creation of reasonably "transparent" land markets, but also the production and reproduction of a cheap labor force desperate enough to be forced to choose between working on a palm oil or sugar plantation, joining a gang, or migrating.

This brings us to what has been called by many the "narco-state," of which Honduras has become the quintessential example. The notion of narco-state obfuscates more than it illuminates, as it conflates an economic activity with the general identity of an institutionalized, and territorialized, framework of domination (Morton 2012; Chouvy 2016; Gillies 2018). It points at the alleged inability, or failure, of various postcolonial states to uphold the Weberian imperative that the state secure the claim to the monopoly of violence and control over its entire territory. This, of course, is not exclusive to the notion of "narco-state," but rather a repetition and continuation of other monikers such as "failed state" or "banana republic," all of which reproduce "a view of postcolonial states that is imbued with the imperial representations of the past based on a discursive economy that renews a focus on the postcolonial world as a site of danger and darkness, anarchy and disorder" (Morton 2012, 1635).

To move away from these types of simplistic approaches, we need rather to draw attention to the historical and geopolitical contexts within which state formation has taken place in regions such as Central America. In the case of Honduras, during the Cold War period, particularly from the 1970s onward, while rural unrest and armed conflict raged in the rest of the region, the country remained relatively stable in political terms, with a very limited presence of rebel groups and relatively low levels of outmigration toward the United

States. However, by the time Zelaya was flown to Costa Rica in his pajamas, and particularly in the aftermath of the coup, Honduras had become internationally known for the active presence of *maras* (violent street gangs). It was now a hotspot of the new drug trafficking routes between South America and the United States and one of the most "dangerous" countries in the Western Hemisphere, characterized by a migrant exodus of massive proportions.

In the mid-2000s, with the squeeze on drug trafficking by the U.S.- sponsored "war on drugs" in both in Mexico and Colombia, "a cocaine tsunami hit Central America.... For the next ten years, smugglers sent, on average, more than 1,000 shipments—about 800 metric tons—annually into the region, a majority of the global cocaine supply" (McSweeney 2020, 159; Paley 2018).

With the rise in prominence of Central America in the global narcotics' political economy, the traffickers' business became ever more intertwined with political structures, as narco dollars began to flow toward electoral campaigns, bribing officials, and fueling processes of deforestation, peasant and Indigenous dispossession, and land grabs across the isthmus. At the same time, the narrative of the "Colombianization," or the supposed invasion of the region by "foreign" drug traffickers, helped justify the militarization of the region, increasing both social control over populations and territorial control of resources, as part of the war on drugs (Ballvé and McSweeney 2020; Paley 2014).

While the process of militarization and narco encroachment into the political structures began in the 1980s within the context of the U.S. strategy of containment of the Sandinista government in Nicaragua (Rosenberg 1988; Marshall and Scott 1991), the 2009 coup came to accelerate the process and generate a newfound interest in Honduras (Dudley 2016).[2] Be it at the level of academic inquiry (Meza et al. 2010; Kerssen 2013; Shipley 2017; Frank 2018), or at the level of everyday life (Miranda 2010; Phillips 2015; Levy 2020), the coup was an unveiling, bringing to light what had been an open secret up to that moment: that Honduras had become the quintessence of what Sarah Chayes dubs a "kleptocracy": a political system where "corruption is the operating system of sophisticated networks that link together public and private sectors and out-and-out criminals—including killers—and whose main objective is maximizing returns for network members" (Chayes 2017, 2–3).

While thinking about the current crisis of Honduras specifically, and of Central America in general, as the result of the colonization of the state by organized crime is suggestive, doing so neglects the fact that both structures—organized crime and state institutions—are the result of the same process of state formation. Phrased differently, the conditions of possibility of these "kleptocracies" or "narco-states" were not born in the 2000s with the "war on drugs"; rather, they emerged many decades before through a process of modernization and state formation that privileged the interests of capital accumulation above the well-being of the Honduran population.

Taking all of this into consideration, this book explores how the relationship between land and power informed the process of state formation in Honduras, which in turn created the conditions of possibility for the 2009 coup d'état and the current crisis. To do so, I follow Gillian Hart and propose exploring "the multiple, divergent, but interconnected trajectories of sociospatial change taking place in the context of intensified global integration" that brought Honduras to this point (2002, 13).

In her work on South Africa, Hart (2002; 2014) approaches the post-apartheid transition by paying close attention to both the gendered and racialized relations of force between different actors, and the articulation between the sphere of the everyday life and the political and economic imperatives of global capital accumulation in particular conjunctures. Further, she proposes that we think about how the conditions of possibility for the present as historically constituted in relation to the past, as well as about how the histories and memories of dispossession and struggle continue to resonate and inform the present and the possibilities of creating other futures. The result is a rich narrative about the process of formation of the post-apartheid state that goes beyond catch phrases such as "globalization" or "neoliberalism." To do so, Hart draws upon the work of the Italian communist Antonio Gramsci, particularly his usage of the notion of "passive revolution."

To summarize, passive revolution is both a tactic to secure a conservative modernization with limited mass participation and a historical project. We can point to three dynamics that help secure the domination of one class over others, in contexts in which either the sweeping away of the ancien régime is impossible and/or the dominant classes are unable to secure the moral and intellectual leadership of society as a whole. First, it refers to a "revolution from above," where the transformation of society follows the initiative of the dominant classes but is instrumentalized through the state and thus presented as neutral and above the different groups (Morton 2010). Second, it can be understood as the "depoliticisation of politics," a defensive measure converting "formerly expressly political debates into purely bureaucratic or technical questions" (Thomas 2009, 151), as well as promoting small reforms or concessions from "above," as a way of defusing or blocking more general transformations from "below." The third dynamic involves the co-optation and demobilization of some of the more radical elements and ideas from the subaltern classes, by means of their molecular absorption into the dominant project. In this vein, Massimo Modonesi (2016) has proposed that we can think about passive revolution, in subjective terms, as the process of subduing the initial radical impulses of the masses and securing their passivity—their condition of subalternity, as it were.

This book builds on and contributes to the expanding body of works that have used this approach to think about the processes of modernization and state formation in different parts of the world (De Smet 2016; Hart 2002; 2014; Allinson and Anievas 2010; Davidson 2012; Mallick 2017). In Latin America, for example, it has been used to explain the process of formation of the post-revolutionary state in Mexico, at both the national and subnational levels (Morton 2013; Hesketh 2017). It has also been used to think about the neo-extractivist politics of the "pink tide" governments in South America (Webber 2016; Lapegna 2017; Andreucci 2017; Roio 2012), as well as the post-civil war period in Guatemala (Short 2016).

Gramsci's framework allows a mode of posing questions about modernization and the state that resist and go beyond the tendency of liberal thought to, on the one hand, separate the political from the economic, and, on the other hand, differentiate and contrapose the "local" or "domestic" against the "global" or the "international." In other words, Gramsci's ideas on passive revolution become a great antidote to the logic of convening space in temporal terms that Doreen Massey (1999) warned us about.

With these notions at hand, we are in a better position to offer an account of the 2009 ousting of popularly elected Manuel "Mel" Zelaya by the Honduran military that pushes against the narratives of either failed transitions or "captured" or "infected" states. Rather, I argue that to understand the Honduran present, framed as it is by high levels of poverty, inequality, and the violent articulation between plantation and narco economies, we must turn our eyes to the past and explore the historical process of production of its conditions of possibility. In other words, instead of trying to explain how the Honduran transition to democracy and development came to *fail*, I hope to shed some light on how the crisis, and its spatiality, came to be *produced*.

## A Comment on Methods

*The Coup and the Palm Trees* is based on over twelve months of ethnographic fieldwork in the Aguán between 2012 and 2014. During that period of time I carried out interviews with more than a hundred members of peasant organizations, such as MUCA, former members of the agrarian reform cooperatives that were created in the Bajo Aguán during the 1970s and 1980s, current and former state officials, current and former representatives of NGOs, and representatives of the Catholic Church that accompanied both the process of organization of the agrarian reform cooperatives in the 1970s and the efforts of peasant organizations during the cycle of peasant mobilization of the late 1990s and 2000s.

Moreover, during 2013 I lived in Tocoa, the largest town in the Bajo Aguán region, but spent a significant part of each week in one of four different peasant settlements in the region that resulted from that same cycle of land occupations. Using participatory techniques, such as "memory workshops" (Riaño-Alcalá 2008) and participatory mapping (Vélez Torres, Rátiva Gaona, and Varela Corredor 2012), I reconstructed with residents of these settlements the history of their communities and of the Aguán in more general terms; I also discussed with them the current circumstances of the country.

During that same period, I accompanied informally the work of the Permanent Observatory of Human Rights of the Aguán (OPDHA). Created in November 2011, the OPDHA is a peasant-run organization that defends the life and well-being of the various peasant organizations in the region from constant attacks by both state (military and police) and private armed actors operating in the area in the aftermath of the 2009 coup and the agreements between Porfirio Lobo's government and MUCA in 2010, a topic I will return to in chapter 6. I was able to accompany OPDHA on various occasions, as they monitored the eviction of peasant communities and organizations, followed up on murder cases and disappearances, and gave support to women who had been victims of domestic violence. Through these trips, and the relationships that I built with the organization, I was able to not only visit many locations all over the Aguán (and beyond) but also to learn about their personal histories: how they arrived to the Aguán and why, against all odds, they decided to remain and fight for a better present for themselves and a future for their sons and daughters.

Finally, I also carried out fieldwork in Tegucigalpa, where I met with members of NGOs, social movements, and scholars who have followed from close and afar what was happening in the Aguán. I also did archival work on the creation of the Bajo Aguán and collected as much written information as I could on the formation of the peasant cooperatives and the demise of many of them in the 1990s. However, this is above all a work of oral history that places the particular histories of the people that I met, and was told about during my time in the Aguán, within the broader context of processes that remain beyond their control and in dialogue with a set of theoretical discussions.

Analytically, I propose a reading that interrogates the Honduran present (particularly the conjuncture around the 2009 coup) in relation to the country's spatiotemporal trajectory of agrarian change. In this, I am loosely adopting Gillian Hart's (2002; 2018) own take on Henri Lefebvre's regressive-progressive method. According to the French thinker, this approach "takes as its starting-point the realities of the present" to then act "retroactively upon the past, disclosing aspects and moments of it hitherto uncomprehended. The past appears in a different light, and hence the process whereby that past becomes the present also takes on another aspect" (Lefebvre 1991, 65).

Hart (2018, 19–20) uses this idea of searching for the conditions of possibility of the present by exploring the past to propose what she calls "Marxist postcolonial geographies" that "are grounded in conceptions of different regions of the world as always already interconnected, both as an ontological position and as an epistemological procedure." As procedure, the South African geographer proposes five moments or moves, of which the first three are as follow: First, we identify important processes or practices, rather than a bounded unit, that can be used as a vantage point from where to begin to grasp the "coming together and interconnections" of key processes (the 2009 coup d'état and the current Central American crisis in our case). Second is the moment of inquiry, in which we use "critical ethnography" and "spatiohistorical analysis" to interrogate and follow the threads that connect the past to the conditions of possibility of the present (in our case, the production of the Bajo Aguán). Next, in the third moment, we use our newfound knowledge of the past to interrogate the present and imagine the production of different futures.

The fourth moment proposed by Hart is that of exposition and the difficulties that presenting this sort of dialectal analysis poses. In this regard the reader of this book will find a tension between my mode of analysis and my mode of presentation. Analytically, I understand the data presented in this book as a set of spatiohistorical constellations that result from the dialogue between oral and written sources, with theoretical discussions that speak to broader contexts.[3] In terms of the mode of presentation, my writing shifts throughout the text. The chapters are organized in chronological order, starting with the rise to power of Tiburcio Carías in the 1930s and ending with the aftermath of the 2009 coup and the regime of Juan Orlando Hernández (current at the time of writing). Each chapter explores a different facet of the process of state formation in Honduras as we move through different scenes. Thus, while the chapters in part 1 ("The Prehistory of Neoliberalism") are constructed mainly through the testimonies of peasant organizers and members of the agrarian reform cooperatives in the Aguán, part 2 ("The Assault on Power and the Coup") broadens the lens to the national scale, exploring the articulation between localized processes in the region and the national dynamics of political contestation. Thus, while the first part is richer in terms of detail of particular trajectories, the second one aims at understanding how those trajectories were brought into, and helped shape, the country's current conjuncture.

Finally, my approach aims at protecting the identity of my informants. Honduras is a country that is very much still coming to grips with its violent past. While the 1990s tends to be presented as a period of transition toward democracy and leaving behind the horrors of the past, many, if not all, of the old wounds continue to fester. For example, on various occasions people would tell me about events that took place during the 1980s and 1990s, to later emphasize that I should not quote them: "See that guy walking down the road over there? My neighbor? He used to be an informant of the 3-16 Battalion. Because of him we never saw my brother again."

Trained by both the U.S. and Argentine armies, the 3-16 Battalion was an army death squad created in the late 1970s that carried out most of the 184 disappearances and executions that were attributed to the armed forces during that period of time (Gill 2004). The fact that few of its members ever faced criminal charges, combined with the generalized levels of rampant and produced impunity that exist in the country (HRW 2014; Chayes 2017; Lakhani 2020), makes it very hard for people to talk freely about the past and about their grievances in more general terms (Cruz 2011). As a result, my account of the recent Honduran history only includes those elements that I felt could be presented safely, without revealing the identity of my sources. I also use pseudonyms for both people and locations, unless they are well-known and what I am telling has already been made public through other outsources.

**Scope of the Book**

Borrowing various insights from the important and exciting debates that have raged around the work of Antonio Gramsci in the last few decades, I develop in this book an analytical framework that stitches together time and space to approach the questions of state formation, and political change and action (Hart 2014; Thomas 2009; Hesketh 2017; Morton 2013; Gidwani and Paudel 2012; Kipfer 2012; Crehan 2016). Besides adding to a growing body of literature that explores the question of capitalist modernization from the perspective of passive revolution, this book contributes to our knowledge base in three other directions. First, thematically, it contributes to the understanding of the 2009 coup and shows how the relationship between land and power is crucial for comprehending the Central American current political and economic crisis. More specifically, by thinking about the Honduran present in relation to its past and the process of state formation, it proposes an entry point into the current conjuncture that is not predicated upon the shorter time scale of the "transition to democracy" literature.

Second, and connected to the previous point, while there has been an increasing academic interest in Honduras, most of it has tended to concentrate on the plight of Indigenous groups and around topics of identity, tourism, drug trafficking, and megaprojects (Anderson 2009; Brondo 2013; Loperena 2017; Mollett 2011; Lakhani 2020). Much less has been written on the political geography and history of the Honduran agrarian reform and counterreform, and the impact that it had on the process of state formation and the historical configuration of subjects and landscapes that have become so crucial for explaining the country's present. This is a particularly glaring omission for a region like the Aguán, whose relationship to some of the most important political events in the country's recent history has not been accompanied by the same level of academic interest (but see Kerssen 2013; Önder 2018). At the same time, except for Jennifer Casolo (2004; 2009), whose important work has informed my thinking on the region and particularly on the gender dynamics around the struggle of land, the Bajo Aguán has been all but ignored by geographers.

Finally, methodologically, the book proposes that land can be a thread upon which to read the process of state formation in Honduras, specifically, but which could be extended to other contexts in which passive revolution is dominant. By following how land is understood, used, and struggled over in different historical moments, we are able to glimpse the different class projects in dispute and how they coalesce in the form of the state. Also, it allows us to bring the geopolitical together with everyday life by showing how more general projects, such as the transition to democracy or neoliberalism, are literally grounded into particular landscapes.

The rest of the book is organized into two sections and six chapters. Part 1 (chapters 2, 3, and 4) focuses on the assembling of the palm oil plantations in the Aguán, prior to the 1990s, through the process of agrarian reform. It is titled "The Prehistory of Neoliberalism" because it explores the production of the conditions of possibility for the way in which neoliberalism was deployed, and disputed, in the country from the 1990s onward. Chapter 1, "Dictatorship and Reform: From Carías to Military Reformism," follows the period between the sixteen-year dictatorship of Tiburcio Carías Andino in the 1930s and the rise to formal political power by the armed forces in the 1970s. It explores the roots of a set of political economic arrangements that have had important reverberation in Honduran history, all the way up to the present conjuncture: from the rise to political power of the armed forces, to the heavy-handed influence of U.S. geopolitical projects on domestic politics; from the fragmentation of the country between the north coast and the interior to the relationships between the two-party political system and the rest of the country's political landscape.

Chapter 2, "Disciplining Peasants, Disciplining the Land: The Political Economy of the Honduran Agrarian Reform in the Bajo Aguán (1962–1980)," examines the Honduran agrarian reform (1960s to the 1980s) as a dual process of disciplining humans and the land to produce a palm oil producing peasantry and the palm oil plantations. It proposes that the way in which these two elements were fused through the agrarian reform created a set of contradictions that would inform the subsequent process of agrarian counterreform in the 1990s.

Chapter 3, "The Hidden Abode of Primitive Accumulation: Agrarian Counterreform, Gender, and Neoliberalism," analyzes the process of agrarian counterreform in the 1990s from the perspective of the internal dynamics of the cooperatives that were created during the agrarian reform period. It places particular attention on the perspective of women of this process, as it analyzes how dispossession was "domesticated"; that is, how the relationships within the domestic unit informed, at the same time that they were transformed, by the process of agrarian counterreform.

Part 2, titled "The Assault on Power and the Coup" (chapters 4, 5, 6, and 7), shifts the attention to the period between Hurricane Mitch (1998) and the coup of 2009. It analyzes the wave of increasing subaltern mobilization that, combined with Zelaya's own attempts to consolidate his political power, came to challenge the dominant bloc that was created through the process of neoliberalization and disaster capitalism in the country. Chapter 4, "Democracy as Disaster Capitalism: Land and Neoliberalism in the Aftermath of Destruction," starts with the arrival of Hurricane Mitch to Honduras in 1998, discussing how it mixed with the dynamics of the palm oil plantation economy in the aftermath of the agrarian counterreform in the Aguán. At the national scale, this chapter looks at the process of disaster capitalism that ended up bolstering the neoliberal project, as well as at the new set of subaltern actors who began to organize against it. Locally, it explores the new set of land occupations that aimed at reviving the agrarian reform in the Aguán.

Chapter 5, "The Failed Assault on State Power," analyzes Zelaya's government, the process that led to the coup, and the ways in which these dynamics played out in the Aguán. Locally, it looks at the struggles between the peasant organizations and the palm oil barons to control the region, and at how this connected to what was happening on the national scale.

Chapter 6, titled "Militarization, Rent Capture, and the State-Narco Relations," shows how land, and the disputes over it between dominant and subaltern actors, has much to say regarding the mess that Honduras specifically, and Central America in more general terms, is in at the current conjuncture. More specifically, by following the overlaps and continuations between the palm oil plantation economy and drug trafficking in the Bajo Aguán, it proposes that it is along the thread of militarization and the spatial logics of rent capturing that we find a connection between the quintessential "banana republic" of the twentieth century and the quintessential "narco-state" of the twenty-first.

Chapter 7, titled "Honduras, Neoliberal Workshop or End of a Cycle?" briefly covers the period between the 2009 coup and the more recent 2021 elections in which Xiomara Castro, Manuel Zelaya's wife and one of the leaders of the political party Libertad y Refundación (LIBRE) in her own right, was elected as the first female president of the country. Finally, the conclusion brings together the different arguments presented throughout the book.

## PART I

# The Prehistory of Neoliberalism

A young woman holds an oil palm fruit, Bajo Aguán region, 2021. Photo by Martín Cálix/Contracorriente.

**CHAPTER 1**

# Dictatorship and Reform
*From Carías to Military Reformism*

On October 3, 1963, at around four-thirty in the morning, Alejandra Bermúdez, the then-first lady and wife of Ramón Villeda Morales, called U.S. ambassador Charles R. Burrows to inform him that a coup d'état was taking place and that the armed forces were taking control over the country.[1] Also, she informed him that her husband, the constitutional president of Honduras, wanted Burrows to gather up the diplomatic corps and request that the United States send help as soon as possible. The ambassador did not carry out Villeda Morales's request, allegedly due to the lack of means of communication and official information regarding what was exactly going on. It later emerged that not all the armed forces had taken part in the initial military uprising: the air force had to fly over various military bases to convince troops to join, or at least to dissuade them from moving against the coup.

Further, the military had to deal with the armed resistance of the Guardia Civil (the Civil Guard), a police-like force under the control of and loyal to the president and the Liberal Party. In places such as Tegucigalpa, this resistance was mild to nonexistent. However, in all the north coast, home of the banana enclave and characterized by higher levels of support for the Liberal Party, the armed clashes were bloodier, and the butcher's bill higher. In the end, according to the estimates of the U.S. embassy in Honduras, around four hundred people were killed. Most of the victims were Civil Guards, many of whom had been stripped of their uniforms and quickly buried in mass graves.

The coup was a quick affair. Except for individual pockets of resistance—where the Civil Guard and sympathizers of the government were able to hold out until October 7—by midmorning of the third, the country was under military control. According to various members of the U.S. mission in Honduras, the coup was "efficiently executed, as the result of careful planning and solid military leadership" (Argueta 2009, 235).

After being put under arrest by the army, Ramón Villeda Morales was flown and deported to Costa Rica that same day by the Honduran air force. He was accompanied by a group of members of the Liberal Party, including Modesto Rodas Alvarado, who had been recently elected as the party's candidate for the upcoming November elections. As we will see later on in this chapter, this ousting and the rise of the military dictatorship stemmed in part from Rodas Alvarado's all-but-certain electoral victory and his strident antimilitary discourse (Argueta 2008; 2009; Holden 2004).

As military coups go, the overthrowing of Villeda was an odd one. It took place just a few weeks before the upcoming elections. Further, according to Mario Argueta's (2009) study on Villeda's government, the U.S. government had tried to dissuade López Arellano, the commanding officer of the armed forces, from carrying out the coup. Thus, the coup plotters were going against the common assertion that you must have U.S. approval to carry out this sort of action in Latin America and get away with it. Also, although transnational companies such as the UFCO had been openly against some of Villeda Morales's policies, particularly the agrarian reform law of 1962, they were also against the perspective of a coup, as it could politically destabilize the country even further, which would be bad for business. Additionally, less than two decades before, in 1947, the Honduran armed forces were considered to be in shambles, with little to no central organization and lacking the capabilities to orchestrate such a coordinated effort (Holden 2004). Finally, just six years before, in 1957, Villeda Morales, as leader of the Liberal Party and López Arellano, as leader of the armed forces, had struck a deal in which the latter would support a Liberal government in exchange for receiving significant autonomy from civilian government in the new constitution being discussed at the time (Argueta 2009). Thus, abstractly, none of the conditions of possibility for a coup seemed to be in place for the ousting of Villeda Morales. However, when read against the historical process of state formation in Honduras during the twentieth century, it is evident that the 1963 coup d'état was something to be expected. In it, and in the way in which the forces that led to it were assembled, we find some clues and a thread to follow up to the 2009 ousting. First, it presents neatly the rise of the military from a ragtag ensemble of poorly trained men with obsolete equipment to the most important political actor in the country in the second half of the twentieth century. Second, the cracks and disputes within one of the oldest two-party electoral system in Latin America, and the constant overflow of the electoral dynamics into the use of force and politics by other means, allows us to see the disruptions and continuities in the process of Honduran state formation, within the broader process of capitalist modernization in Latin America. Third, it brings to the fore the complicated marriages between the National Party and the armed forces on the one hand, and between the Liberal Party and organized labor and the peasant movement on the other, marriages that were born, as it were, during the sixteen-year dictatorship of Tiburcio Carías Andino (1933–49), which did much to stabilize the country's political situation and culture but did just as much to stunt the modernization of both state and civil society.

The ousting of Villeda Morales is then a point of amalgamation between the more traditional caudillo politics that had marked most of the postcolonial process of state formation in Central America and the process of liberal modernization that was both promoted and imposed in the region in the aftermath of World War II by the U.S. geopolitical project (and its discontents) in the context of the Cold War. This was a process of modernization that, after yet another coup in 1972, saw the Honduran armed forces rise as overseers of the nation and the process of state formation, under the rubric of what López Arrellano came to call the "historical actualization" of Honduras.

This chapter follows the period between Tiburcio Carías Andino's sixteen-year dictatorship in the early 1930s, and the formalization of military rule in the early 1970s. This is a long period of dictatorship, punctuated by the ongoing attempts by an incipient alliance between the emergent bourgeoisie on the north coast and subaltern groups—particularly the peasant and labor movements—to have some say in the process of state formation and question the amassing of political and economic power by the local elites and their transnational allies. As I show in this chapter, it is a period in which the new social groups created in the process of peripheral capitalist modernization questioned and constantly attempted to wrest political and economic control away from the traditional elites. This eventually resulted in a set of reformist policies that included some of the demands of the subaltern groups—particularly the incipient north coast bourgeoisie—while maintaining the structures of power basically intact.

This is a very important period for both stories that I am weaving together in this book. In the case of the Aguán, the production of the region that we will begin exploring in the next chapter took place under the aegis of the agrarian reform that was directly shaped by the attempts from above to arrest the increasing combativeness of the peasant and labor movement during this period. Regarding the 2009 coup, as we will see, there were parallels between the ousting of Villeda Morales in 1963 and Zelaya Rosales, both in terms of the process of state formation and the role played by the land question. We begin following the thread that connects both historical moments in the 1930s, with the rise of Carías Andino.

### Order and Peace

The 1932 elections pitted against each other two quintessential Honduran political strongmen of the twentieth century: Tiburcio Carías Andino of the National Party and José Angel Zúñiga Huete of the Liberal Party. Both presented the perfect traditional caudillo résumé: lawyers, undisputed leaders of their respective parties, and former government officials. The electoral results gave Carías a landslide victory over Zúñiga and as was the tradition, the Liberal Party and its followers rose in arms trying to stop the elected president from taking office. The rebellion was quickly suppressed and, finally, after being denied the presidential chair in the two previous elections, Carías was able to assume the presidency in February 1933, which would eventually extend into a sixteen-year-long dictatorship, legalized through two constitutional reforms in 1936 and 1939.[2]

The Carías dictatorship constitutes a watershed in Honduran history on various levels. Regionally, it was part of a wave of conservative and highly repressive authoritarian regimes rising to power in the five Central American republics and other places of the Caribbean (e.g., Rafael Trujillo in Dominican Republic). These regimes emerged in reaction to the rise of new social groups in the region—mainly organized labor, peasant organizations, and the commercial petite bourgeoisie—that came to challenge the traditional dominant blocs, as well as the severe post-1929 economic and fiscal crisis in all the countries and the collapse of both coffee and banana prices. Victor Bulmer-Thomas (1993, 348) notes that "in exchange for the preservation of their class interests, the elite in the four republics of the north [Guatemala, El Salvador, Honduras and Nicaragua], were prepared to renounce all of their accustomed privileges and benefits, which at least, since the 1920s, had given the superficially democratic appearance to the political process."

The Carías regime's social base consisted mainly of large landowners, the UFCO and the U.S. government (Argueta 2008). The army had a clear role in the process, too. Knowing how easily military leaders could turn into political contenders, Carías kept the officer corps on a short leash. He relied heavily on the air forces, which he called the "support of the national peace" (Barahona 2005; Bulmer-Thomas 1993). The rest of the armed forces continued to be an ill-equipped and poorly trained grouping of people, extracted from the most deprived social sectors of the country.

In fact, according to Argueta, it is a mistake to think that the political stabilization that the Carías regime brought to Honduras was the result of the modernization of the state and an absolute centralization of power around himself. Rather, Carías's government was organized both on a spatial decentralization of political power, and a hierarchical chain of command, which at the same time operated as a funnel of rents. It began with him at the top of a pyramid that rested on a set of regional military strongmen who imposed their leader's iron will, with vast political and economic autonomy; below them existed a set of trusted high-level state bureaucrats. Both these groups managed to enrich themselves at the expense of the state, capturing rents through their control over commerce and the designation of public officials, as well as by acting as middlemen between foreign businessmen and the state.[3] This structure would become an enduring feature of the Honduran political system, with regional strongmen and the logic of the state as bounty continuing to resonate to this day, as we will see further on.

Thus, while Carías owed his power to the actions of these regional strongmen and high-level bureaucrats, for which he rewarded them with high levels of autonomy, their capacity to plunder the public purse and capture rents accrued from international trade were dependent on the dictator's continuity in power. This whole system of checks and balances depended on none of these actors accumulating enough power to threaten Carías's dominant position. The already mentioned lack of modernization of the armed forces was one mechanism in place to prevent this outcome; the other was making sure that there were not enough public funds lying around for anyone to enrich themselves above the rest. For example, Argueta (2008) notes that the dictator was against signing foreign loans, fully knowing that his associates would pocket a significant portion of any such funds received.

Furthermore, Carías's alliance with the banana companies was the target of much criticism, and it is here that the idea of Honduras as the quintessential "banana republic" really took off. Carías and the UFCO were two sides of the same coin, and their fates were tightly knit into the Honduran political fabric.[4] Nonetheless, it would be a mistake to think that under Carías only the banana industry flourished. While the north coast and its banana plantations became the nucleus of capital accumulation with San Pedro Sula as its capital (the "industrial capital of Honduras," as it is commonly known), Tegucigalpa, in the interior but historically oriented toward the south and the Pacific Ocean, continued to be the seat of the state powers and most of the bureaucracy. Both political landscapes were the outcome of the dynamics between the local military strongmen and other significant actors. At the same time, there were certain constant features throughout the country, such as the continual siding of the government with the interests of foreign investors and a recalcitrant anticommunist perspective that informed a geographically differentiated approach to subaltern protest and political mobilization. On the north coast specifically, and particularly in the case of the banana and railroad workers, we see the bloody repression of any revolt, strike, or public demonstration confronting labor conditions, the banana companies or the government. This was the space of capital, and "order and peace"—Carías's government motto—would be understood in its terms. At the same time, Carías's approach to the rest of the country was paradoxically different. For example, he responded to Tegucigalpa artisans' and government officials' claims with negotiations and moderately progressive policies and distributed a certain number of national lands to poor peasants (Barahona 2005; Argueta 2008). Finally, Carías succeeded also in pacifying the country and bringing to a halt the constant revolts and armed clashes that had wrecked and bled the country since independence.[5]

In their study of the development of agriculture during the Carías regime, Cáceres and Zelaya (2005) try to capture the impact that Carías's spatially differentiated policies had in economic terms, dividing the country into two spaces: the "banana republic" and the "non-banana republic," which refers to rest of the country outside of the banana-producing departments of Colón, Atlántida, Yoro, and Cortés. According to their data, before the arrival of Carías, constant warring had impoverished the non-banana republic in terms of both production levels and demographic growth. In response, Carías implemented a heavy-handed approach to reactivate and promote agricultural production in these regions. Local army commanders were required to make sure that peasants dedicated a portion of their land to the cultivation of beans, maize, other staple crops, and small-scale animal husbandry. Carías also began to distribute national and *ejido* lands—municipal lands, not to be confused with the Mexican institution—to poor peasants in usufruct (Cáceres and Zelaya 2005; Argueta 2008).

However, this political stabilization and economic revival or awakening should not be overstated. The non-banana republic continued to be a space dominated by the contradiction between large estates, not particularly efficient in production terms, and (mainly) self-provisioning small producers, with nothing close to a dynamic domestic market. At the same time, in political terms, this lack of economic dynamism was a blessing in disguise for the

Carías regime. Since only the banana republic was articulated to the global market, the impact of the 1930s financial crisis was circumscribed to that space. As such, although the government saw a steep decrease in its income, due to the falling banana exports and attendant increasing layoffs of banana workers, the living conditions of most of the Honduran population remained the same (Argueta 2008).

Carías managed to remain in power for sixteen years by this combination of authoritarian rule and economic stabilization. He exacerbated and controlled to his advantage certain contradictions and tensions that were already present in the country. While he did not create the national fragmentation between the banana and non-banana republics, he was able to capitalize politically by differentiating his approach to these two spaces. On the one hand, military support to the banana companies on the north coast meant that the conditions of reproduction of the most important economic activity in the country—from the elites' perspective at least—would remain stable in the banana republic. On the other hand, quelling social and armed unrest in the non-banana republic and promoting agricultural production had a similar effect, but by different means. For the traditional elites, the separation between class and state meant that they could dedicate themselves to other activities—such as cattle ranching or commerce—without having to worry about their intra-elite opponents capturing the state.

Importantly, Carías was able to use the large reserves of available ejido and national lands to securely fix a sector of the peasantry on the land without affecting the elites, thereby settling down the population and making it difficult for opposing caudillos to conscript unhappy peasants for armed campaigns. This policy also increased production of staple crops and thus lowered the price of labor on the national scale, as well as stimulating commerce and economic activity. However, at the same time, consolidating the access to land of the peasantry meant that both their labor and the lands they occupied were not available for other economic activities, stunting and delaying the development of a capitalist agricultural sector, as seen in other countries of the region. Finally, it exacerbated the spatial and social fragmentation of the country. All these elements would be explosively combined toward the end of Carías's rule, showing just how precarious the balance of power was in the country.

## "Honduras's Paris Commune": The Rise of Organized Labor

Toward the mid-1940s, the opposition against Carías began to mount. The dictator did not have much to fear from within, as none of those opposing him had the capacity to dispute his political and military might. Nonetheless, the regional context, as well as the United States' approach to the regime, was shifting significantly. After 1944 the Central American dictators' club was down to Carías and the Somoza dynasty in Nicaragua, which emboldened the Honduran opposition; it took to the streets in both Tegucigalpa and San Pedro Sula, demanding Carías's resignation. From 1945 onward, the opposition—a combination of the urban middle class, the industrial and commercial petite bourgeoisie, and the labor movement—began to organize in political parties to push for reform. Probably the most important oppositional party was the Revolutionary and Democratic Honduran Party (PRDH), whose members would eventually recreate the defunct Honduran Communist Party and attract the left-wing faction of the Liberal Party from the 1950s onward.[6]

The U.S. approach to the region and particularly to dictatorial regimes was also changing. After World War II, coinciding with the arrival of Harry Truman to the presidency and in the context of the Cold War, the discourse of the United States shifted toward the promotion of democracy, as a way of curtailing the communist influence that the Soviet Union supposedly irradiated in the region. In the case of Honduras, from 1946 onward, the United States began to make clear that it preferred a change of government in Honduras. In early 1948 Tiburcio Carías announced that he would be stepping down and elections were planned for October. The initial optimism of the Liberal Party dwindled as it became evident that the dictator would impose his own successor. Thus, José Angel Zúñiga Huete, the Liberal Party's candidate, pulled out of the contest amid complaints regarding the electoral rolls, and Juan Manuel Gálvez—minister of war under Carías and the UFCO's former lawyer—was elected president.

Carías's peaceful stepdown must also be understood against the backdrop of various structural changes. In the aftermath of World War II, the international prices of bananas slightly recovered, increasing the size of both the land dedicated to the crop and the labor force. It also meant an improved fiscal situation for the government. At the same time, the U.S. war effort during World War II had also created a market for Honduran products, such as beef, cotton in the south, palm oil, cocoa and Manila hemp in the north, and coffee, mainly in the west, helping diversify the national economy, particularly after the 1950s. Consequently, the dependency on the bananas industry declined, diminishing the political leverage of the companies (Bucheli 2003; 2006). However, at the same time, it meant that Carías's policy of protecting ejido and smallholder lands and his suspicions against public indebtedness now became barriers against the further expansion of the new agricultural export activities.

Gálvez's government was envisioned as one of transition toward democracy and economic and political modernization. From day one, the former UFCO lawyer claimed that his government would focus on developing the agricultural sector and the internal market. The idea was simple: improve infrastructure to connect the foodstuff production in the interior with the larger cities and markets in the north coast. Also, under the tutelage of the IFIs (World Bank and IMF), Gálvez's government began a process of institutional modernization that included the development of a national banking system to stimulate the economy, education reform, and a labor code, among other reforms. It also meant the beginning of the non-banana republic articulation with the global market.

Although Gálvez continued with the heavy-handed approach to dissent, this was a period of growth for the labor movement, particularly on the north coast. From the early 1950s onward, despite intense repression, several strikes and strike attempts took place not only in the different banana plantations but also in related branches such as the railroads. At the same time, nationalist feelings and anti-imperialist denunciations against the banana companies and particularly against "The Octopus"—as the UFCO was popularly known—continued to mount. In early May 1954, the tensions peaked, as thousands of UFCO workers launched a strike led by communists, left-wing liberals of the PRDH, and with the moral and financial support of the San Pedro Sula bourgeoisie (Euraque 1996). The strike was not a spontaneous or surprising event. It was the result of a long arch of over forty years of workers' grievances and organizing against the total lack of economic or social rights in the plantations and the intransigent positions of both the companies and the government.

The initial reaction from the government was a combination of carrot and stick, as both military troops were deployed and a negotiating commission was named. However, the discipline and determination of the more than twenty-five thousand striking workers, so vividly depicted by Ramón Amaya Amador's (1988) novel *Destacamento Rojo* (Red Detachment), did not falter; the workers took over the banana towns and brought the industry to a halt. Among their demands were the right to unionize, a significant increase in wages, and better working conditions. The company's initial response was to try and delay the negotiating process and break the strike.

In July, two months into the strike, it became clear that the workers would not merely give in to the company's pressure. Gálvez was forced to intercede and negotiate an agreement between the representatives of both the UFCO and the workers. For the labor movement, this was more a political than an economic victory, as only a bare minimum of the strikers' demands was satisfied. Still, the banana workers had shown that they could stand up to capital and force some concessions from the state. For example, the strike's outcome opened the door for the legalization of labor organizing in the entire country. It also meant that they would now be considered as a significant political force. The strike also showed other actors, such as the peasant movement, how to negotiate with the government. It comes as no wonder that Ramón Amaya Amador, one of the most prominent Communist Party intellectuals of this period, would later characterize the strike as Honduras's "Paris Commune" (quoted by Euraque 1996, 71).

Meanwhile, in Guatemala, President Jacobo Arbenz was ousted by a CIA-orchestrated coup. Known as part of the "Guatemalan Revolution," the Arbenz government had promoted a set of reformist policies, including probably the most far-reaching agrarian reform in Central American history up to that moment and a labor code that emboldened the labor movement, which began to push for better labor conditions. While initially the United States did not show much fear regarding a communist turn in Guatemala, the UFCO began a high-level lobbying campaign to convince Washington that the government was infested by communists and that its policies went against the interests of U.S. capital and were unfair to the company. Eventually, Washington's preoccupation with communism in Guatemala grew, and in 1953, the CIA armed, funded, and trained a force of over four hundred men, led by the exiled former general Carlos Castillo Armas, which invaded the country from Honduras on the June 18, 1954. While this force by itself represented no real threat to the Guatemalan armed forces, the fear of further retaliation by the United States led them to refuse to fight, and, on June 27, Arbenz resigned, bringing Castillo Armas to power and the "Guatemalan Revolution" to a crashing end (Gleijeses 1992; Tischler 2001; Handy 1994; Grandin 2011).

In Honduras, the UFCO and the traditional land-owning elite had been following Arbenz's government and worrying that its influence could spread across the border. Further, they were quite adamant in their communications with the U.S. embassy that Arbenz's regime, not the abhorrent conditions in the banana plantations, was somehow behind the Honduran banana strike of that year (Argueta 2008). Gálvez's government supported the Guatemalan coup, allowing Honduran territory to be the launching pad for the Guatemalan counterrevolution. In exchange, the Honduran army received increasing U.S. support and, as Barahona (2005, 173) points out, it also "inaugurated a tradition in which Honduras would take on the role of the territorial base of the Central American counter-revolution." Also, in more general and geopolitical terms, it showed that, under the excuse of the "red menace" and rooted in the Roosevelt Corollary, the United States would be open to allowing the toppling of democratically elected governments that threatened the interests of U.S. capital.

**Villeda Morales and the Political Ascendency of the Military**

After the 1954 strike, it became evident that "for things to stay as they are, things [would] have to change" (Di Lampedusa 2007, 19). The 1954 banana strike had shown that coercion by itself was no longer enough to maintain the dominance of the ruling elites in the country, and the signs were there that a substantial change was taking place. First, the 1954 strike had signaled the entry of new actors onto the political stage. Second, the Liberal Party's leadership was revitalized around the figure Ramón Villeda Morales, who reflected the ascent of these new social groups and a political discourse favoring a more active role for the state in the national economy. Third, the Honduran armed forces were also in the process of modernization and a new group of better-trained leaders was coming up the rank and file, due to U.S. support of the Central American armies (Holden 2004). Fourth, during August and September of that same year, heavy rains and flooding had destroyed a significant part of the banana production in the country. The banana companies responded by abandoning large amounts of land and introducing technological changes that led to the dismissal of around thirteen thousand workers (almost half of the total workforce). This combination of idle land and massive landlessness set the stage for combative peasant movements that not only sought to access land but also protection for their tenure against the attempts of landowners to evict them (Posas 1981; Carney 1985). Finally, the National Party, the dominant political force since Carías and a traditional ally of U.S. interests in the country, was clearly in decline.

In October 1956, after Julio Lozano Díaz—who had taken over the presidency after Gálvez retired in 1954—rigged the elections to remain in power, the military decided to stage a coup and a constituent assembly was convened. This was an excellent opportunity for the Villeda Morales-led Liberal Party to finally return to power and take advantage of their growing popularity in the aftermath of the 1954 strike. However, at the same time, due to the traditional marriage between the National Party and the armed forces there was a lingering fear that a Liberal candidate would not be allowed to reach the presidency, no matter how many votes he received. Utilizing its overwhelming majority in the constituent assembly (thirty-six representatives, against eighteen of the National Party), the Liberal Party struck a deal with the armed forces: in exchange for allowing Villeda Morales to reach the presidency, a specific chapter was included in the new constitution (chapter 13), granting a set of concessions to the military. For example, although the president was the one in charge of electing the supreme leader of the armed forces, he had to do so from a slate of three defined by the Supreme Council of National Defense, formed by the heads of the different branches of the military. Further, the armed forces had a broad berth of freedom to define their budgets. This constitutional change and the coup allowed the military's rise as the new political arbitrator and created a dual military and civilian government that would forever change the Honduran political landscape (Argueta 2009; Holden 2004). Moreover, the military, not the National Party, would become the new local partner of the U.S. government.

During this period, and particularly after the Cuban revolution of 1959, the U.S. approach to Latin America shifted significantly. In August 1958 Eisenhower made an emphatic statement in favor of representative governments in the region. Later that year, he approved the establishment of the Inter-American Development Bank (IADB), and in early 1959 he extended his backing to the Central American Common Market (CACM), albeit using the IADB as a financial lever to press for policies compatible with U.S. interests (Euraque 1996). With the election of Kennedy, these policies crystallized in the Alliance for Progress in 1961. The alliance promoted a set of development goals (economic growth, decreasing poverty, and macroeconomic stability), as well as institutional transformations (democratic governments and agrarian reforms) that together would supposedly bring sociopolitical stability and thus undercut the communist threat that allegedly was hanging over all the countries in the region. Therefore, the anticommunist strategy in Central America included both coercion and consent: strengthening the armed forces and training them in counterinsurgency (Gill 2004; Schrader 2018) while promoting modernization under the mantle of development.

If the autonomy granted to, and the strengthening of, the military was the most glaring transformation brought up by the 1957 constitution, the other not less important aspect was the new mandate given to the state of politically and economically modernizing the country, in the process bringing under control the structural causes of dissent. As a result, from the beginning, the state took a much more active role in the economy, passing an industrial promotion law and the 1959 labor code and creating in 1961 the National Agrarian Institute (INA). Levels of repression diminished as the government moved closer to organized labor in a bid to co-opt it, by promoting those unions close to the moderate Inter American Regional Organization of Workers (ORIT) and suppressing those closer to the Left. By late 1961 Villeda established a local counterpart to the Alliance for Progress, called "The March toward Progress." With financial support from the IADB, a group of technocrats drawn from the San Pedro Sula bourgeoisie controlled this project and turned toward a deepening of the modernizing agenda. However, in 1963 this experiment in political modernization under democratic rule would come to a halt.

### The 1963 Coup: Revolution with No Revolutionary Change

From the beginning of his rule, Villeda Morales showed a clear commitment, an obsession really, with maintaining an equilibrium between his civilian government and the military's rising political clout. According to Mario Argueta (2009), this commitment was the result of Villeda Morales's interpretation of recent Honduran history, wherein the military had been crucial to Carías's extended government and was now fundamental to the Liberal Party's bid for power. However, or rather because of this position, his government had to deal with opposition coming from three fronts: from within the Liberal Party, the military, and the National Party. Internally, the decision to negotiate and give such concessions to the armed forces was regarded with disdain by various sectors within the Liberal Party. Particularly vocal was Modesto Rodas Alvarado, the president of Congress and eventually the Liberal Party's presidential candidate in the 1963 November elections. Villeda Morales was very critical of Rodas Alvarado's antimilitary and anti-conciliation discourse and considered that a less antagonistic and polarizing candidate was needed to extend the Liberal Party's sojourn in power. As we will see, time would prove him right.

The National Party, in turn, viewed the rise to power of the Liberals negatively; unsurprisingly, its leadership constantly looked for ways to return to power. For example, Tiburcio Carías, who continued to loom large within the party, was particularly active and vocal against Villeda Morales and the Liberal Party, which he considered a nest of communists. As such, members of the National Party were very active mobilizing against the government, with activities that ranged from organizing rallies against the government to writing public protests in newspapers; denouncing the government's political and economic incompetence or claiming to the U.S. embassy that it had been seized by "communists"; to imploring that the military remove the Liberal Party from power.

A particularly critical event took place on July 12, 1959, when Colonel Armando Vásquez Cerrato, with the support of members of the national police and the National Party, as well as the financial and logistical aid provided by the dictators Anastacio Somoza of Nicaragua and Rafael Trujillo of the Dominican Republic, tried to oust Villeda Morales by taking control over the Military School and various police posts in Tegucigalpa. In the end, the resolute action of the Presidential Guard as well as armed commandos of Liberal Party militants who took back the police posts stopped the would-be coup. Meanwhile, Oswaldo López Arellano, supreme leader of the armed forces, remained outside of Tegucigalpa, and the military only intervened when it became clear that the coup had failed. The involvement of the police in the uprising led to its dissolution and the creation of the Civil Guard, a new police-like armed force that was loyal to the Liberals and the government, exacerbating the frictions between the government and the military in the process (Holden 2004). This episode is also a good example of how the political disputes between different groups, those agglutinated around the National and Liberal Parties in this case, informed the process of state formation, as they both angled for control over the police forces—a struggle that in turn led the military to proclaim who really had the "legitimate" monopoly over violence in the country.[7]

Under the control of López Arellano, the position of the military concerning the Liberal government oscillated between condescension and barely concealed contempt. For example, Mario Argueta (2009) quotes various U.S. diplomatic cables in which López Arellano refers to Villeda Morales as a weak president, whose administration had not done enough to fight against the communist menace. Also, in December 1958, various members of the armed forces—but not López Arellano—signed and published a letter protesting the alleged anti-military postures of the Liberal Party, as well its lack of commitment in the fight against communism. These maneuvers seemed to be part of a larger chess game in which the military was testing how far it could push the government and consolidate its own political power. At the same time, López Arellano's political ambitions were also in play. Just before the October coup, he had probed his possibilities of being chosen as the National Party's presidential candidate for the upcoming elections. In the end, seeing how slim his chances in the party's convention were, he decided to retire his name from contention.

As a result of these mounting tensions, 1963 was a year of profound political and social turmoil. Not only did the government have to walk a tightrope between the just mentioned fronts, it also had to deal with decreasing levels of popularity, due to its incapacity to fulfill its electoral promises of modernizing the state and improving the living conditions of the population, particularly those of the working classes. However, as the year went by, and particularly after the selection of Modesto Rodas Alvarado as the Liberal presidential candidate, it became apparent that the Liberal Party was the country's principal electoral force. And thus, if the elections were to take place cleanly, it would mean the continuation in power of the Liberal Party and the arrival to the presidential chair of the antimilitary and polarizing figure of Rodas Alvarado.

In the end, on October 3, 1963, a few days before the end of his term and under the excuse that he was leading the country toward communism, Villeda Morales was ousted by the military and exiled to Costa Rica by Oswaldo López Arellano. This was a bloody and preemptive coup aimed at stopping Rodas Alvarado from becoming president and menacing the delicate balance that Villeda Morales so desperately had tried to sustain with the military. Further, and more importantly, it was an attempt to curtail the increasing influence that the subaltern sectors, particularly the worker unions and peasant movement, had on the government, as we will see in the case of the agrarian reform in the next chapter.

Furthermore, the coup temporarily resolved the question of dual power between civil and military government in favor of the latter. Just as in 1932 with Carías, the concentration of power around a single actor who could operate as a political arbitrator and upheld the powers that be, namely the military, emerged as the "solution" to the national political crisis. However, this was far from a permanent solution. The contradictions that had first led to the 1954 strike, and later to the 1957 constituent convention and the 1963 coup, continued to vibrate.

### The Football War and the Regime of National Unity (1969–1972)

If, as I have been arguing, the 1963 coup was an attempt to curtail the political power and involvement of the Honduran subaltern classes, it quickly became evident that it had changed nothing in that regard. Far from weakening the opposition of the nascent nationalist industrial and commercial bourgeoisie and their unlikely alliance with the reformist wings of the labor and peasant movements, the ousting of Villeda Morales and its aftermath pushed these actors together against the concentration of power around the National Party and the military. A clear example of the galvanization of the opposition came on September 17, 1968, when the industrial bourgeoisie and the labor movement planned to jointly carry out a general strike in San Pedro Sula and the north coast. The official reason for the strike was the signing by the government of the San José Protocol, an attempt to revamp and strengthen the CACM. This protocol negatively impacted Honduras's young industries—

some of the weakest on the isthmus—as it lowered tariffs within the Central American region, affecting the industrial production from the north coast and strengthening the traditional landowning elite, as agricultural commodities such as sugar and beef from the south enjoyed a competitive advantage with the rest of the region.

López Arellano and his allies learned about the planned strike beforehand and intimidated critical representatives of the San Pedro Sula elite. As a result, the industrial bourgeoisie backed out of the agreement, leaving the labor movement frustrated and isolated and showing the limits of cross-class alliances. As the labor movement announced a general strike on the morning of the eighteenth, the military declared a state of exception and dispatched troops to the region. By the twenty-third the strike committee had been captured, and the striking workers repressed (Euraque 1996). As such, the failed strike came to show that what was keeping the traditional elite in power—articulated around the National Party and the dominant figure of Ricardo Zúñiga Augustinus—was their alliance with the armed forces, particularly the older guard born during the Carías dictatorship.

As these events were taking place in the heart of the banana republic (north coast), agrarian conflicts continued to flame in the countryside all over Honduras. Particularly in the interior and southern sectors of the country, the new processes of land concentration and dispossession related to the cotton and beef industries that were beneficiaries of the CACM fueled a new wave of peasant mobilization (Boyer 1982; Jansen 1998; Parsons, Buchard, and Paz 1976). As such, toward the end of the 1960s, Honduras was entering a period of what Antonio Gramsci (1971, 275–76) dubbed as a "crisis of authority," where "the ruling class has lost its consensus, i.e., is no longer 'leading' but only 'dominant', exercising coercive force alone, this means precisely that the great masses have become detached from their traditional ideologies ... The crisis consists precisely in the fact that the old is dying and the new cannot be born."

In the Honduran case, the "new" began to unfold in 1969. Since the initial expansion of the plantation economy in the north coast, Honduras had become a magnet for a steady flow of poor Salvadoran peasants in search of the land or work that they could not find back home, a migration that comprised approximately 250 to 300,000 Salvadorans by 1969 (Anderson 1983). By late 1967 organized landowners in Honduras began to call for the expulsion of the Salvadoran squatters as a way of freeing land and dealing with the national peasant movement's increasing political activity. The evictions began toward mid-1969 and quickly resulted in the deportation of around twenty thousand Salvadorans.

At the same time, at least one sector of the Salvadoran oligarchy was calling for an invasion of Honduras as a way of dealing with the domestic agrarian problems that would be exacerbated by the returnees (Euraque 1996). The tensions between the two countries continued to mount, and in June 1969, their respective national football teams met in a two-leg qualifier for the 1970 FIFA-World Cup. The first match took place in Tegucigalpa on June 8 and ended with fighting between fans of both countries. On June 15 the return game took place in San Salvador, ending with even more violence. A few days later, El Salvador broke diplomatic relations with Honduras, claiming that it had done little to curb the brutality unleashed against Salvadorans living in Honduras. On July 14, 1969, the Salvadoran army invaded Honduras in what came to be known as the "Football War" or the "Hundred-Hour War" (Kapuscinski 1992).

Initially, the invading army was able to push deep into Honduran territory. However, as the Honduran military, and particularly the air force, recovered from the initial surprise and the population moved en masse to protect the country's sovereignty, the conflict was brought to a stalemate. By July 18 the Organization of American States (OAS) had negotiated an end to the fighting, and by early August the Salvadoran troops had left Honduran territory. However, the political and social effects of the war would linger for the years to come.

First, the armed conflict mobilized Honduran nationalist sentiment, papering over most of the internal antagonisms and bringing further together the industrial bourgeoisie and the labor movement. Second, the war brought the popular sectors—the Honduran Labor Central (CTH), for example—closer to the armed forces, now seen as the guardians of the nation, as against the traditional parties—the "oligarchs"—whose policies had led the country to this debacle. In other words, the war pitted "state" and "nation" against each other, with the military taking on the role of protecting the latter from the shortsighted interests of the elites festering within the former. Third, the war was seen as a failure by the Honduran armed forces, particularly by the younger officers who placed the blame on the older leadership and were deeply influenced by what they saw in Panama and Peru, where military governments had taken an active role in the modernizing of their countries in the name of social justice. Further, the conflict allowed this younger generation to enter in contact with the population in general.

In the aftermath of the armed conflict, the military took on the commitment of holding elections and ceding power to a civilian government in April 1971. Immediately, both the labor movement and the industrial bourgeoisie began to push for a government of "national unity" that would go beyond the petty interests of the elites and put the nation's interests first. Particularly outspoken were the CTH and the Honduran Council of Private Enterprises (COHEP), representatives of the reformist wing of the labor movement and the nascent industrial bourgeoisie. On December 8, 1970, a "minimum political plan of national unity" was presented by López Arellano and agreed upon (January 7, 1971) by the only two registered parties (Liberal and National) for the upcoming elections (Posas and Del Cid 1983).

The elections took place on March 28, 1971, and the lawyer Ramón Ernesto Cruz of the National Party defeated the banker Jorge Bueso Árias of the Liberal Party. From the beginning, Cruz's administration was tarnished by accusations of corruption and the distribution of government appointments and the national budget between the two traditional parties (Liberal and National Parties), in what came to be known as the *pactito* ("the little pact"). At the same time, Cruz was accused of not moving forward with some of the reforms that the country needed the most: an agrarian reform, resolving the border conflict with El Salvador, and adopting a more favorable trade policy in the CACM. All these elements had been agreed upon just a few months earlier as part of the "minimum political plan of national unity." It was clear that, behind the electoral facade, the same problems of political legitimacy continued to reverberate in the form of protests, accusations in the media, and the increasing combativeness of the organized peasant movement. The straw that broke the proverbial camel's back was the threat by the National Association of Honduran Peasants (ANACH)—one of the largest peasant organizations in the country—of mobilizing their bases all over the country to carry out a "hunger march" (*marcha del hambre*) on the capital unless the government heeded their demand for an immediate agrarian reform (Barahona 2002). One day before ANACH's deadline, López Arellano and the military decided to act, ousting the tottering civilian regime by force.

### The "Historical Actualization" of the Honduran State (1972–1979)

The 1972 coup changed Honduras's political landscape. On the one hand, it showed that the traditional landowning elite, organized around the two-party system, was unable or unwilling to go beyond its petty interests and think of Honduras as anything other than its birthright. On the other, it cemented the position of the military as the country's supreme political arbitrator and the only actor with enough clout to sustain some equilibrium between dominant and subaltern groups. As I have shown in this chapter, it is more precise to speak of the coup of 1972 as the culmination of a period of crisis of authority that began with the 1963 coup and the unraveling of Carías's rule and hegemonic project. What could not be done in 1963 became possible in a new context in 1972: a reformist regime organized around an alliance between the military, the incipient industrial bourgeoisie, and the reformist sectors of the labor and peasant movements.

In general terms, the political framework of the reformist military regime that began in 1972 was a continuation of the political project that Villeda Morales proposed in the late 1950s. The objective was to modernize the country from above, understood as an expansion of the conditions for capital accumulation, without necessarily changing the balance of power, and with the military as the overseer. There was little new or unique about this plan. It was a national adaptation of what the United Nations Economic Commission for Latin America and the Caribbean (ECLAC) had been preaching to the governments of the subcontinent since the 1950s. However, Honduras's particular history and correlation of forces mark a set of particularities worth mentioning.

On January 1, 1973, some three months after toppling of the civilian government, the Honduran military began to outline its political project. In his New Year's Eve message, López Arellano presented the basic concerns of his government: the agrarian reform as its "fundamental task," protecting the forest resources and securing their place as part of the "nation's patrimony," strengthening the manufacturing sector, promoting an education reform, "tidying up" the public administration (*"adecentar la administración pública,"* as in eliminating corruption and client-patron relations), as well as pushing forward a fiscal and foreign policy reform, among others (Posas and del Cid 1983, 270–72) The project had two central pillars: (1) a more direct involvement of the state, understood as both an enabler of capital accumulation—articulating the local with the global—and a buffer of class struggle, in the country's economic life; and (2) the "honduranization" of the economy, pointing to the goal of strengthening the role of Honduran capital in the country's development.

The plan laid out by López Arellano and his allies had two parallel phases. Initially, the government approved a set of "emergency" decree-laws aimed at pushing forward the reformist agenda around the aspects mentioned above but also at consolidating the alliance between the military, the industrial bourgeoisie, and the reformist sectors of the labor and peasant movement. In parallel, an overarching National Development Plan (NDP) would be prepared and launched in the next six months. In the end, what was supposed to take just one semester took over two years, and the NDP was finally presented in 1975. This delay was the result of the resistance from the traditional ruling elites, who immediately pushed back against most of the new policies, using their control of the media to decry the government as both populist and pro-communist.

At the same time, the labor and peasant movements complained that the reforms were not moving fast enough, resulting in escalating tensions with the government and the elites, with the military taking every so often a heavy-handed approach to dissent. Pressure also came from foreign companies based in the country. For example, the UFCO negotiated and threatened to stop new investments in Honduras if a proposed tax on bananas exports was not axed. Finally, the traditional Liberal and National Parties also pressed for the return to electoral life.

As a result, by the time that the NDP came into practice in January 1975, it was a watered-down version of the all-encompassing project of "historical actualization" that López Arellano had promised in 1973. By early April 1975, it was also clear that changes were taking place within the military government. First, López Arellano ceded his position as the leader of the armed forces to Juan Alberto Melgar Castro, while remaining the head of the government. Later, on May 16, the *Wall Street Journal* published a note reporting that López Arellano had received bribes from a banana company. When he refused to grant access to his banking accounts in Switzerland as part of the ensuing investigation, López Arellano was deposed as head of state and substituted by Melgar Castro. With this change, a younger generation of officers, many of whom had studied abroad in the U.S.- run School of the Americas (Gill 2004), rose to power and the reformist project came almost to a halt. While López Arellano had relied on the support of the subaltern groups to gain legitimacy and push forward his plan, Melgar Castro and the renewed military government imposed their will in more vertical terms and aligned themselves closer to the interests of the traditional elites.

The ousting of López Arellano and the watered-down version of the NDP also came to show the general balance of forces in the country, as the pressure exercised by the traditional elites and foreign capital had succeeded in stifling the most radical aspects of the reformist agenda, eliminating or dialing down those policies aimed at changing the balances of power and tackling social and economic inequalities, while maintaining those aimed at promoting economic growth.

On August 8, 1978, amid various scandals of corruption and collusion between Melgar Castro and the National Party and the supposed involvement of the military in drug trafficking, the head of the armed forces and the government was forced to step down and was replaced by a governing military junta led by Policarpo Paz García, head of the army. Soon after, the junta vowed to convene a national constituent assembly in 1980 and call for general elections in 1981, formally signaling the end of the reformist military regime and the beginning of what is usually known as the "transition toward democracy," a topic that we will explore in the subsequent chapters. However, before doing so, we will turn our eyes toward one of the proposed central technologies for the modernization of the Honduran nation: the agrarian reform.

**CHAPTER 2**

# Disciplining Peasants, Disciplining the Land
## The Political Economy of the Honduran Agrarian Reform in the Bajo Aguán (1962–1980)

> Well, my dad is from there [Copán], and they told him to come here, right? Always searching, because the lands over there were barren [*quemadas*], very little money to be made ... So, they came, searching for the Coast, that is how they call it here, "Let's go to the Coast."
> —Gonzalo

> So, he [the INA organizer] told us: Look, here we cannot give you these lands, but we already have lots ready for you in Colón. There—he said—we are going to give each family ten hectares of land to work individually.... That really made us happy, because we did not have anywhere to work. The problem began when we got here.
> —Marcelo

> The organization started with [Hurricane] Fifí because we were left with our arms crossed [idle, unemployed], after the river flooded, and we lived close to the river. Aha, we were left then with almost nothing. And then, after a time, I came to Colón with the idea of having some land.
> —Eugenia

To say that Gonzalo, Marcelo, and Eugenia's lives did not pan out as they had hoped is an understatement. Born into poverty in the country's western highlands, they have existed in constant struggle and motion: motion, as they migrated toward the fertile lands of the Aguán, and struggle against "nature"—as they brought down forests to grow maize and oil palms from the 1970s onward. It was also struggle against the state, which persistently tried, and in a sense succeeded, in transforming them into something other than what they wanted to be. In brief, they experienced constant struggle against poverty and dispossession that not only marked their personal histories but also illustrates the shared experience of the waves of peasant families that flocked toward the Aguán from the 1970s onward in search of a piece of land they could call "theirs" and a better life.

Exploring these lives, and particularly those of Gonzalo, Marcelo, and Eugenia—whose experiences are the narrative threads of this chapter—provides us with a privileged window into the inner works of the Honduran agrarian reform that began formally under the government of Villeda Morales but picked up steam and traction in the 1970s, under military control. Our focus here will be the Bajo Aguán Project: a colonization scheme that was supposed to turn the "empty" and fertile lands of the Valley of the Aguán into a modern development hub and transform a bunch of unruly and "traditional" peasant households into productive (and consuming) citizens.

By the 1980s, when the Honduran agrarian reform was running on its last steam, it became evident that it had failed on both accounts. Not only were most of the households that had embarked on the colonization scheme as poor as the rest of the rural population in the country but the cooperatives and other forms of peasant collective enterprises created were struggling economically. However, at the same time, the agrarian reform had been quite successful in curbing agrarian conflict in the country, as well as creating a new set of agrarian landscapes, oriented toward commercial agriculture, be it for the domestic market or exports. At the crux of this dual process stands the creation of a new social actor: a form of peasantry cultured in the production of palm oil and collective labor.[1]

We find in Antonio Gramsci's (1971) thoughts on Americanism and Fordism some useful cues for thinking about this process. While most of his discussions on passive revolution in the *Prison Notebooks* focus on the historical past, in the notes organized under this title the Italian communist explores a set of dynamics taking place in his lifetime. For him, the basic question was the possible impact that the inclusion of the mass standardized production model that Ford had implemented in his factories, as well as the rationalization of labor proposed under Taylorism, could have for contemporary Italian society. While certain parts of his discussion are quite dated (particularly his comments on sexuality, feminism, and the family), his explorations of "the biggest collective effort to date to create, with unprecedented speed, and with a consciousness of purpose unmatched in history, a new type of worker and of man" (Gramsci 1971, 302) show neatly how the transformation of both the production process and the private lives of workers necessarily results in new conceptions of the world. In other words, Gramsci posits that for social and historical change to be durable, it is necessary to articulate—bring together and enunciate—new relations both of production and of social reproduction.

For Gramsci, in the Fordist United States, this new form of hegemony was born in the factory.[2] This was possible due to the lack, in the United States, of the "parasitic" or rentier rural classes that still had a dominant position in the "Old World" (Gramsci 1971, 285). As such, under Fordism, the shift toward mass production came with significant changes in the economic, cultural, and psychological fabric of society, ensuring the subordinate position of the working classes.

While Fordism as a concept is a questionable one, plagued with problems of inconsistency and vagueness, particularly when applied to agriculture (Goodman and Watts 1994), many of the questions that Gramsci poses regarding the factory resonate with the function that the agrarian reforms, as a set of technologies, were supposed to have in the Latin American rural areas. If progress was to be attained and revolution subverted, a dual transformation was needed: "traditional" peasants needed to be molded into market dependent and productive modern citizens, while self-provisioning peasant farms, unproductive large estates, and forests needed to be turned into industrialized fields and processing plants that produced for the market.

The production of particular subjects and landscapes is the necessary corollary to this process. There is nothing "natural" about a prevailing conception of the world that is the result of earlier historical struggles that become sedimented, quite literally, in space (Mitchell 1996; Wainwright 2012; Fontana 2012). In other words, the process of disciplining and creating a new type of men and women is inscribed spatially, highlighting or making visible certain elements while rendering others invisible. These politics of visibility are crucial for the exercise of domination and control. According to James Scott (1998, 2), the production of a political gaze that simplifies society and its landscapes to make it "legible" is one of the central characteristics of the modern process of state formation. The transformation of spaces understood as unruly and fallow into spaces of order, and the inscription into these spaces of social relations perceived as productive and/or desirable, also becomes a process of shaping people into behaving in specific ways (Sioh 2004).

In this chapter, I follow the migration trajectories of Gonzalo, Marcelo, and Eugenia to look at the process of producing both landscapes and subjects, as it took shape through the implementation of the BAP. My main argument is that the agrarian reform was a profoundly gendered process through which a new peasantry was produced. This production was oriented toward the creation of the conditions for capital accumulation and securing the passiveness of the peasantry. As I will show, far from improving the living conditions of the targeted population, the agrarian reform placed peasant households in a set of relations of dependency to the palm oil plantation economy, expressed in the monetization of the relations of social reproduction.

## Agrarian Reform in Latin America and the Social Function of Property

From the 1950s onward, there was a consensus in Latin American political circles that times were changing. As global capitalism reconstructed itself around developmentalist policies and governments and the United States and the Soviet Union struggled for global supremacy, modernization came to be seen as the cure for every society's ailment. The diagnosis for Latin America, as presented by the highly influential Economic Commission for Latin America and the Caribbean, was very straightforward: the region had a subordinate position in the global economy due to an economic structure based on exporting raw materials and importing everything else. Thus, the solution was to promote industrialization to add value to exports and substitute some of the imported commodities for domestic goods. This model came to be known as imports substitution industrialization (ISI), which took different shapes in different parts of the region and was also embraced by those sectors of the Left closer to "dependency theory," as it fit with their interpretation of the relations between center and periphery regions (Grosfoguel 1997; Kay 2011).

One of the central elements of this model was the land question. Most of the literature discussing the problem of development and progress in this period agrees that one of the main reasons for Latin America's underdevelopment was the agrarian structure inherited from the colonial period, organized around the hacienda system (Stein and Stein 1970; Thiesenhusen 1995). This system was deemed as highly inefficient, relying mainly on unpaid labor and extensive land use, with minimal use of technology. Spatially it was characterized by large haciendas or latifunds, owned by the local elites and occupying the best lands, which were surrounded by a sea of impoverished Lilliputian estates (minifunds) located mainly in marginal lands. As a result, besides being inefficient, the system was also highly unequal in terms of land tenure. Thus, it followed that in political economic terms the first step on the road to progress was to get rid of this system through a process of agrarian reform that would democratize tenure and improve productivity.

These explicit objectives coincided with two more implicitly political ones. On the one hand, at its core, the hacienda system represented the concentrated political power—in the form of the control of land as a source of wealth, prestige, and influence—of a small and rather homogeneous landowning oligarchy. Thus, to break the oligarchy's control over land was to break their monopoly over the state and open spaces for the nascent industrial and commercial bourgeoisie. On the other hand, distributing land to landless peasants was a way of curbing their increasing combativeness and constructing an alliance with the reformist sectors. This second point became particularly salient in the aftermath of the Cuban Revolution of 1959, when the promotion of "democratic" agrarian reforms became the preemptive measure par excellence against the spread of the communist threat.

The Latin American agrarian reforms were deeply informed by the logic of the "social function doctrine," which proposed that property had to be in the service of the common good of society and not exclusively of the owning individual.[3] In practice, what this social function of property meant for agrarian policy, and the exact combination between redistributive justice and productivity that it contained, depended on the outcome of a dispute between three rural projects: (1) an oligarchic project, advanced by the traditional landowning elites who tried to push against the agrarian reforms, which they billed as communist and endangering the sacrosanctity of private property; (2) a reformist project, headed by the new industrial and commercial bourgeoisie, in alliance with reformist sectors of the labor and peasant movements, that promoted agrarian reforms to both undermine the control of the traditional landowning elites over the state and create the conditions for new dynamics of capital accumulation; and (3) a popular project, primarily comprising the more radical sectors of the labor and peasant movement, which saw in the call for agrarian reforms an opportunity to recover that which had been taken away from the working classes and create a new society from the bottom up.

In those limited cases where revolutionary governments embarked on agrarian reform (for example, Cuba or early Sandinista Nicaragua), it tilted toward redistributive justice. In other cases, productivity reigned supreme, in what Cristobal Kay (1998) dubs "modernization from above": under the threat of expropriation unless they put their lands to "work," many large landowners begin to invest in technology to improve productivity. At the same time, since land could not be left fallow, many of them expanded the scale of production and introduced new products.

In the case of Central America, for example, from the 1960s onward cotton and cattle farming began to expand in the region, with the introduction of new dynamics of production (Williams 1986). The state was central in all these processes. Kay concludes that, although the overall balance of the agrarian reforms in the region is mixed, the most significant changes aimed at creating the institutional conditions for the modernization of the countryside, thus promoting capitalist agriculture, with the large capitalist farmers as the main winners.

Moreover, most of the Latin American agrarian reforms relied more on colonization schemes than on a transformation of the agrarian structure. The appeal of colonization over restructuring was twofold. First, it was cheaper and easier for the state, as no expropriations needed to be paid, and no powerful actors were aggrieved. Second, the inclusion into the national economy of lands deemed as "empty wastelands" created and expanded productive landscapes, without expanding productivity. This is clearly an example of the tendency toward convening space in temporal terms noted by Massey. Under the logic of modernization, other ways of being in the world, and of conceiving the relationship between society and nature, could only be understood as backward and anachronistic. As such, good intentions aside, the process of agrarian reform in Latin America must be understood in relation to a longer project of racist and imperial dispossession and extermination of Indigenous, peasant, and Black communities in the name of progress and development.

To sum up, the implementation of the agrarian reforms in Latin America of the 1960s through the 1970s was a form of passive revolution. Under the promise of transforming the agrarian structure and creating a democratic and inclusive future, the agrarian trajectory of most of the region's countries was imposed from above. This is not to dismiss the role of pressure from below, as the speed and depth of the reform was very much informed by peasant mobilization. However, as the objective of productivity superseded the goal of redistributive justice, this path of agrarian modernization allowed the traditional landowning elites to retain their economic and political privileges in exchange for the inclusion of the incipient commercial and industrial bourgeoisie within the ruling class. At the same time, peasants and workers, enticed by the motto of "the land to the tiller,"[4] struggled against the old powers, forging alliances with the emerging ones, only to end up being betrayed by all by the 1990s. Nonetheless, both the peasantry that entered the processes of agrarian reform from the 1960s onward and the landscapes in which they dwelled and worked were very different from those that emerged in the neoliberal period of the 1990s, as we will see in the next chapter.

## Agrarian Reform and the "Historical Actualization" of Honduras

Honduras's agrarian reform stemmed from three intersecting processes that I characterized in the previous chapter: (1) the increasing political activity and levels of organization of the peasant and labor movements in the aftermath of the 1954 strike; (2) the rise through the military ranks of a new generation of reformist and foreign-trained officials, particularly after the 1969 military debacle against El Salvador; and (3) the U.S. foreign policy shift toward the region after the Cuban Revolution of 1959.

The process of reform proceeded in different phases that began to take shape in the 1960s under the Villeda Morales truncated government, picked up traction and speed in the early 1970s with the rise to power of López Arellano's military government, and finally came to a standstill in the 1980s. As befits a policy dubbed the "fundamental task" of the process of "historical actualization" of Honduras, the explicit aims of the agrarian reform were very grand. According to the agrarian reform law of 1974/5 (Decree-law number 170, approved on December 30, 1974), its objectives were (1) to transform the country's agrarian structure by replacing the latifund-minifund system with a land tenure and exploitation system that would guarantee social justice in the countryside and augment the agricultural sector's productivity (article 1) and (2) to secure the active and equal participation of the peasantry in the process of social, political, and economic development of the nation (article 3). The agrarian reform became the centerpiece of the nation's development strategy; as such, the rest of the government's political and social policies had to be formulated and executed accordingly. This included particularly those policies related to education, health, housing, employment, infrastructure, commercialization, technical assistance, and credit (article 2).

However, there was also a clear sense that distributing land was not enough, as the Honduran peasantry was deemed by the reformists as too backward-minded due to its squalid living conditions and lack of education (see IDHER 2018). For the agrarian reform to be successful in its modernizing intent, it was necessary to civilize the peasantry. At the crux of the reformists' concerns was the peasants' supposed tendency toward individualism and isolation, as they allegedly preferred to produce for themselves rather than for the market.

There was also a problem of scale. According to the modernist perspective of those in charge of the agrarian reform process, large scale agricultural enterprises, which combined collective labor with technology, were far more productive than smaller, family-exploited individual lots. Thus, from the beginning, the idea of agrarian reform was accompanied by a pedagogical concern: how to turn traditional and backward peasants into modern and productive citizens, while turning Lilliputian and unproductive lots into large modern and productive estates?

Before the 1970s no one in the government knew how to tackle this question, which led the military to seek the support of the United Nations. As a result, in March 1973 the Agrarian Reform Peasant Training Program (Programa de Capacitación Campesina para la Reforma Agraria—PROCCARA) was created with the support of the Food and Agriculture Organization, under the direction of the Brazilian sociologist Clodomir Santos de Morais.[5]

The training provided by PROCCARA was based on Santos de Morais's methodology of experimental workshops on the theory of organization, grounded in his interpretation of historical materialism. In his view, different types and experiences of work engendered different work cultures. He proposed a spectrum of workers that ranged from "artisans" to salaried "workers." While the former were engaged in the entire seamless production process from top to bottom, the latter's activity involved the social division of labor and was superior in terms of productivity. Further, as society developed, the artisan mode of life was destined to disappear. Thus, the only way forward for those artisans and small producers being cornered by modernization and development was to become "entrepreneurially literate" (trained) in the mode of production and organization based on the division of labor. This training would allow them to overcome the individualizing "deviations" of the artisan mode and acquire a new collective "organizational consciousness." According to Miguel Sobrado (2000, 18), one of Santos de Morais's most prominent followers in Central America, the workshops organized along these lines were

> a practice in organizational capacitation [sic] that unleashes a prodigious amount of social synergy. Inside this practice "the worker" will emerge as a new positive social value and force. Being a "worker" means to have learned to cooperate with others; to be modest (to know one's place in the whole), but, at the same time, to be disciplined and systematic in the planning and execution of the set tasks of the enterprise. Setbacks and failures are usually attributable to the "simple" (non-complex) and self-sufficient "artisan" ways, which are dysfunctional in the context of a complex organization, as well as to the "opportunist" artisan character and behavioural traits that will tend to subordinate the needs for proper planning and organization by the group to immediate, short-sighted individual(istic) needs. Thus, in the context of the workshop as envisioned by de Morais, the "artisan way" will soon acquire negative connotations because of the pettiness and self-centredness of the individualistic spirit that is typical here. "Organizational vigilance" is therefore required to counteract and continue to overcome those artisan "deviations." The need for group vigilance is an important topic during the seminars on theory of organization that are run throughout the length of the workshop.

PROCCARA operated for forty-six months, between 1973 and 1976, when the new government led by Melgar Castro decided to close it. Accused of promoting pro-communist ideas, Santos de Morais was also forced to leave the country. During its time, a total of 17,400 peasants participated in the program, roughly 39 percent of all agrarian reform beneficiaries up to that point. At the same time, this was not the only effort directed toward the production of this new subject. For example, the Catholic Church, with the support of the national peasant organizations, carried out literacy campaigns via radio. What these programs had in common was the attack against the supposedly ingrained individualism of the peasantry and the exaltation of cooperation, following orders, and working for others as the way toward the modernization of the country. In other words, they aimed at convincing peasants to leave behind their traditional individuality and become members of a larger and abstract collective: the Honduran nation.

While male peasants took part in training programs like the one promoted by PROCCARA, their wives attended "housewife clubs," where they learned about hygiene, how to prepare food, and the importance of sending their children to school (Ooijens et al. 1990). In this vein, it is important to remember that the central unit of the agrarian reform was supposed to be the heteropatriarchal household: while men played the role of breadwinner, women were supposed to take care of the reproductive work and children were supposed to learn these roles to repeat them in the future. What these arrangements did in practice was to exclude most women as beneficiaries of the agrarian reform, while deepening their economic dependency on their male counterparts (Deere and León 2004; Montoya 2003; Jacobs 2009; Yie Garzón 2015). As we will see further on, this model also came to divide the spaces of "men" from those of "women," which had an important impact in the capacity of the Honduran organized peasantry to resist the process of agrarian counterreform of the 1990s.

This pedagogical and disciplinary exercise had an institutional correlation. In Honduras land was distributed mainly collectively in the form of cooperatives and peasant associative enterprises, because collective work was understood as the precondition for the creation and exploitation of the productive landscapes that were being envisioned. Further, cooperative enterprises were easier to control, since they came with mechanisms of self-discipline, such as the obligatory internal vigilance boards mandated by the agrarian reform legal framework. Thus, under the logic of collective land tenure and the alleged superiority of collective work, a whole disciplinary program was deployed, aiming at producing a set of new productive landscapes, exploited by a (male) "collective worker" well-attuned to the necessities of capital accumulation. However, as usually happens with what James Scott (1998) dubs "high modernist projects," there is a big difference between how they are imagined and the reality that they end up conjuring.

### Mission 105 and the Bajo Aguán Project

As early as 1960, a year before the famous Conference of Punta del Este at which the Alliance for Progress was officially launched, the Honduran government had requested support from the OAS to design an extended agrarian reform plan. The initial letter of intent went beyond land redistribution and proposed a set of broader reforms that together seemed to point toward a grand agrarian development program that included both agricultural and industrial development. Toward the end of 1960, the OAS sent a multidisciplinary group of specialists to Honduras, which came to be known as Mission 105. Due to the lack of the necessary technical information (climatic, hydrological, and morphological, among others), Mission 105 limited itself to proposing two colonization projects: one in the south of the country and the other in the Aguán River basin in the northeast.

Regarding the Aguán, the initial objective was an integrated development project that would include the entire river basin. However, since the country did not have the minimal necessary financial and human resources to develop such a grand project, and since foreign banana companies controlled much of the land in the higher sectors of the river basin, it was decided to focus only on one section, the Bajo or Lower Aguán. The idea was that after the completion of this first part, it would be possible to expand toward the middle and upper parts of the basin. On March 4, 1964, the general secretary of the OAS, Uruguayan José Mora, handed the Honduran government the resulting document titled Proyecto Bajo Aguán (Lower Aguán Project; BAP). The Honduran Rigoberto Sandoval Corea, who was then working for the IDB and later become the mastermind of the country's agrarian reform process, presented the report.

The original BAP proposed by Mission 105 was very ambitious. It suggested creating all the necessary infrastructure and the financial and technical conditions so that "following an ordered plan, the river basin . . . [could] be in full production in approximately 10 years" (OAS 1964, 2). The envisioned project was expected to inscribe civilization and development into a region that was rich in natural resources but allegedly "empty" and "idle." For example, early in the document we are told that "these lands, most of which were very fertile, had been returned to the State by a banana company that exploited them for several years. However, due to the deterioration of the infrastructure, these lands are currently semi-abandoned and populated in part by occupants whose activities do not contribute to fulfilling the economic potential of the region" (OAS 1964, 4). On the next page, the document asserts that the Aguán "possesses the [country's] most abundant and practically unexploited natural resources" and that "the project will be the first step in what could be called the 'the march toward the East'" (p. 5), that is, toward the colonization of the region of the Mosquitia.

During the 1920s and 1930s, the Aguán had been the home of the Truxillo Railroad Company, which cut down vast quantities of valuable hardwoods to plant thousands of hectares of bananas. The fact that in the early years it bought most of its bananas from small local producers speaks not only of the transformation of the landscape—from tropical forest to banana plantation—but also of some social organization, involving groups of small producers and railway and plantation workers (Soluri 2009). By the 1940s, the company had abandoned many of the banana farms due to the spread of the Panama disease. In the postwar period, the companies had all but left the Aguán, giving way to scattered settlements of ex-banana and railway workers, Garifuna communities, landless Salvadoran immigrants, and local landowners (either former banana producers or cattle ranchers), all of whom remained largely outside the purview of the state (Casolo 2009). In terms of tenure, the region's land was divided into farms ranging from one to five hundred hectares, with a predominance of small farms (around 60 percent) (Castro 1994). However, according to the 1966 and 1974 censuses, 3.6 percent of the local population, mostly cattle ranchers and timber merchants with family links to the neighboring Department of Olancho, owned 87 percent of the land (Macías 2001).

Thus, the BAP should not be understood as the inscription of a development project in a socially empty space. Rather, it was part of the broader logic of the "long Green Revolution" that proposed to transform a set of lands that were deemed as inefficient and unproductive into a collection of productive landscapes while changing the balance of class forces, reconfiguring the relations with nature and the dynamics of production and reproduction in the process (Patel 2013).

The main explicit objective of the epic march toward the east was to colonize around seventy thousand hectares and "to incorporate to the money economy and improve the living conditions of 6,059 peasant families . . ., reaching a level that will allow them to produce enough food to improve their diet, as well as producing surpluses for national and international markets" (OAS 1964, 4–5).

The BAP aimed to bring the peasant families into the logic of the market in two main ways: on the one hand, by promoting the production of export-oriented cash crops, such as oil palms, cacao, and citrus trees and on the other, by providing financial and technical support to improve the productivity of staple food production—mainly maize and beans—to supply both the domestic and Central American markets. In the initial plan, beneficiaries would receive individual lots, whose size would depend on their location and would range from ten to sixteen hectares, depending on the fertility of the soil. Through the INA and the state banking sector, the beneficiaries would receive financial and technical support, and the farms would be furnished with basic improvements, such as irrigation ditches and water wells. Housing projects would also cover all the beneficiaries. The construction formula was easy: the state would provide the needed materials, and the beneficiaries would provide most of the (unpaid) labor.

The selection of the beneficiaries was not left to chance, either. In addition to the selection criteria in article 79 of the agrarian reform law—beneficiaries had to be Honduran, male (or female head of household), at least sixteen years old, own no or minimal land and have as an occupation agricultural labor—the BAP presented a set of "specific characteristics, which define the individual and family group aptitude of the future beneficiaries" (OAS 1964, 152). These characteristics included "working capacity" and "general conditions." Regarding working capacity, "it will be measured through the point system proposed by the sociologist Arrigo Serpieri. . . . In this system, points are accorded to the man-work unit, the consumption relation, and the future consumption relation" (OAS 1964, 153). It is worth noting that Serpiere was undersecretary of the Ministry of Agriculture under Mussolini in 1923. In the case of general conditions, four elements were considered: conduct, habits, health, and education.

As this quick overview suggests, the project proposed by the OAS report was not only quite ambitious but also all-encompassing. It included almost every aspect of the beneficiaries' future life: from what and how to produce to where they should live, from what their homes should look like to the type of attitudes that they should have. All of these were to be under the control of the state in the form of the colonization authorities. The project drafted by Mission 105 imagined the BAP as an institutional and development hub that could later be replicated in other parts of the country. Within this vision, peasant families would become efficient cash crop producers and promoters of the country's development.

In practice, however, the BAP took a very different shape. The final US$7.7 million agreement between the OAS and the Honduran government was signed on October 2, 1969, nearly a decade after the original letter of intent was signed. The total cost of the project was estimated at US$13.1 million, leaving the government to provide the other 41 percent. However, the project suffered significant delays due in part to the 1969 war with El Salvador; furthermore, at the time, there were no clear legal procedures regarding land tenure. Thus, in practice, the project only kicked off at the end of 1971, twenty-four months later than initially planned. Also, the BAP got off to a slow start and only began to gain momentum with the signing of Decree no. 8 (1972) and Law-Decree no. 170 (1974/5). Because of these delays, as well as the destruction caused by Hurricane Fifí (September 1974), the budgetary disbursements were pushed back another twelve months, to April 1977. A final element that also influenced these delays was the decision in 1972 to change the original plan from a focus on individual farms toward the framework of peasant cooperatives.

The approach of the state, and specifically that of the INA, to the region evolved in two stages. First, from 1971 to around 1975, the BAP got off to a rocky and shaky start as the money from the IAB still had not rolled in and the military had not yet seized formal control of the state; this was a moment of slow advance. Second, from 1975 onward, after the 1972 coup and the passing of the agrarian law, the military state approached the colonization endeavor as it knew best: through vertical control and a ruthless exercise of force that left little space for dissent. In 1977 the international funds for the BAP finally kicked in and the actual plan of enrolling participants in different parts of the country began.

In the first period (1971–75), the original Mission 105 text of the BAP mentioned the local population of the region and included them as potential members of the future cooperatives. However, once the project picked up steam, it became harder and harder for locals not only to participate in the cooperatives but also to hold on to the land they had lived on up to that moment. From the perspective of the state, since all these lands had been abandoned by the banana companies, they were state-owned and not fulfilling their social function; thus, most local dwellers were deemed illegal squatters.

Everyone I met who had been living in the Aguán prior to the arrival of the INA and the BAP remembered this period with bitterness, as they were told that the land on which they had lived all their lives was not really theirs, and that they must now understand themselves not as poor landowners but as poor landless peasants.[6] Three elements saturate their "memories of dispossession" (Hart 2006): first, that although they agreed with the idea of giving land to the poor, they were against how it was done; second, that the state had lied to them; and third, that the whole process was tilted in favor of the "foreigners" and the local *terratenientes* (large landlords), and against the poor "locals."

Luis is a schoolteacher who was born and raised close to the town of Tocoa in the middle of the Aguán Valley. When I asked him about how the town was before the cooperatives arrived, he responded bitterly:

> Before the cooperatives arrived, Tocoa was a hard-working agricultural town with little education, very few schools... Here each independent peasant enjoyed having up to eight milk cows, and there was no enclosed property in the hands of the poor. Only the rich had barbwire fences to keep their cattle, but for the poor, it was a free space. And everything was abundant: maize, beans, rice, pork, cattle, milk, cream, everything in abundance. The daily wage was a lempira [around US$0.50 at that time] ... It was, we could say, a more individual [independent] lifestyle.

"The process of intrigue began once the cooperatives arrived," Luis continued. As our conversation shifted to that period, he said,

> The agrarian reform brought peasants from the south, from Intibucá [in the west]; groups of many trucks would come into the settlements with the military and evict the owners of the land. Then the peasant [that was living in the region before the BAP] began to emigrate; their sons began to migrate to other places... So, we had a rivalry, and the *cooperativista* [cooperative member] hated the independent peasant because the latter resented that his patrimony had been taken away.... It was then, after the agrarian reform with the settlements, that the independent peasants began to move to the *cerros* [the surrounding hills]. Because they didn't have any other option, because they saw that [oil] palms covered everything and it was a labyrinth, and major discords began, and there were a lot of deaths.

For Luis, the independent peasant's world was opposed to that of the cooperatives, with their collective labor and support from the state. With the cooperatives, the variety of crops gave way to the monoculture of oil palm and its labyrinthine and monotonous landscapes. The only seeming constant was that of the large landowner, of the valley's rich.

It should come as no surprise, then, that during the first year of the project, the message "*INA fuera del Aguán*" (INA leave the Aguán) was scribbled in walls all over Tocoa, or that trucks and other machinery were vandalized at night. This resistance to the agrarian reform and the INA was not limited to poor peasants, such as Luis's parents, but also involved the valley's local elites.

However, according to the testimonies that I was able to collect, the rich managed to keep their lands or to be relocated to other places. Don José, for example, a member of La Norteña Cooperative, remembers how his father had a thirty-hectare farm on the hillsides close to Tocoa. The functionaries of INA informed him that he should either join a cooperative or lose his land. He "opted" to join but later learned that his former farm was given to the Nájera family, one of the richest and most influential in the Aguán to whose history we will return later in the book, in return for a piece of land that they had lost in the valley's lowlands.

These sorts of negotiations between local elites and the government highlight the fact that capital accumulation—and hegemony for that matter—is never promoted or conducted in a vacuum. The BAP was installed in a place that, far from being "empty," was at the time filled with political dynamics and tensions and particular relations of domination which—as Luis so eloquently describes—articulated the local cattle ranching elite with the poor peasantry that also inhabited the region. Thus, more than simply imposing its will upon the region, the state had to negotiate with the local dominant groups, in order to lubricate the sociopolitical landscape and allow the agrarian reform to gain traction on the ground.

This local history upon which the BAP was imposed was also informed by a clear differentiation between the Aguán River's left and right banks. Already during the period of the banana plantations, there was an apparent concentration of both infrastructure and production in the river's right bank, which also affected population patterns once the companies left, as most people concentrated around the town of Tocoa. This situation also came to inform the design and implementation of the BAP, as the right bank had better infrastructure and year-round accessibility; thus, the first cooperatives created in the region—Salamá in 1971, quickly followed by La Confianza, Central Aguán, La Zamora, and La San Isidro—were all located on the right bank, relatively close to Tocoa.

### The March to the East from Below

From the point of view of the state, the BAP started with the negotiations with the OAS and the promise of national development. However, the reasons that led to the arrival of so many families to the Aguán during this period were many years in the making. I already mentioned how the 1954 general strike had sparked a set of agrarian conflicts all over the north coast and the "banana republic." At the same time, in the area outside the influence of the banana enclave, toward the south of the country, accelerated proletarianization and land dispossession led to a cattle elite controlling most of the land and labor, which encouraged the expansion of the cattle, sugar, and cotton industries, resulting in an increasing number of conflicts between landowners and peasants (Williams 1986; Boyer 1982). In the west, in the lands where Marcelo, Eugenia, and Martino were born, there was a strong Lenca Indigenous component, and communities were under siege by local elites and the influx of impoverished peasant migrants and Indigenous Chorti families from Guatemala and El Salvador, which in turn led to a significant land squeeze (Anderson 1983; Chapman 1985; Jansen 1998). As a result, most of those who arrived in the BAP before the mid-1970s did so through the effort of national peasant organizations and because of the agrarian conflicts in their hometowns.

Here, the differences between the various organizations mattered. In 1962 the more radicalized sectors of the peasant movement created the National Peasant Federation of Honduras (FENACH). Anti-imperialist in discourse and heavily inspired by the Cuban Revolution, the FENACH mainly promoted the "recuperation" of lands that were under control of foreign owners, such as the banana companies.[7] Further, they understood their fight as not only for the betterment of peasant families but for the transformation of the country as a whole. The same year of 1962 also saw the formation of the ANACH, with the support of Villeda Morales's government and the blessing of the U.S. American Federation of Labor-Congress of Industrial Organizations (AFL-CIO). In contrast to FENACH's incendiary discourse, ANACH was from the beginning much more moderate and willing to play within the framework of the reformist military regime. This cleavage within the peasant movement was clearly informed by the logic of the Cold War, as FENACH aligned closer to the radical Left and the ideas of anti-imperialist revolution, and ANACH with a reformist and anticommunist position. This is not to say that ANACH has always been passive and obedient to the designs of the state; I already mentioned how their threat of staging a "hunger march" led to the 1972 coup. Rather, the point is that it is clear that their main function was to co-opt, diffuse, and give a less explosive outlet to the peasant conflicts taking place in different parts of the country. As such, it should come as no surprise that most of the cooperatives that were created within the BAP were affiliated to the ANACH.

For example, Marcelo remembers well that the harsh life that he and his wife had back in Copán forced him to join ANACH and occupy a piece of land that they considered "empty."

There [in Copán], we would each contribute with six lempiras when the daily wage was two lempiras. We got organized; we made a big sacrifice... We applied for the land [that they were occupying], and after two years of waiting, the state tells us that they are going to sell us the land. An INA promoter came and told us that we had to make a contract to acquire the land. However, it happened that there were a lot of precious woods in the land: cedar, mahogany... So he [INA promoter] came back and told us, "Look, we can't give you this land, but we have some other land ready in Colón. There—he told us—we are going to give each associate ten hectares of land to work individually." That made us happy, as we didn't have anywhere to work... But the problems began when we got here.

Most of the cases that I encountered during my stay in the Aguán followed this similar pattern: the peasants would first join a national peasant organization (in this case, ANACH) to continue in their struggle for land, to later be told that they would have to migrate to the Department of Colón and the BAP. It is important to add that before 1977 the role of the state was to enable migration toward the region, but the actual organizing and logistics of the trip were undertaken by the peasant organizations (Castro 1994).

Marcelo remembers that once they were ready, ANACH hired a convoy of trucks to take them and all the possessions that they could carry from their hometown in Copán to the Aguán. They had to go with an armed escort since the local population was against their arrival. Once there, their original group of families was divided up among several cooperatives. When I asked Marcelo about how he remembers the place when he first arrived, he said emphatically, "These really dense forests! There were big trees, really thick bush."

Shortly after Marcelo's arrival on the left bank of the Aguán, in September 1974, Hurricane Fifí struck. In the aftermath of the disaster, the types of families selected into the BAP expanded to include those affected by the hurricane. Further, the state moved from simple enabler to active promoter of the migrations. By 1977, with the inflow of OAS funds, the INA had opened offices in Choluteca (in the south of the country), Comayagua (center), and Santa Rosa de Copán (west) (Castro 1994). The idea was not to create new cooperatives but rather to fill the already existing ones. This was connected to the high levels of desertion from the original cooperatives, which was due both to the region's rough climate, which had higher temperatures than the hometowns of many of the immigrants, and to the disciplining dynamics enforced by the agrarian reform.

We find an example of the relationship between Hurricane Fifí and migration toward the Aguán in the lives of Eugenia and Marino. They had left Copán in the late 1960s in search of a better life on the north coast. After relocating to the municipality of Esparta in the department of Atlántida, they built a *champita* (small hut made of palm leaves and mud-covered walls) close to a river. When Fifí struck, the river overflowed and left them homeless and with their "arms crossed" (without work), as Marino would phrase it. In the aftermath of the hurricane, the peasant organizations began the process of organizing the affected families. Just as in the case described by Marcelo, this process was carried out by ANACH. Eugenia and Morino recall they were told that once they got to the Aguán, everything would be different and they would have land to work and food to eat—that everything was pretty much ready. Then, perhaps five trucks arrived to take them east. Eugenia remembers putting into the truck not only her clothes and other meager possessions but also a few chickens that she owned. However, once they got to the Aguán their difficulties continued:

> When we got here, we arrived with the two girls, we came to eat rotten maize, they gave us rotten fish and wet oatmeal, damp, and with a funny smell, but we had to eat it because there was nothing else... Because of him [Marino], for the land is that we came. Then we started to see that there was no drinking water, and it was then that I felt really uncomfortable, "Damn! Let's better go away from here," I told them. "No," he responded, "we already went and saw the lands, they are excellent lands, and we are going to make *milpa*." And my mom would also support me. She used to tell me, "no, daughter, to better yourself, you have to suffer, there is no water here, but we will find a way." We made *champas* with sheet metal, there we cooked and we took out water with plastic containers from some really deep wells. And most of the people were fighting over the little water that there was. And if we didn't cover the well, the next day that we could come, we would find frogs and rotten logs, everything would fall there, and we would pull out the container with water and frogs would be in there. So, we would throw them away and drink the water. It was awful! I don't even want to remember.

Coming from challenging contexts, framed by dynamics of dispossession and "natural" disasters, these impoverished families arrived in the Aguán with the promise that they would receive plenty of suitable lands and that their lives would immediately improve. However, as we can see from these testimonies, these promises remained unrealized. For Eugenia, her bitterness was very much grounded in her immediate domestic conditions; procuring subsistence became an almost nightmarish task. In the case of Marino, he stood behind the idea of moving to the Aguán, motivated by the hope of accessing land and with it, a better future.

I found this differentiation along gender lines in many of the testimonies that I collected. The women remember the trip in terms of the everyday difficulties of procuring basic subsistence; their lived experience remains very much grounded in their immediate conditions. For example, mentions of the milpa—the slash and burn cultivation of maize, beans, and squash in the same plot—and the ability to produce their own food and nourish and care for their children were constant features in my conversations with them. In the case of men, the process was remembered rather from the perspective of the future hopes of moving away from poverty, becoming landowners, and being able to work for themselves. For example, a saying that would constantly come up in my discussions with them was the hope and pride "*de no darle el pulmón a nadie*," literally, in not giving their lung to anyone else, which meant not wanting to work for some else's enjoyment. Both gendered narratives inhabit, of course, a present of ubiquitous poverty, but while the women tended to judge the past from the standpoint of provisioning and subsistence, the men focused on the ideas of being able to work and of being forever poor.

In general, the memories of most of the people that I spoke to about this period, both "locals" and "outsiders," were saturated by three overarching elements: first, nature and their struggles against it; second, the new dynamics that coming together and working with other people brought; and third, the tensions between milpa production and the introduction of oil palm as a cash crop.

### "Las palmas del BID": Nature, Capital, and a New Laboring Subject

Nature as an external element is a pervasive theme in the memories of those who lived and arrived in the Aguán during the 1960s and 1970s. Words such as *guaimil* or jungle are often found in their narratives. Eugenia and Marino remembered the place where they arrived as wild and socially empty: "There was nothing, only *monte* [high wild grass]," she told me, "there were only mountains and a part guaimil down below." "Most of it was guaimil; other than that, there was nothing at all," Marino adds.

In the different testimonies, nature appears as something both external and opposite, but also as something exotic and potentially nourishing. Mosquito and snake bites, bad water, fevers, and other tropical diseases were just some of the dangers that they had to face. Further, this was a strange nature, one that contrasted with the types of climate, animals, and plants they had been used to in their hometowns in the west. However, at the same time, this nature provided them with new sources of nourishment through gathering and fishing. For example, Eugenia remembers this period as one of suffering, but also as one where she had to turn to collecting to feed her family: "There were a lot of tomatoes. When we couldn't find anything to eat, we would go and cut them down and roast them in the griddle, and that is how we fed the girls."

At the same time, as they transformed this wild jungle into milpa, it became a home. Eugenia remembers, "When I saw our lot, it felt like my life had changed. We now ate good maize, and I would take care of a chicken, now she would lay an egg, we were on our way, it changed, it made a difference." This production of nature—of turning this alien and hostile environment into a home—was deeply intertwined with the idea of making milpa to sustain themselves and their families. This was a very deeply ingrained element in the stories of both the migrant families coming from the west and of those already living in the region before the 1970s. These crops were seen as a form of safety, of making sure that their families would not go hungry. It should come as no surprise then that in most cases, all the ones that I learned about at least, the first thing that the members of the cooperatives did was to clear the forest and plant maize. For example, José remembers preparing and planting one hundred hectares of the crop in the La Norteña cooperative. With support from a state bank, they also bought trucks to improve their productivity. Although they were producing the same crops they had grown most of their lives, the production process was now different. In their hometowns, peasant households were used to producing in small individual plots, oriented mainly toward their self-provisioning. Now, in most cases, the land in the cooperatives was split between individual plots for each family and others to work collectively, which were worked on different days of the week. Further, a portion of the collective production had to be for the market. Here debt played a crucial role. With very few exceptions (such as in Cuba), agrarian reforms do not give the distributed land to the beneficiaries for free (Chonchol 1962). The logic behind this is twofold.

On the one hand, the beneficiaries are expected to help pay back at least a part of the money that the state spent—usually through domestic or foreign debt—in acquiring, preparing, and distributing the land. On the other hand, debt is a powerful political lever. As different authors have argued, debt can be used by creditors to direct the conduct of the indebted in particular ways. For example, the threat of losing the land forces beneficiaries to produce for the market as the only way of creating the necessary cash flow to keep up with the payments. However, this is not only an economic dynamic. Debt is deeply enmeshed with morality, in the sense of defining what is good and bad and how one should behave. Thus, as a general rule, we can claim that the relation between debtor and indebted is one of subordination, where certain particular forms of consent are continually being manufactured and resisted (Bonefeld 1995; Graeber 2012; Lazzarato 2012). In our case in point, the fact that the peasant cooperatives were born in debt translated from the beginning into a process of "agricultural intensification," which—according to Michael Watts and Judith Carney (1991, 652)—"is about getting people to work harder, a process that is social and gendered (getting some people to work harder than others) and that is typically coercive and conflictual."

The gendering of this process was particularly salient. To be a member of a cooperative, one had to work in the fields; thus, membership was dominantly masculine. Women had an indirect membership, and their activities were limited to participating in the aforementioned "housewife clubs" organized by the INA promoters. However, the fact that each household had access to an individual plot, in which the family might or might not be residing, meant that women could work on the side, rising minor livestock and some other crops. As we will see, this tenuous foothold that women may have had on the land, and thus the household's subsistence pattern, would begin to change, as the general strategy of the BAP shifted toward more profitable cash crops.

In this context, women's unpaid domestic labor was not seen as part of the productive endeavor of the cooperative and, thus, rendered invisible. This is, of course, nothing new or particular to the Honduran agrarian reform. As feminist scholars have shown us for some time now, the separation between productive and reproductive labor has been crucial for the dominance and survival of capitalism, as well as the subordination of women to men (Federici 2004; Fraser 2017). Further, as Verena Stolcke (1988, xv) reminds us, "workers" as a generic category, is deeply masculinist: "Besides their class position the women and men are also part of family relations and responsibilities which shape their respective identities as workers."

The point that I want to make is that by looking at how the changes in the relations of production were "domesticated" (Carney and Watts 1990), that is, translated and incorporated into the internal dynamics of the household, we can explore how the disciplining dynamics operated. Further, and this will become a crucial point in the next chapter, by looking at how the agrarian reform cooperatives were assembled along gender lines, we can get a better understanding of the conditions of possibility for the process of agrarian counterreform that would take place in the 1990s. A particularly fruitful way of following this thread is through the process of monetization of the regional economy.

That is, we must look at how money began to colonize the relations of production and reproduction of the peasant households, placing men and women in very different positions in relation to the process as a whole (Crehan 1997; Mackintosh 1989; Mies 1986).

For example, cash crops, and particularly oil palms and citrus trees, figured importantly both in the report written by the OAS and in the letter of intentions signed between this organization and the Honduran government. However, once the actual cooperatives began to work, there was great reluctance by their members to make the shift, due mainly to the lack of knowledge that the peasant families had regarding the new crops. For example, Marino remembers vividly that, initially, people thought that you could eat the palm's fruit directly.

However, in September 1974, when Hurricane Fifí crashed into the northern coast of Honduras, this situation began to change. Fifí holds a central place in the testimonies of most of the people with whom I spoke, who remember the considerable alterations that it made to the landscape: "This used to be a wild forest!" Marcelo told me. "However, Hurricane Fifí cleared it up, and the woods were left sparse. After that, a wildfire started by the Honduras Aguán [village] and burnt all this side [Aguán River's left bank]. It finished off the deer, *tepezcuintle* [lowland paca], the entire zone was left clean since then." Indeed, Fifí's landfall was followed by three days of floods and hard winds that felled most of the trees in the valley's surrounding hills. Later, no one knows if intentionally or not, great fires raged, devouring the trees and bush. At the same time, this destruction opened the door for the penetration and consolidation of cash crops, such as oil palms and citrus trees, in the region.

According to different reports on the BAP, the planting of the palms began as early as 1971. However, for almost everyone that I spoke with, the introduction of this crop was related to Fifí. Not only did the hurricane help topple most of the forest cover—a requirement for planting the palm trees—but it also put the cooperatives' future and production plans in the hands of the INA. Here, once again, debt would play an important role.

As we can recall from José's testimony regarding the beginning period of the La Norteña cooperative, its members had received loans from the national banking system to finance their production and buy machinery. Thus, after Fifí, the cooperatives were left in terrible shape: impoverished, with their fields destroyed and deeply indebted. The INA promoters "recommended" that they shift toward more valuable cash crops as the only way in which they could continue accessing loans and paying their debts. It was in this context that oil palms went from being an unattractive alternative to a necessity.

The introduction of oil palms had a clear transnational component. From the 1950s onward, the research unit of the Standard Fruit Company in Tela had been exploring alternatives to banana in response to the spread of the Panama disease; oil palm emerged as one such alternative. It is hard to directly connect the documentation from company's research department with the decision by the OAS to finance the BAP project in Honduras. However, there was a clear differentiation regarding the financing sources of the different projects of the BAP. In the case of the palm oil industry, its extension and promotion were financed directly by the OAS and deployed by the INA. It is hard to come by reliable data in terms of how much money was spent on the different crops, but according to information from 1980, over US$9 million had been spent in the cultivation of over nine thousand hectares of oil palms (around a fifth of all the land distributed) divided in fifty-four cooperatives (Reyes 1980, 69).

The promotion of the crop from above, the lack of control over what to produce and the scant knowledge of it from below, led to a very low level of adoption and initial appropriation of the oil palms by cooperative members. For example, José remembers that, although the crop was supposed to be "theirs" as it was planted in "their" lands, most members would talk about the palms as *"las palmas son del BID"* (the palm trees are owned by the IADB). Further, when I spoke to various members of the cooperatives, they referred to the planting the palm trees in terms of the low wages that they earned, the difficult working conditions, and how little profit they made. All of this contradicted the formal logic behind the BAP. What the cooperative members saw as low wages was understood from the perspective of the INA as cash advances from a near future when the plantations would come into full production. However, from the perspective of the cooperative associates, this was clearly an exploitative relationship in which their labor was extracted almost for free. For example, Eugenia, reflecting on the process of planting the palm trees, told me:

> They were forced to plant the [palm] trees. Now you see how much the businessmen value the palm trees. It is exaggerated how much they pay for a planted tree. However, they [the cooperative members] didn't get paid for the planting. Making the hole, I don't know how you call it, all that process before production, they didn't get paid. We had to figure out how to have maize to eat, we sold maize to buy salt, sugar, and soap; but from the palm trees they didn't receive any money. So, we had to sell the eggs that the chicken laid to buy sugar, because it didn't leave anything until the production began [oil palms trees take at least two years to begin production]. But then [when the oil palms began to produce] the problem continued because they got paid very

little. I used to tell him "damn! Didn't they used to say that once the palms started to produce, things were going to change?"

Furthermore, the expansion of the surface dedicated to the oil palms created tensions within the cooperatives that were deeply gendered and produced a particular kind of geography. During the first years, as the palm trees began to grow, it was possible to plant other crops. However, after two to four years, this becomes impossible. Marcelo remembers that "when we finished clearing the land, came the issue of the promotion of the oil palms. We took out a loan and with trucks, we finished clearing out all the lands and began planting the palms, and between them, we planted maize. We always lived from eating maize, beans and rice, until the palm began covering the lanes, and we couldn't grow maize anymore."

Most women remember the impact that this process had on the nourishment and living conditions of their families. For example, Eugenia recalls the moment when the expansion of the production of the oil palms began to displace the production of staple crops:

> When the oil palm project arrived, they ran over the maize with bulldozers, without harvesting it. No, there was a lot of stupidity. I would say, "No! Women, see how they are destroying those milpas. Why are they destroying those milpas? Why didn't they harvest them?" "No"—the men would answer—"this project [the oil palm] must be, and it must be now."

Marino jumps in and adds, "They ran over the milpas, they toppled everything. Afterwards with the project, three hectares of oil palms were planted. Then a time passed, around three years, before the first harvest. Then we saw that the product that we took out of the palm was very cheap."

As we will see in the next chapter, these elements—the lack of appropriation of the process, low wages, and lack of control over what to produce—are at the center of many of the explanations regarding the selling of the cooperatives in the 1990s. However, little mention is made of how the turn to oil palm production was informed by the discipline imposed through the application of the agrarian reform. In this way, what should be seen as the effects of a particular form of understanding and using the land is instead taken as the causes. As the extension of the area dedicated to the production of oil palms grew, there was less space to produce staple crops. This meant that the reproduction of the households depended more on cash, which was in general hard to come by but practically impossible for women, who did not work in the fields and were only indirectly members of the cooperatives. As such, the new productive landscapes were controlled by men, with women losing their tenuous grip on provisioning activities, such as the cultivation of their gardens.

The necessary corollary to this process of gendered spatial transformation was the disciplining dynamics needed to enforce the move from individual or independent to collective labor. It was not easy for those families that came from the west, as well as those already located in the valley before the arrival of the BAP, to organize in a cooperative and work collectively. As we saw in Luis's testimony, the forms of organization were viewed as oppositional and related to different social relations. In the cooperative, peasants were told what to produce, when to work, and what could be done or not. For example, in the first years of the cooperatives, although many families experienced high levels of poverty, the members could not work as day laborers outside of the cooperative. Eugenia remembers this situation vividly:

> He couldn't go and work in any other place, although there was work in Guanchias [an older banana cooperative]. Those who went to work there had problems [with the cooperative's vigilance board] because they couldn't work in another place other than the cooperative. He obeyed, he didn't go, but others would sneak out and go make their *pesos* over there because if they got caught, they were sanctioned. The problem was that Guanchias would pay them five lempiras [US$2.5] per day, while there [in the cooperative] they only made two lempiras.

As we will see, these forms of discipline were too much for many of the families, who decided to abandon the cooperatives and either stay in the valley as day laborers or migrate to the surrounding hills.

### From "Virgin" to "Productive" Lands, from Guaimil to Oil Palms

By the late 1970s and early 1980s, the landscape of the Aguán valley had been radically transformed. Abandoned infrastructure was resuscitated, and families had been brought from other parts of the country to bring down the guaimil. They planted staple crops first and citrus trees and oil palms later. The weight of this transformation was carried mainly by the impoverished immigrant peasants, who thought that in the Aguán their lives would improve dramatically and quickly. The reality was different from the expectation, and their struggles against poverty and dispossession continued, but in a different setting and under different conditions. For the men, joining the cooperatives meant adapting to the "time-discipline" (Thompson 1967) of collective labor. They had little control over what was being produced and their relationship with the land that they supposedly owned was limited to a form of wage that barely covered their needs. For women, this situation meant looking for alternative ways to secure their family's nourishment, from foraging to different forms of husbandry (pigs, chickens). However, as time went by and the palm oil industry extended its chokehold across the land, these possibilities of diversifying their provisioning became harder.

This was a profoundly alienating experience. The way in which the cooperatives had been assembled did not create a sense of belonging in many of the beneficiaries, whose relation to the land seemed to be limited to working for others and receiving little to show for it. For women, the alienation was compounded by other factors, as they valued the land in terms of the forms of nourishment that it provided for their families rather than its function as a money source. However, at the same time, their position in relation to the cooperative left them in a position with less leverage to defend it. We can understand their estrangement from the land in two ways. On the one hand, their reification into housewives in charge of the reproductive labor of the household produced a sense of the land in terms of nourishment and safety. On the other hand, their relation to the land was mediated by their husbands, both in terms of ownership and the monetization of the household's provisioning.

At the same time, the cooperatives, and thus the valley, particularly the right bank of the Aguán River, came to be associated with a set of practices and forms of social control. This was the place of the oil palms labyrinths but also the seat of the INA, a place where you could find better access to services, such as education and health, as well as markets and infrastructure, but also tighter social vigilance and control. This concentration of elements and services around the city of Tocoa created a set of binary relations, and geographies, with other parts of the valley. For example, while the more successful palm oil-producing cooperatives concentrated around the right bank, most of the staple crop-producing ones were located on the left bank. This differentiation also reflected the way in which the state approached each bank. As I mentioned, the most important state institutions were based either in Tocoa itself or around the city.

Another and even more crucial spatial differentiation was that between the valley—with its better infrastructure, access to market, public services, and state support—and the surrounding hills, which had less access to these elements. At the same time, due to that same social distance from capital and state, the hills provided a greater sense of freedom and autonomy.

James Scott (2009) has argued, based on the Southeast Asian case, that historically there has been a tension between the state—with its processes of subject formation and economic taxation—and certain "zones of refuge," a notion that he borrows from Mexican anthropologist Gonzalo Aguirre Beltrán (1967). These regions are at the margins and beyond the reach of the state, inhabited by various social groups that have organized themselves in opposition to the states from which they have fled, an idea that Scott develops from his reading of Pierre Clastres (1989). He argues further that this tension usually takes the form of an opposition between the lowlands—as the place of control of the state—and hills and mountains, as privileged zones of refuge due to their remoteness and the difficulties of controlling them.

In a situation close to the one described by Scott, and which can also be found in other parts of Latin America (see for example, Gordillo 2004; Herrera 2002; Turits 2004), in the Aguán a deep contrast came to be produced between the valley and the surrounding hills. This differentiation was informed, firstly, by the social and physical distance from state power and sites of capital accumulation, and, secondly, by the climate conditions, as people coming from the west preferred the cooler temperatures of the hills to the warmer climate at the valley.

Further, as time went by and the grip of the INA and the state more generally tightened, this differentiation expanded and extended to include a set of migration movements between valley and hills. In his book on the BAP, the Jesuit priest and anthropologist Ángel Castro (1994) dedicates a whole section to those families that had decided to move and settle in the hills. He was particularly interested in understanding why anyone would choose to live in such a remote and isolated place. For him, this movement from valley to hills in the mid-to-late 1980s was directly related to the high desertion levels characterizing the cooperatives: "Besides the hard work, a peasant discipline was needed, to which you had to add the ecological conditions that weighed down on their health, particularly that of the children. Due to this, in the cooperatives there were numerous desertions" (61).

Castro identified various reasons as to why people decided to leave the valley and move up the hills. One of his informants mentions, "I remained in Tocoa for three years. I was affiliated with a construction cooperative. But it was not successful because the treasurer stole the money . . . Only a few remained. There were attempts to work the land, but we couldn't, as it was already occupied" (113). According to another testimony, "A relative of mine who knew the place encouraged me to come. I sold what I had and bought in Jazmines [in the hills] a 30-hectare farm. I bought the house of someone who now lives in the valley. The land here is good; those who come love it here" (114).

The first thing to notice from these microvignettes is the importance of kin relations in the migrating patterns: most of the people Castro interviewed came to the hills because a relative told them there was free land to be had. Second, the hills appear as an alternative to the problems in the valley, where access to land was inexorably becoming harder. According to Castro, "Those who came [to the hills] between 1979 and 1984 . . . share not having belonged to any organized group, either in the valley or their place of origin. Those who had participated in a peasant settlement or in a cooperative had done so briefly and only while an already settled relative or friend provided them with a place. Also, for many, the hills appeared initially as a place of safety, because they can experience the satisfaction of working for themselves, where nobody bothers you, and you can cultivate everything."

However, Castro continues, "this safety is shattered because, either the land has to be bought from those who arrived first and enclosed large extensions . . . or they had to take possession of a piece of land deeper in the mountain; in this case, they ran the risk of being expelled legally, as it happened to a whole village that was evicted since the State declared a good part of the mountainous territory national property and a forestry reserve" (115).

Here we see the hills again as a space of freedom and survival. However, they were now interacting directly with the closing of the agrarian frontier, which at the same time signaled an open conflict with the state and its forestry policy. In this vein, according to Castro, the later migrants to arrive the hills, from the 1980s onward, were limited to three options: first, "working in someone else's land that was yet to be cleared down, in exchange of having a single harvest," since, if they wanted to keep the land they had to buy it; second, "move deeper into the mountain and clear a piece of land"; and, finally, "there were those who decided to go down to the valley, even if only in search of a free space to build their home" (115).

It is also important to add that this differentiation between valley and hills did not only respond to a temporal dynamic. The hills presented themselves as an alternative for those searching for safety and a sense of freedom, which made living there more appealing than working in the cooperatives. One of the peasants interviewed by Castro in the hills affirmed, "I don't agree with the cooperatives, because you are under the charge of someone else and get fooled by the bigger ones. In the cooperatives, I am the owner of my wage, not of my work and sometimes not even of the salary. That is why I looked for the hills. One is used to working, and here, there is no money, but there is plenty to eat" (117). Similarly, another of Castro's informants mentions that "people go off to the mountain so that they are not dominated and can do their own thing every day. In the cooperative, however, they must work daily and follow mandatory rules. In the mountain it is better; the hard thing is to take out the produce" (118).

## The Aguán on the Eve of Dispossession

By the 1980s, the subjects and landscapes of the Aguán reflected three sets of tensions: between production and social reproduction; between the left and right banks of the Aguán River; between the valley and the surrounding hills. All these tensions were the result of the way in which the grand project of "historical actualization" of the country took shape in a place that was understood, from the standpoint of the state, as an empty wasteland. But, as I have shown, it was anything but that. Into this previously occupied space, unruly and impoverished peasant households were brought from different parts of the country to create a set of cooperatives expected to become the spearhead of the country's development project.

This economic process was also a civilizing project. Here, land operated as the intersection of a set of different disciplining and subject making techniques. First, land was the hook to attract unruly peasants. Once they were hooked, it was combined with a set of pedagogical technologies—Santos de Morais's experimental workshops, the housewives' clubs, and radio schools, among others—oriented toward the demonization of individuality and independence and the exaltation of collective labor and discipline. Furthermore, when combined with debt, land became a powerful disciplining lever. Under the threat of losing their hold on the land that had supposedly been given to them, the cooperatives began to implement relations of production that would probably have been unthinkable to their members a few years before. When nature—in the form of the Hurricane Fifí "disaster"—was added to the mix, the doors were opened for commercial agriculture, and particularly the oil palm monoculture, to take hold in the region.

As I have shown, this process of disciplining and producing certain kinds of landscapes and subjects was deeply gendered. The Honduran agrarian reform, and Latin American agrarian reforms in general, envisioned a modernized peasantry based on a patriarchal subject: the male-led household. In this vision, men, affiliated to the cooperatives, would work collectively in the fields and use the fruit of their labor to provide for their families. Women were supposed to stay home and take care of all the affective and material reproductive work needed for the continuity of the process. In other words, it was not that feminized reproductive work became irrelevant; rather, the ways in which it subsidized and sustained the work of men in the oil palm plantations were rendered invisible.

In the Aguán, we can follow the imposition of this model along the thread of monetization. As the extension of the cooperatives' land dedicated to the palm oil monoculture grew, the spaces that women could use to produce other crops or to keep animals such as pigs or chicken, diminished. As a result, more and more of the household's provisioning came from the market, strengthening the men's position within the household and, consequently, weakening that of the women. As we will see in the next chapter, this process of domestication of the capitalist relations of production through the agrarian reform would inform the process of agrarian counterreform that emerged in the 1990s.

**CHAPTER 3**

# The Hidden Abode of Primitive Accumulation
*Agrarian Counterreform, Gender, and Neoliberalism*

In the last chapter, I explored the transition from a patrimonial understanding of land to a modernization-oriented one. In theory, the former reflected and articulated the idea that (landed) property was supposed to be under the absolute control of the owner, be it an individual, a family, or a corporation, as in the case of the UFCO, with few limits placed on its usufruct and enjoyment. In practice, the tensions between more conservative and liberal sectors of the elite led to a struggle over the role of the state and the limits to property, which marked most of what is known as the liberal period (1870–1930). In contrast, the second understanding of land, which began to take shape in the 1940s, was inspired by ideas of the social function of property and proposed rather that since people in society are interdependent, property should be oriented toward the betterment of society as a whole.

Above all, these ways of understanding land are political assemblages. In the first approach, land represented both the status, power, and differences within the old landowning elite that inherited their position from the colonial period and the expanding influence of U.S. capital in the region. The second understanding reflected the dispute between this old elite and a new set of actors created by the process of political and economic modernization in the context of the Cold War: organized labor and a developing industrial bourgeoisie. However, far from a supersession, the transition between these conceptions of land was an amalgamation of a patrimonial understanding and the expansion of capitalist relations of production and monetary exchange in the market. As I have shown, the result was a process of modernization from above—a passive revolution—with agrarian reform as a central technology. Toward the 1980s, this process of modernization and the state formation that it supported—the military reformist project—began to unravel.

This unraveling was neither just local nor global but rather a complex articulation of processes, logics, and technologies that shifted the positions of actors and institutions to produce new social, economic, and ecological orderings. Usually known as neoliberalism, these new orderings became prevalent toward the turn of the century, when different national expressions of the previous developmentalist state-oriented model entered a crisis in various parts of the globe.

A large and heated debate has raged throughout the last three decades over what neoliberalism is or is not. For some, neoliberalism should be understood as a class strategy (Duménil and Lévy 2004; Harvey 2007); for others, as governmentality (Brown 2015; Gago 2015; Rose 1999); and yet for others, as an environmental project (Bakker 2010; Castree 2010; McCarthy and Prudham 2004). By themselves, each of these approaches are both correct and limited. According to Gillian Hart (2008, 680), "the challenge, rather, is coming to grips with how identifiably neoliberal projects and practices operate on terrains that always exceed them."

Focusing on the agrarian counterreform of the 1990s in the Aguán, this chapter will show how the neoliberal project began to gain traction on the ground by taking advantage of the ways in which the agrarian reform was first assembled and then undone. To do so, I return to Eugenia's story (chapter 2) to show how the process of formation of the oil palm plantations by the agrarian reform was "domesticated" along gender lines (Carney and Watts 1991; Casolo and Doshi 2013; Crehan 1997; Mackintosh 1989; Stolcke 1988) and how this domestication set the conditions of possibility for the agrarian counterreform of the 1990s. Thus, rather than looking at "neoliberalism in general," we will focus on how it operates in more "ordinary" spaces (Hart 2008; Berman-Arévalo and Ojeda 2020), by looking at what, following Nancy Fraser (2017), Silvia Federici (2004), and of course Marx (1992), I am dubbing the hidden abode of primitive accumulation.

## The Aguán's Reformed Sector Just before the Neoliberal Storm

Between 1990 and 1994, more than half of the land that was distributed nationally during the Honduran agrarian reform was sold. In the case of the Bajo Aguán, this number rises to a staggering 73.8 percent, roughly 15 percent of the total area of the region (COCOCH 2010, 24).[1] This was a ruthless process of dispossession, combining the loud compulsion of force with the silent one of the markets. However, it would be shortsighted to frame it merely as a raid conducted from outside and above. Many of the conditions of possibility were already present in the region.

As we saw in the previous chapter, the initial idea of the BAP was to bring poor peasant families from all over the country into the cash economy, mainly through the oil palm cooperatives. For this to work, they had to be able to produce for the market and generate enough monetary return to pay their debts to the state—loans for production, to acquire tools, trucks, seeds, etc. and the payment for the agrarian reform land—and still have enough to sustain themselves. Schematically, from the perspective of the cooperatives, the model looked something like this: the state, using international loans, injected money (M) into the reform sector; that money was then used to buy the means of production (C) for the cultivation of the crops; which later were sold to make a profit (M') that would allow the cooperatives to not only pay off their loans but also to sustain themselves and start the process anew. Formally then, the system looked like this: M-C-M', resembling the formula of the circulation of capital presented by Marx (1992) in volume 1 of *Capital*. In Marx's model, capitalists use their money to buy means of production in the market, to then produce commodities that are sold in the market for a profit, where at least a portion of this profit is later reinvested in expanding the scale of the operation.

However, Indian economist Kalyan Sanyal (2013) persuasively argues that other types of economic enterprises operate under this same model but are ruled by different logics. Dubbed by Sanyal as "need economies," these enterprises begin with a monetary fund (the INA-funneled loans in our case), which is used to buy means of production, which in turn are then sold for a surplus. Unlike capitalist ventures, the need economies use just enough of this surplus to restart the process anew, and the rest is spent on consumption. Thus, if for the capitalist venture accumulation for accumulation's sake is the final goal, for the need economies the goal is full employment and making enough money to assure each member of the venture has a good enough income to survive. In other words, while the former is oriented toward competition and profit, the latter is motivated by survival.

According to the three book-length studies that have analyzed the process of agrarian counterreform in the Aguán during the 1990s, one of the most constant complaints by the cooperative members was how little revenue they received from the production of palm oil and the alarming levels of embezzlement by those in positions of leadership (Rubén and Funez 1993; Castro 1994; Macías 2001). Moreover, there were also tensions around the uneven distribution of income between the different cooperatives, with the palm oil ones receiving the lion's share of the profit produced in the region, to the detriment of the staple crop ones.[2] The resulting landscape was riddled with tensions and points of friction within and among the cooperatives, as well as between the reform sector and state institutions. These conflicts centered mainly on how the surplus produced by the cooperatives was extracted and distributed.

In general, there were two main mechanisms through which the value created by the cooperative members was taken from them: (1) exploitation of their labor (both collective and individual) by other classes, such as the cattle ranchers, the banana companies, or even the IADB; and (2) rent extraction in the form of embezzlement by leaders of the cooperatives. These two mechanisms—exploiting labor for the benefit of others and corruption—became a way of talking about the different types of class relations as well as the processes of internal differentiation within the reform sector.

Initially, the reform sector in the Aguán shared an egalitarianism born out of poverty, as both immigrants and local communities had very similar class backgrounds. However, as time went by, differentiation within poverty arose both inside the cooperatives and among them. By looking at those points from where differentiation arose, we can explore how rent was being captured and by whom, thus getting a better idea of how the valley's landscape was produced.

I identified three principal axes of differentiation/rent-capturing: state-cooperative relations, relations among cooperatives, and relations within the cooperatives. The state-cooperatives axis was the main and most evident point of friction in the region, which was first and foremost experienced as the low "wages" that the members received for their work in the cooperatives, as well as the debt payments that they had to make for the land they worked on.[3]

Another point of friction between the state and the cooperatives was the process of industrialization and commercialization of palm oil. Since the initial plan of the BAP, the idea was that an industrial sector would be developed to add value to the production of the raw material and thus vertically integrate the industry. In 1979 the governing military junta issued two decrees (774 and 810) giving birth to the Agro-Industrial Cooperative of African Palm (COAPALMA) on February 18, 1980, with an initial capital of more than 35 million lempiras (around US$18 million) (Castro 1994).

Initially, the extracting mills and COAPALMA were administered directly by the state, leaving the cooperatives at the margins. Supposedly, once the state recovered its investment and paid off its loans to international creditors, it would gradually cede control to the cooperatives. This idea was rejected by their leadership, who felt that they had little or no control over their production and went on a two weeklong strike in September 1980. As a result, on March 31, 1981, the National Congress voted and approved decree 52, giving full control of COAPALMA to the cooperatives (Macías 2001).

This movement was significant on at least two accounts. First, it allowed the cooperatives to vertically integrate into the palm oil value chain, increasing the differentiation between palm oil and staple crops cooperatives. Second, it allowed them to gain further political autonomy in relation to the state, as they acquired more control over both the profits generated and what was done with that money. As a result, with more money flowing into the cooperatives, there were higher chances for embezzlement and rent capturing by those members in positions of leadership.

In terms of the second axis of rent capture, the relations among cooperatives, COAPALMA was also crucial. As Catherine de Fonteney (1999) shows in her study of COAPALMA, a limited set of cooperatives was able to control the board of directors, concentrating in the process most of the profits. "Such 'inside' groups tended to be those closest to headquarters and the largest town [Tocoa] (with some exceptions), perhaps initially because they had more contact with COAPALMA, and their families had better access to education to qualify for clerical jobs at the plant" (17).

Further, according to internal documents that de Fonteney was able to analyze, the "inside" cooperatives were transferring a significant part of their debts to the "outside" ones by paying them slightly lower prices for the oil palms fruit. The result was a three-tier system with the inside cooperatives on top, the outside ones below, and the staple crops cooperatives, external to COAPALMA and the palm oil economy, at the bottom (Önder 2018).

Finally, the cooperatives were also differentiated internally along gender and age lines, as well as in relation to the labor process. The industrialization of the production of palm oil meant a much more complex division of labor than the one found in staple crops. Thus, with the creation of new more specialized technical and administrative jobs, income differences began to rise between workers. Since this differentiation was informed by education levels, the better-paying posts tended to flow to members, and the sons and daughters of members, of the inside cooperatives, located closer to Tocoa and the better education centers.

Another internal differentiation arose from the legal framework of the cooperatives. According to the law, all the members had the possibility of occupying administrative and leadership positions. However, it also stated that members of the board of directors needed to know how to read and write, creating a form of differentiation between base and leadership that was particularly pronounced in outside and staple crops cooperatives, as their members had less access to education. Also, it translated into practices of bossism, in which a few members could decide what to produce as well as engage in rent capturing practices.

Forms of gender differentiation were also written into the cooperatives' legal framework. According to the law, the legal title and membership in the cooperatives were exclusive to the head of the household. This meant that apart from widows and single mothers, women were effectively excluded from direct membership, and thus, highly dependent on their male partners.[4] As we will see, these forms of gender differentiation and subjugation were inscribed into the region's landscapes and would play a significant role in the context of the land sales.

Finally, the children of the members did not have any direct entitlement in the cooperative, other than the individual inheritance of the membership. Also, very often, the cooperatives did not have the opportunity to include them as members and thus, once they reached working age, they either had to move to another organization with available member spots, look for a job outside of the agricultural sector, or work permanently as day laborers.

## Structural Adjustment and the Debt Lever

In the 1980s and 1990s, Honduras—following the trend of most Latin American countries—entered a process of structural adjustment (Robinson 2003; Barahona 2005; Cáceres and Zelaya 2011). Usually seen as the withdrawal of the state from direct involvement in the economy, this process can be better understood as the institutionalization of profit-making by the private sector as the state's primary function. What we find is the subservience of much of the structures of government to the logic of the market, as both distributor of resources and the promotion of the private sector. As such, a useful way of thinking about structural adjustment is through the institutional spaces and logics "adjusted" to assure the "proper" function of different markets. I use quotation marks to signal that the ideas of adjusting and propriety must be understood as part of a logic of discipline, in which people and landscapes are subjected to new forms of control and dependence and their associated spatialities. Here, the primary and crucial discipline mechanism was debt.

For Latin America, the history is well known: the attempts of breaking free from the chains of dependency through ISI were funded with public debt. In some countries more than others (Mexico and Brazil, for example), this process translated into the creation of an important, albeit dependent, industrial sector (Morton 2013). However, for the Central American region it sparked an escalating maelstrom of public indebtedness that focused on diversifying the product basket of the plantation economy through agrarian reform projects such as the BAP, and that, while financing critical public projects such as hospitals and schools, was also the target of misappropriation and embezzlement by the countries' elites and transnational companies (Robinson 2003). Further, with the creation and growth of the public sector and relatively higher incomes, the import of luxury goods, indirectly funded by public debt, also increased, wreaking havoc on the already negative payment balance and thus begetting more public debt.

During the 1970s, with the organized hike in oil prices and the subsequent massive inflow of "petrodollars" from the Organization of Petroleum Exporting Countries (OPEC) into the global financial system, very cheap loans could be found to continue feeding this system. However, when in the 1980s Reaganomics and Thatcherism emerged and captured the IFIs and the global economic common sense, monetarist politics—basically that the focus of the government should be to adjust the amount of money in an economy and limit both deflation and inflation—led to the rise of interest rates and the subsequent devaluation of local currencies, forcing various countries to default on their debts (Mattei and Nader 2008). Probably the better-known example was Mexico in 1982, but already in 1980, Costa Rica was forced to announce that it was incapable of paying its financial obligations, opening the gates for the imposition of structural adjustment projects (SAP) (Edelman 1999).

In the Honduran case, we find a very similar pattern. Between 1976 and 1979, the country experienced a spectacular growth of the GDP of nearly 9 percent,[5] accompanied by even more spectacular growth in public debt. According to British economist Ian Walker (1990), the country's historically cautious approach to external borrowing was thrown out the window during this period, with debt rising from US$183 million in 1970 to $502 million in 1975 and $1.388 billion in 1980. This situation made the country's economy very vulnerable and thus when the international prices of its agricultural exports fell, and the cost of its imports of inputs and capital goods (over 75 percent of the total imports in the 1980s) increased, Honduras's terms of trade and its ability to stay up to date with its debt payments took a big hit. What kept the country's economy somewhat afloat was its geopolitical position in the Central American region.

During the 1980s Honduras played an essential role within the U.S. strategy of containment of both the Sandinista government in Nicaragua and the armed conflict in El Salvador; the country thus received massive amounts of economic and military aid from the U.S. government.[6] However, toward the end of this decade, the situation became unsustainable, as Honduras's foreign debt surpassed the US$3 billion mark in 1988, around 70 percent of the country's GDP. In the 1990s Honduras would come to negotiate and sign three SAPs to secure new loans that would allow the government to keep up with its payments and finance its activities: a first agreement, on March 1990, during Rafael Callejas's government, with the signing of Executive Decree no. 18-90, which came to be popularly known as the *paquetazo* (literally the big package); a second one under Callejas's successor, Roberto Reina (1994–98), known as the Grand Project of National Transformation; and a third one during Carlos Flores Facussé's (1998–2002) government (Robinson 2003).

As Ugo Mattei and Laura Nader (2008, 57) write, "structural adjustment is essentially the contractual agreement by which developing countries give up economic and legal sovereignty in consideration for financing." Here, "agreement" stands as a euphemism for imposition, as the "adjusted" countries had little leverage to negotiate the conditions. In practice, it meant following a set of prescribed policies oriented toward harmonizing the domestic economic framework with those dominant globally: liberalization and deregulation of markets, cutback on universalist social policies and the move toward focalized ones, and the privatization of not only various public companies but also of several spaces of governance and control (Hibou 2004). In Honduras, some of the specific policies implemented were: devaluation of the lempira, tariff reduction, sales taxes increase, fiscal incentives to attract foreign investment, promotion of nontraditional exports, the creation of free trade zones, and the liberation of bank interest rates (Cáceres and Zelaya 2011). In practice, the SAPs translated into a process of plunder and concentration of assets and resources that used to be in the hands of the state and other forms of noncapitalist organization, such as the agrarian reform cooperatives, by a limited set of local capitalists and transnational capital. Nowhere was this more evident than in the case of the agrarian sector.

**Legalizing the Plunder of the Land**

The neoliberal project can be understood as one of expansion of what can, and should, circulate as a commodity. Crucial for the whole project is the privatization of assets and resources and their packaging or repackaging as commodities that can enter the market and be distributed in the most "efficient" way possible. Efficiency here is understood in monetary terms; thus, the allocation of these assets and resources should go toward those who will be able to pay for them and use them to make a profit (Fraser 2017).

In terms of how property is understood, circulates, and gets spoken about, the emergence of neoliberalism provoked quite a radical shift. During the previous period there was, at least formally, a sense of society as a collective, and of property having to support or bolster that collective. Now, the idea was that individuals should use that property for their enjoyment and betterment, and the market would take care of the rest. Here, one of the victories of neoliberal thought has been to create a common sense in which "freedom" is directly related to property, and where "private property" stands for property as such. This is particularly clear in the case of land.

According to authors such as Hernando de Soto (2001), the differences in wealth between the West and the rest have to do with property. People in poor countries have assets and resources, but they cannot turn them into capital because they do not have legal ownership rights (probable ownership) over them. As such, they cannot use them as collateral in negotiating bank loans, nor can they sell them in the market as there is no legal security. Thus, the solution to the problem of economic inequality is to find ways in which the poor can "represent" their property as capital. In the case of land, the objective is then to promote titling programs meant to provide legal security for would-be investors and lending institutions. In the 1980s this mode of thinking translated into a radical rethinking of what an agrarian reform should look like. From this perspective, it was essential to move away from state-controlled programs, which distributed the land inefficiently, and instead, to create the conditions for the market to take over. The result was the promotion by the World Bank of a set of market-led agrarian reforms in the 1980s and 1990s (Lahiff, Borras Jr., and Kay 2007).

It is within this framework that we must understand the agrarian aspect of the structural adjustment in Honduras, which took shape in two bills: The Land Titling Program (LTP) of 1982 and the Agricultural Sector Modernization and Development Law (AML) of 1992. The LTP project—mainly bankrolled by the USAID—partly resulted from the escalation of the agrarian conflict in the country toward the end of the 1970s and the open defiance and opposition of the right-wing National Federation of Farmers and Cattlemen (FENAGH) to the government's agrarian policy (Jansen and Roquas 1998). The main objective of the LTP was to allocate land more efficiently to producers, thus opening up access to credit and technical assistance, as well as granting legal property rights over land (Salgado 1994). In practice, LTP spiked the prices of land, thus making it harder for land-poor and landless families to have access. Also, although it was oriented toward those sectors not included within the scope of the agrarian reform, by granting full and individual title to occupants of national and municipal lands it weakened the peasant movement and brought lands that used to be outside its scope into the market (Salgado 1994).

This legal counterreform deepened in 1992 with the AML, which came to be known as the Norton Law due to the active participation in the drafting process of U.S. economist Roger Norton. The AML came to dramatically transform much of the agrarian reform framework that had been in place since the 1970s. The causes for acquiring private land for redistribution were reduced to two: private estates that extended over the landed property ceilings or had been idle—not in production—for the eighteen consecutive months. Also, AML expanded tenure security over land. For example, national and municipal lands sold to private individuals had to be titled within six months. Further, small farms could be titled, regardless of their size. When and if the INA now assigned land to beneficiaries, it was in the form of a title with a mortgage lien and individual plots could be titled as part of the distributed land. Also, cooperatives could title their land and the indivisibility of their property was abolished, allowing the division into individual plots of the cooperatives' lands among their members or their straight-up sale in the market (COCOCH 2010; Macías 2001). Another significant change was the abolition of the "land to the tiller" principle that had been present in both the 1962 and 1974 agrarian reform laws, allowing for the separation of ownership from working on the land, as now, according to article 64, land had to be only "adequately exploited," whatever that might mean. Further, the definition of a smallholding was reduced from ten hectares to one hectare (Noé Pino, Thorpe, and Corea 1992).

Taken together, the LTP and the AML present us with an entry point into the place of land within the neoliberal logic: land, like any other asset, should be distributed by the market, not the state, and even when it is distributed by the state, this should be under the logic of the market. Further, property rights should be extended to expand the amount of land available for market transactions, thus assuring that it will reach the hands of those who will make the most of it. This is, of course, a reiteration of Lefebvrian abstract space, where space is understood as homogeneous, devoid of differences, partitionable, and produced through a set of state technologies aimed at its simplification (Lefebvre 1991). In other words, abstract space is commodified space that can be oriented in different directions depending on the needs of capitalists.

However, a problem arises when this logic is applied to land. Unlike other would-be commodities, a title over land allows the owner to accrue a certain amount of the profit produced in the form of ground rent, "whose very existence is a barrier to the investment of capital and its unrestricted valorization on the land." (Marx 1981, 884). In other words, if landed property exists, it will enter into contradiction with free capital accumulation, due to the amount of surplus that it accrues because of the mere existence of private property. This is, of course, a political problem. Landowners' power is based on the fact that land cannot be moved, that two pieces of land can never be the same (agroecological characteristics), and that one use necessarily excludes the possibility of others (Hall, Hirsch, and Li 2011). Thus, land values, understood basically in terms of the rent land can accrue, can never be homogeneous.[7]

Further, land is multifaceted. In economic terms, it is both a means of production and the location of production itself. At the same time, from the perspective of financial capital, it is a form of fictitious capital, as monetary loans and investments are calculated on future expected revenues. Socially, land continues to be a source of prestige and political sway, as shown in Honduras by the effectiveness of FENAGH's pressure on influencing the country's agrarian policy. At the same time, as we saw in the last chapter, land was also understood by peasants in Honduras as a means of subsistence and a way of improving their lives. Moreover, although the idea of the social function of land was watered down, and the economic and legal resources to enforce it had diminished, it did not completely disappear from the country's legal framework. Further, while the idea of "land to the tiller" did leave legal talk, the discussion as to whom should own the land and what they should do with it continued to animate the political debates of the country. As such, as Casolo and Doshi (2013) so eloquently show, land, and the struggles over it, articulate the relations of production, the visible economy of capital accumulation, with the dynamics of social reproduction, the invisible economy of the forms of provisioning, caregiving, and interaction that produce and maintain the social bonds necessary for the labor force to reproduce.

It is within this context that we must understand the process of land dispossession that took place in the Aguán of the 1990s. However, to make sense of how the global dynamics of neoliberalism and structural adjustment were articulated domestically and locally, we must first take a longer view at a process of class formation that was unleashed by the reformist military regime, and which created a new "transnationalized" elite that became the main character opposing the peasant movement in the agrarian counterreform tragedy.

## "Los Turcos": The Formation of a Transnational Elite

According to Honduran historian Darío Euraque (2019), there is a myth in the country's historiography that, unlike the rest of Central America, Honduras never truly developed a national bourgeoisie, due to the late development of coffee production and the stranglehold that the banana enclave had on the national economy (see for example: Mahoney 2001; Pérez Brignoli 1989; Torres-Rivas 1981). Accordingly, the process of elite formation in the country was dominated for many years by a set of economic and political family networks, weaved around doing business with the enclave and plundering the state. However, according to Euraque, this reading is misguided, as it renders invisible the commercial bourgeoisie that grew in the shadow of the state and around the city of San Pedro Sula, from the 1960s onward.

The process of class formation of this commercial elite, commonly known as "los turcos," the Turks, as the people of Levantine descent are popularly known as in Honduras, was the result of two intersecting tendencies. The first was the support given by the Honduran state to the industrial development of the country. For example, in 1958, the Industrial Development Law was approved, offering incentives for the creation of new companies. Shortly thereafter, the establishment in 1960 of the Central American Common Market was accompanied by the inflow of financial support by the newly minted Central American Bank for Economic Integration (BCIE, 1960) and the USAID.

Second, during the 1920s and 1930s, Latin America in general and Honduras in particular received a significant number of Palestinian immigrants, mainly Orthodox Christians, running away from the military conflict in the Middle East. Many of them arrived at the country with some economic and cultural capital that allowed them to insert themselves into the local economy as merchants and build commercial relations around the banana enclave. However, since most of them thought that this was a provisional stop, this community of immigrants initially had limited interactions with the Honduran society as a whole (Gutiérrez Rivera 2014), a situation compounded by the ingrained racism of Honduran elites and the government's stringent immigration policies. This began to change in the 1950s, in part due to the declaration of the state of Israel in 1948, which foreclosed their dreams of returning to Palestine, but also due to the ascent of these Palestinians within San Pedro Sula's economic elite, which would eventually translate into marital ties with the local elites.

By the 1980s, various economic groups controlled by Palestinian families were among the richest in the country, with an important presence not only in the manufacturing sector but also in the financial, agribusiness and mass media, just to mention a few (Euraque 2009). Thus, by the time the SAPs rolled in the 1990s, this new elite was in prime position to take advantage of the novel situation. Since the 1950s, they had cultivated strong relations with transnational capital, first with the banana companies but later with other firms. Thus, they already had the know-how and cultural capital to become prime domestic partners and take advantage of the liberalization of the economy and the promotion of foreign investment. At the same time, although they did not necessarily have a direct presence in the two main political parties, they were able to wield enough influence through their economic power (i.e., financing political campaigns) to influence policy and position themselves favorably in the new institutional and political context.

To get a better understanding of how these different elements came together during the process of structural adjustment, it is useful to look at the case of Miguel Facussé and his rise as one of the richest men in Honduras, whose company Corporación Dinant is one of the central players within the palm oil industry. Facussé's trajectory from U.S.-educated aeronautical engineer to one of the wealthiest persons in Central America is somewhat shrouded in mystery. Before his death in 2015, he preferred to remain away from the public eye and, with very few exceptions (Wilkinson 2012), never gave interviews. Thus, what we know about his career is mainly through sometimes contradictory journalistic pieces. However, due to the importance that Corporación Dinant has had in the development of the palm oil industry, I would like to present a brief profile of Facussé's business trajectory, based on some of the more reliable sources (Agüero Starkman and Naum Ávila 2014; Cáceres and Zelaya 2011; Estrada 2018; Wilkinson 2012).

The son of Palestinian immigrants, Facussé founded the Corporación Cressida in the early 1960s, dedicated to the manufacturing and commercialization of light industrial products, ranging from prepared foodstuff to detergents and soaps. Cressida's operations included a small soaps and detergent plant known as Químicas Dinant, founded with a US$7 million loan from the Bank of America and Lloyds Bank International, with the National Investments Corporation (CONADI) serving as guarantor.

Created in 1974 by Oswaldo López Arellano's government, CONADI's objective was to attract and promote industrial investment in Honduras by connecting local entrepreneurs with foreign financial capital. By the 1980s Dinant had grown from a small plant to a much larger corporation dedicated to the production of foodstuffs, detergents, and soaps, with palm oil as a crucial raw material. At the time, most of the palm oil came from mills such as

COAPALMA. Attracted by the profits that could be made by moving down the production chain, Facussé began building an extraction plant in the Aguán. However, as de Fontenay writes, "the State, under pressure from Coapalma, revoked Facussé's building permit for the Aguán, and he had to build halfway between the Sula and the Aguán valleys" (1999, 11).

This first failure did not deter Facussé; rather, it made him understand that if he wanted to tap into the palm oil industry, significant political and legal changes were needed. Specifically he felt that control over the state must be wrested away from both the traditional elites, and any remaining reformist spirit that might be found in any of the public institutions needed to be eliminated. It is around this same period that he joined the Honduran Progress Association (APROH), an organization made up of businessmen and army officers who were interested in opening the country's economy and profiting in the process.[8] This association was the political brains and muscle behind the rise of neoliberalism in the country (Paz 1984); one of its main objectives was to direct the transition from military to civilian governments that began in 1982 with the declaration of a new constitution and the election of Roberto Suazo Córdoba as president.

During Suazo Córdoba's government, Facussé served as a presidential economic counselor. In this capacity, he recommended that the country strengthen its economy by limiting capital and currency drain. Also, he suggested that the foreign debt that many of the local companies had assumed under the mantle of CONADI and other public corporations—and which had brought them to the brink of bankruptcy—should be converted into domestic debt. Afterward, the government could recover the money spent paying off these debts by selling the assets of the recovered companies to the local private sector. In the case of CONADI, these debts rose to around US$2.5 billion, distributed among sixty-eight companies, including Facussé's Dinant. Between 1986 and 1988, these assets were sold in public auctions for pennies on the dollar and in some cases, promissory notes were accepted. One of the biggest winners was Facussé, who, through a set of under- and over-the-table maneuvers, managed to maintain control over his companies.

The biggest loser was the Honduran public, as in 1989 the National Agricultural Development Bank (BANADESA) was instructed to buy the actions of CONADI and pay the debts that the corporation had with foreign banks. This turned the foreign debt into domestic debt and erased, as if by magic, the obligations incurred by Facussé and others in the 1970s. This plundering of the state ended on September 29, 1990, when Rafael Leonardo Callejas issued a decree (no. 106–90) cancelling and liquidating the CONADI.

By the early 1990s, Facussé maintained a presence all over Latin America as the official distributor of brands such as Colgate-Palmolive and Maseca—a brand of industrial maize flour—among others, grouped under Corporación Cressida. In 2000 the transnational company Unilever bought Cressida for over US$420 million (Interactive Journal News 2000). The only company that Facussé kept under his direct control was Dinant Corporation.

With the money accrued from these moves and the legal changes implemented by the AML, Facussé, Dinant Corporation, and other similar actors were now able to enter the Aguán, acquire lands, and deepen the vertical integration of their enterprises: from the growing of the oil palms, through their processing mills and into an assortment of finished commodities, including foodstuffs and cleaning products. His story also serves as a general blueprint for how the conjuncture of the 1980s crisis and the structural adjustment process created the conditions for the privatization of many public assets and the lifelines of need economies such as the agrarian reform cooperatives.

### The Birth of the Capital of the Agrarian Counterreform

Once it began, the sale of the agrarian reform cooperatives spread like wildfire. After the cooperative of Isletas sold its lands to the Standard Fruit Company on May 5, 1990, the transfer of agrarian reform lands to a handful of Honduran landowners and transnational companies began to spread rapidly. As the AML opened the legal floodgates, money devalued by the same process of structural adjustment began to flow into the Honduran countryside in search of profits and cheap assets.[9] In a context framed by a reformed sector lacking production incentives, heavily indebted and with little or no support from state institutions, there were plenty of willing sellers and cheap lands to be found. And when they were not found, they were manufactured through bribery, threats, deceit, and blood.[10]

According to the prevailing narrative, the main forces behind the process of dispossession were the "foreign" large landowners Miguel Facussé, Reinaldo Canales, and René Morales. Although their "foreignness" is very questionable,[11] their racialization as an external force came to distinguish them from the "real" Hondurans: the poor peasants, who should be the rightful owners of the land. This nationalist discourse was mobilized against the apparent transnational nature of the neoliberal project.

According to Macías (2001, 94), the three bigger buyers of agrarian reform lands were Facussé (Dinant Corporation; who acquired 34 percent of the land sold), Morales (Grupo Jaremar; 23 percent), and the Standard Fruit Company (8 percent). This data is probably an underestimate, as in many cases the larger purchasers would also use surrogate buyers, as Harald Waxenecker (2019) shows in his analysis of the lands bought and concentrated by Dinant Corporation (see also Rubén and Funez 1993).

As I showed earlier, the expansion of the palm oil industry during the developmentalist period in the Aguán had created a set of contradictions and conflicts that in turn produced various forms of differentiation and located the different individuals and groups in particular positions regarding both the cooperatives and the palm oil industry in general. Once the AML lifted the restriction on selling reform sector lands, vast amounts of capital entered the region and circulated within and among the cracks left by these previous processes of differentiation. Without it being a mathematical rule, it is clear that staple crops cooperatives had a greater tendency to sell their land and assets than those producing palm oil and closer to COAPALMA.[12] This is in part why many cooperatives preferred to sell to external investors than to local ones: not only were stipends distributed and skulls crushed, there were also prior resentments that informed their decisions.

The rhythms of the global palm oil ensemble also had their say in the matter. The period of the BAP, from its beginning in the early 1970s to its closing in the mid-1990s, is framed by two cycles in the international price of palm oil. The first cycle is one of growth and instability, which peaked in 1984. That year, a new cycle began, in which prices maintained their volatility but remained lower, as the global production of palm oil expanded significantly. Locally, the down period coincided with the transfer of COAPALMA's control to the cooperatives, the withdrawal of the INA's support from the cooperatives, and what most cooperative members remember as a very hard time, with little profits. This, of course, placed the organizations in a very vulnerable situation, which was deepened by COAPALMA's profit squeeze (high rent capture with low prices).

For investors such as Facussé, this down cycle was a blessing in disguise. Since he had sold his companies in dollars, he was able to take advantage of the double devaluation that was taking place in Honduras. First, due to the SAPs the lempira had been deeply devalued and there was rampant inflation, meaning Facussé could buy land in the Aguán at low prices. Second, in public discourse, there was an offensive against the reform sector, presenting it as both the domain of lazy farmers and a thing from the past that did not have any longer a role to play in the development of the country: it was now time for the forces of the market to take over.[13] Finally, since Facussé and others buying the palm oil plantations were deepening their process of vertical integration, they could absorb losses for a while, unlike the cooperatives. From this perspective, then, the sale process could be seen as the effects of the coercive laws of competition that Marx so eloquently refers to in volume 1 of *Capital* (1992). However, it is essential to remember that this was not a case of capitalist firms competing against each other but of large and subsidized capitalists raiding deeply impoverished and fragile need economies. Here the transfer and concentration of assets took more the form of primitive accumulation than of "market rationalization." Let us now turn to how this process played out on the ground.

### Of Cows and Oil Palms: The Hidden Abode of Primitive Accumulation

Eugenia's testimony regarding the sale of the cooperatives' land is a particularly useful window into the shared experience of many women who witnessed their husbands, brothers, and fathers sell the land that they had received and fought for through the BAP.[14] In terms of content, there is nothing exceptional about her story. I heard many similar ones told by very dissimilar women all over the Aguán. However, what makes Eugenia's testimony unique is her very profound retrospective reading of the loss of the cooperative's lands, which disrupts the dominant narrative presented above, as it locates most of the reasons for the sale behind the closed doors of the cooperatives. My aim in this section is to use her story as a way of characterizing and bringing to life the process of land sales, as it was experienced by many of the women I spoke to during my stay in the Aguán.

In other words, with Eugenia's story we will leave the "noisy sphere" of the land market, "where everything takes place in the surface an in full view of everyone" and enter the "hidden abode of dispossession," where we will see not only how the privatization of the palm oil economy came to be but how, and why, the lands of the cooperatives were in a position to be dispossessed.[15]

For Eugenia, the sale of the land and the dissolution of the cooperative occurred in three strikes, all of which were connected to the introduction of the palm oil industry. In the first, their living space was separated from where the oil palms were located. In the second, they lost the cows that the cooperative had bought a few years before. In the third and last one, it was the turn of the land to be sold. These three strikes, which may appear disjointed, had a deep connection and were part of a broader process. And, as we will see, this was a profoundly gendered process as well (see also: Casolo 2009).

In the previous chapter, I described Eugenia and Marino's journey to the Aguán and the difficulties they encountered once they arrived at the cooperative. Initially, they lived on the land that had been designated for them. There was no real difference between the place where they lived and the place where they began producing milpa, later mixing it with oil palms and finally shifting to an oil palm monoculture. These were lowlands close to the Aguán River and thus both highly fertile and vulnerable to frequent floods. A few years after their arrival, in the late 1980s, the cooperative's board of directors informed them that, as a result of the land being prone to flooding, they could no longer live beside the oil palms and that a new housing project was being created nearby on higher ground. In retrospect, for Eugenia, this was not such an innocent move. She tells me, "Now I understand. The directors used to say to us: 'Look, we cannot stay here.' But we had been living there for a long time. I gave birth to my children there. And they would say: 'We are no longer going to live here because the river can sweep us away, it is better to move up there, we have to buy land and move up there.' So, they bought a piece of land and divided up into lots and we all moved up here."

The separation of their place of residence from the palm oil plantation meant two things for Eugenia. First, it would be easier to sell the land if no one lived there, and second, it spatially separated women's work from men's work and this, as we will see, had a profound effect. As the cooperative transitioned toward the palm oil monoculture, the household's provisioning rested more and more on the wages received by the men for their work in the fields, making women more dependent on their partners. Meanwhile, their domestic work was rendered invisible, as it did not produce any significant amount of money. What the housing project did was to inscribe this differentiation on the landscape of the cooperatives.

The relocation also influenced women's land uses. Before the housing project, there was no separation between each household, which led to women spending time together, taking care of the little livestock that they had, growing and harvesting vegetables, picking up wood, collecting water, looking after the children, and doing laundry. However, once they moved up to the new housing project, each family's plot was separated from the others by barbwire fences. As a result, the spaces for women's solidarity and collective work became fewer, deepening the differentiation between the private and the public areas and who could do what in which.

Then came the second strike: the sale of the cows. In the mid-1980s, the cooperative had bought a few cows, which would rotate between the different families. The relocation opened the way for the selling of the livestock. Not only did keeping cows distract cooperative male members from their monoculture dreams (more area dedicated to oil palms equaled more money), but also, in their new place of residence, there was less space available to keep the animals. Eugenia remembers that when she first heard that the cooperative's cows were going to be sold, she protested against the decision:

> They began talking about selling the cows and I fought against it. Now I understand that this was hopeless. I wasn't a member; he [Marino] was the member. I told them "no, you are not going to sell the cows." I spoke with the president and asked him, "why do you want to sell the cows? Don't sell the cows. Look how many children are going to be left without milk." "Look, what has been decided, has been decided, and no one can stop it," he responded.

She continued to mobilize and got the other women of the cooperative together to discuss the issue. "I went and spoke to some women. I told them, 'Women, we cannot let them sell the cows. Give me money because I am going to go and denounce this on Radio Tocoa.' Now I laugh because I went to do nothing. I spoke on the radio about how the cooperative was selling the cows." In the end, her efforts were unsuccessful, and the cows were sold for half of what they were worth.

After the sale of the cows, there was a change in the board of directors and if the former one had sold the cows, the new one was intent on selling the land with the oil palms through a process that was clearly gendered. Following a similar pattern of other land sales, the members of the cooperative began discussing the possible selling of their land a few months before the actual deed. The reason, according to Marino, was that since the cooperative's debts had been forgiven during Callejas's government, they could now follow in the steps of other cooperatives in the region that had already sold and see how much they could get. Internally, things were not looking good. The price paid for the oil palm fruit was low and many felt that COAPALMA was taking advantage of them. Further, there was a feeling that not everyone was working as much as they should. Marino remembers the discussions: "That there were people that didn't want to work and just pretended to do so. That there were a lot of people just trying to live off the others. Others said that some of the members were too old and didn't get any work done. So, then it was decided that it was better to sell."

These discussions would take place among the "palm trees" (*las palmeras*) as they referred to the plantation, to make sure that the women would not find out about them. This was another effect of the separation between their residence and working spaces. According to Eugenia, they were worried that if the women found out, they would oppose the sale. This comment was clearly self-referential, as she was the most vocal voice against their plans. Marino also remembers that of the forty or so members of the cooperative, only eight were against the sale and all of them were threatened.

> Eight of us didn't agree with the sale. If they wanted to sell the cooperative, it was better to divide up the land and give each member the twelve hectares that they were entitled to. But one of them said: "No, with this gun that I have here, we are going to cut down (*pelar*) anyone who tries to get in the way of the sale. It won't do that just because one or two are against, we all lose out. That is all that I have to say."

At the end, due to these threats, the decision was taken to sell the land. Once Eugenia heard from Marino that the men had made up their minds, she decided to do something about it. Sensing that gender differences were important regarding the relationship with the land, she turned to what she saw as her natural allies, the other women: "I gathered about five women and told them: 'Look here, we can't allow the sale of the cooperative. We must stop it. What are we going to do? What are we going to do with all these children? What are we going to eat? Where are we going to find a place to plant maize to sustain our children? Look at how many boys and girls we have!'"

For her, the land had nothing to do either with COAPALMA's corruption, or with the prices received for the fruit, or with the critiques regarding the unequal payment or amount of work done by the different cooperative members. For her it had to do with the self-provisioning of subsistence items and the possibility of sustaining their families. This sense grew out of a different relation with the land, one that was not as mediated by money as that of the men and thus more interested in those other uses and relationships that it could, and did, sustain. The way in which she remembers and narrates this episode contrasts not only with Marino's but in more general terms with most of the male testimonies that I heard. Just as I mentioned in the previous chapter regarding the migration process, the memories of the land sales tend to split into the male perspective of money and work, and that of women, much more oriented toward the dynamics of provisioning and subsistence. This difference should not be naturalized. I believe it to be the result of the differentiated positions from which men and women lived the shared experience of dispossession. Stuart Hall et al. (1978, 394) argue that "race is the modality in which class is lived." In the case of the Aguán, I would make a similar case: gender was the modality in which class was lived, but also the modality in which dispossession is remembered (Crehan 2016; Hart 2006).

Regarding her crusade against the sales, Eugenia reminisces:

> They [the other women] told me that I was right and gave me 5 lempiras [US$5] each, so that I could go and look for someone that would come and talk some sense into the board of directors. We couldn't find anyone. I went to the neighboring cooperative, and they told me that they couldn't intrude in the business of another cooperative. I went to the church and asked the priest to help me. He drove me all the way out to Progreso, to HONDUPALMA. I desperately spoke to them, asking them for help against the sale, that there were a lot of women who didn't want to lose the lands. They told me that they could not intercede. They of course thought that they could run into some trouble if they got involved, but me, I wasn't aware of this, I never wondered what could happen to me.

Eventually, both Marino's and her lives were threatened, but she continued to look for help, any help she could find, to try to stop the sale. Then, one day Marino told her: "'I am not going to sign. They say that if a single person refuses to sign, that they can't sell the land.' How quickly they won over the rest! Only he remained against!" By then, everything seemed like a lost cause. The only thing stalling the sale was Marino's signature and eventually a more concrete death threat came. Eugenia described the situation to me: Marino was standing by a tree near the corner of his plot sharpening his machete when "a member of the cooperative arrived at our house asking for Marino. I told him where he was and they spoke softly, I couldn't hear what they said. Once he left, I asked Marino what he had told him. 'He said that if I didn't go and sign, they are going to kill me.'"

Eugenia was inconsolable. For her, losing the land meant losing pretty much everything: "I was crying. I wanted to be thousands of women so that I could stop the sale of the land. Those that didn't do milpa, was because they didn't want to! It was God's blessing to harvest maize! Any seed that you planted would grow up thick! We had maize to eat and to raise animals, but no, they sold the land."

In Eugenia's narrative, there is a deep connection between gender positions and the continuum between self-provisioning and wage labor; for her, the sale had been a men's deed. This thread connects the three strikes that I have described. First, with the relocation, came an even more severe separation between the domestic space and the place of the oil palms. This not only paved the way by literally removing them from the land but also separated women's spaces from male ones, deepening in the process the gap between self-provisioning and wage/market dependency and their possibility of making claims upon the land. Second, the sale of the cows not only showed the new differentiations between the households but, more importantly, came to deepen this gap even more. Without the cows—and other livestock for that matter—and with all the land covered with oil palms, the scales were clearly tipped away from self-provisioning and toward wage labor. Finally, the sale was the logical conclusion of this process. Eugenia's reaction to the money that they received from the sale—about US$750—is also revealing:

> I told Marino to keep that money away from the house, to deposit it in the bank. I didn't want to know anything about that money! I tell you, the men took the money and spent it on foolish things, they bought guns, and they went insane! Everybody went insane! I used to tell them when I encountered them in Tocoa, that they should be more careful with their money. What are you going to do when it runs out? And they would respond that I was pestering them because I didn't want to sell. And now, if you go and ask anyone, they will tell you that they were against the sale! You can go and ask! Anyone! Of course, it is because they are left with nothing. It was horrible. I came down sick and everything. And you know? For over a year I would not speak with the directors, maybe more.

For Eugenia, the money represented the loss of the land—her linkage with self-provisioning—and that could not be replaced. For example, their home has concrete block walls, but she was adamant that I should know that they had done that with their own labor and not from the money that came from the sale. She makes a profound reflection on this matter:

> Now life is different; it is different not having a piece of land. It is different and it is terrible. Never, never I tell you; after they sold the land, we don't know what an ear of maize is, what a maize plant is. We buy everything. First, we used to buy Maseca, but now we figured out that it was better to buy an arroba of maize. As they say, nobody dies of hunger, but it is not the same. Take for example the case of firewood. You know what I told them one day that they were gathered to discuss the sale? "Men, stop talking about selling the land! Once you have sold it, you won't even be able to find some firewood! Now, now we can go and bring our own firewood and we can go and fish wherever we want. You are going to remember these things once you sell the land." They told me that I didn't know what I was talking about. And look what is happening now. Whoever goes there [to the oil palm plantations] for a piece of wood doesn't come back. There is fish, I think, but nobody can go fishing because they run into trouble. It was terrible! Life without land is very hard, because

with a piece of land you can at least do a little milpa and grow some beans, and at least one has his maize and beans, but like this, it is very hard. It used to be a gift of God! Imagine we didn't have to buy plantains; we could just go and take them down. It was the most beautiful thing, to have one's land, but without land . . . Look how we are doing now. I tell Marino that he should go and see who would give him a piece of land to make milpa, but he tells me that he is embarrassed to do so, after he had land and sold it.

### What Is Accumulated by Primitive Accumulation?

In the previous two chapters, I analyzed the process by which a group of land poor and landless peasant families from Honduras's south and west left their birthplaces and relocated to the Aguán region in search of a better life through a piece of land. This journey was marked by various changes in their class positions: from land-poor and landless peasants to cooperative members or mountain settlers, to landless rural workers or some combination of the above. At the same time, however, this was a journey of continuous impoverishment framed by an ongoing process of primitive accumulation and class differentiation that ran along gender lines.

Primitive accumulation can be understood as the process by which labor is separated from the means of production and accumulated (De Angelis 2004; Perelman 2000). According to Marx (1993), in the *Grundrisse*, this accumulated labor takes two distinct—albeit interconnected—forms: dead labor and living labor. Dead—or past labor—refers to labor already spent in the production of commodities and the transformation of landscapes (Mitchell 2003). Living labor, instead, refers to living subjects who have the capacity to labor and thus are potential workers (Gidwani 2008). Both forms of labor are crucial to our story.

The 1990s agrarian counterreform in the Aguán tends to be seen mainly as a process of dispossession and concentration of land. However, this is only a part of the narrative. A large amount of dead labor had been grounded in the region by the agrarian reform, in the shape of roads, levees, houses, extracting mills, wells, and so on. For example, in the case of the BAP, it is estimated that eleven thousand hectares were planted with oil palms, for an initial total cost of US$100 million, involving around of seven thousand producers, which represented more than forty-four thousand direct dependents (Noé Pino, Santacreo, and Dunnaway 2002, 2). Meanwhile, significant public funds were invested in preparation of the oil palm plantations, including both the infrastructure necessary for the industry to develop and the plantations themselves. Let us remember from the previous chapter that this planting was done basically for free by the cooperative members. All this past labor came to produce the regional landscape and laid down the conditions of possibility for the development of the palm oil industry in the Aguán and Honduras in more general terms.

Living labor was also accumulated in the process. However, this was not only a case of separating the potential laboring bodies from the means of production and their ability to self-provision. For living labor must be turned into a subject willing and able to produce under the control of others. In the case of the Aguán and the palm oil industry, it was necessary to create a subject different from what was understood by the state and the modernizing elites as the traditional Honduran peasant. The worker had to be fixed to in place, able to work collectively and accordingly to a particular discipline and temporality determined by the plantations. This was the result of the disciplinary and production forms introduced and exercised in the creation of the cooperatives, both in terms of the workers and their families, and the landscapes that they produced. It was important that this new subject knew and understood oil palm cultivation and accepted it as his own. Having workers who knew the terms used and the forms of planting, harvesting, and taking care of the oil palms provided ideal conditions for the industry to flourish. Thus, it was not only the plantations that accumulated in private hands with the sale of the lands. This knowledgeable and disciplined subject was also "freed," and with it, a cycle of primitive accumulation that had commenced with these land-poor and landless peasant families' journey toward the Aguán had come around full circle: from landless and poor, to landless and poor, but now versed and placed in, and shackled to, the (mono) culture of the oil palms.

At the same time, this cycle coincides with the more general one of agrarian reform and counterreform (1972–92), a cycle also framed by the discussions regarding who should own the land and what they should do with it. Silvia Federici (2004, 63) has argued that primitive accumulation is not only about the concentration of labor and capital but " *also an accumulation of differences and divisions within the working class,*" including those along gender lines. This holds true for the Aguán, where not only did men and women experience the agrarian counterreform differently but the process itself also came to transform the relationships between genders and to recreate a division between productive (paid) and reproductive (unpaid) work, subordinating ever more women to men, both in the household and in the context of the cooperatives. As a result, when the assault against their collective lands came in the

1990s, cooperative members were already deeply divided and differentiated among themselves. For example, Eugenia's story points toward the role that differentiated positions regarding land had in foreclosing the possibility of a united front against the sales.

We can read this form of gendered differentiation along two threads: monetization and property. Regarding the former, the way in which the cooperatives were organized meant that the reproduction of households rested ever more on wages. This deepened the dependency of women on their male partners or relatives in a twofold movement: on the one hand, women were blocked from wages; on the other, with monetization came the separation of production and reproduction, which shaped the landscape, as the story of Eugenia illustrates so well. As money became the cooperatives' highest priority, every piece of land that could be covered in oil palms became important. Thus, the places of "residence" and of "work" were separated and having a place to keep the cows became less important. This differentiation also changed the relationship between the members of the cooperatives and the land. For men, it became more and more a means to access money, making the sales more palatable. Indeed, it allowed them to make more money than they had ever seen before, from a venture—the cooperatives—that had never lived up to its promises. For women like Eugenia, however, it meant losing their fragile foothold on the conditions of self-provisioning, and thus, at least the illusion of autonomy, as the loss of their shared spaces and spatial mobility so forcefully shows.

Therefore, if we follow Marx and think about the commodity as the combination between use value and exchange value, the agrarian reform, in the form of the cooperatives, came to inscribe spatially their separation in relation to land, effacing the tangible use values (self-provisioning plots, maize, the cows, among others) in favor of more abstract exchange values (palm oil first, land sales later).

This differentiation was also inscribed legally. Law separated women from property, as their relationship with the cooperatives tended to be mediated by their husbands, brothers, and fathers. Here, the law came in a way to discipline and impose a much larger transformation in terms of property relations. I argued before that, with the development of capitalist relations and modern state formation in Honduras, a shift in how land was being understood also began to take place. Further, I have posited that this should not be seen as a complete transformation but rather as an overlap between patrimonial, liberal, modernist, and capitalist understandings of land and space. Recall that the introduction of the social function doctrine of property in the Honduran constitution in the 1950s opened a new space for a legal and political dispute regarding the place and uses of landed property. What Eugenia's story shows us is how these disputes over property were actualized and imposed on the ground. Her family's arrival to the Aguán and the creation of the cooperatives was part of an agrarian reform process that was trying, however timidly, to reconfigure the country's economic and political project. At the same time, the attempts to modernize the Honduran peasantry, which were intrinsic to the agrarian reform, pointed toward the monetization of social reproduction and the promotion of Lefebvrian abstract space.

This transformation was not absolute, as gender came to inform different positions regarding land. However, since the law, and political practice in general, divided the households hierarchically, women were in no position to mount an effective opposition to the new neoliberal property and land regime. In other words, it was through violence, monetization, and law, that capital—understood as a social relation—was "domesticated" (Carney and Watts 1990).

More explicitly, men were threatened into selling their lands. More subtly, but also more pervasively, the relations between men and women were reorganized and rearticulated in relation to value, property, and land. Together, these changes came to produce a long-lasting transformation of the region's landscape, including very ordinary places, like the household. As we will see in the next chapter, the actors and forces that were produced and unleashed together with this new landscape—the "freed" landless peasantry and the privatized palm oil plantations—would combine in explosive ways in a new cycle of agrarian conflict. It is this cycle that will bring us to the doors—and foundations—of the 2009 coup.

## PART II

# The Assault on Power and the Coup

Banner in the Guadalupe Carney Community, 2013. Photo by the author.

## CHAPTER 4
# Democracy as Disaster Capitalism
*Land and Neoliberalism in the Aftermath of Destruction*

On August 7, 1998, the Pastoral Social—Social Care (PS)—of the Catholic Church sponsored a forum in Tocoa titled "Together Let's Strengthen the Agrarian Reform."[1] Although it might appear odd to talk about strengthening something that had been dead for the last half-decade, the forum came with an aura of optimism. In the 1990s the neoliberal economic agenda deepened through the application of the SAPs discussed in the previous chapter. At the same time, there was a political opening, due to the partial retreat of the armed forces from the country's political life and the development of a formally democratic framework, based on the language of the rule of law and human rights.

For example, if 1992 was the year in which the Agrarian Modernization Law was approved, 1993 was the year in which, for the first time in many decades, an openly left-oriented party, the Democratic Unification Party, was legally registered and allowed to run for elections. The result was a tense stalemate, in which the depth and speed of the imposition of the neoliberal project began to slow down, while important social actors, such as the left-leaning sectors of the church and what was left of the peasant movement began to maneuver and take advantage of the new opportunities.

The forum was an effort to capitalize on the renewed interest that part of the national Left had in the agrarian reform as a way of furthering electoral prospects. It also intended to take advantage of the appointment of Aníbal Delgado Fiallos, a figure sympathetic to the peasant movement, as the new executive director of the INA by the newly elected President Carlos Flores Facussé, the nephew of Miguel Facussé, who came into office in January 1998.

The forum brought together different regional actors who shared their experiences of the processes of agrarian reform and counterreform in the Aguán. The first speaker to take the stage after the welcoming words was a regional representative of INA, who emphasized how land could not be seen merely as raw materials and needed to be understood as the foundation of life itself. At the same time, he highlighted the importance of efficient and competitive production, wherein the peasant had to be, above all, an important actor within the market. Moreover, following the liberal mantra of personal accountability, he laid at the feet of the peasant families the responsibility for their development and improvement (Altiok 1998).

The two next speakers, both important members of the Pastoral Social, took the stage and questioned the interpretation presented by the INA representative. According to them, the blame was not so much on the peasant families of the cooperatives as on the types of policies that the INA had promoted. For example, for Peter Marchetti, a U.S.-born Jesuit economist and at the time general coordinator of the PS,

> The agrarian reform in Honduras was not planned or driven by Hondurans. It was one of the ten conservative and counter-insurgency agrarian reforms that were planned by the USA under the Alliance for Progress... In the Bajo Aguán... it was designed and financed by the Inter-American Development Bank, a bank under strict U.S. control. It is fair to say that the Agrarian Modernization Law and its planning were part of the great Agricultural Transformation Project of Miguel Facussé, one of the great Honduran entrepreneurs.
>
> This alien model implemented a top-down technocratic agrarian reform, in which the actual members of the cooperatives had little say. It had fostered multiple levels of corruption and coercion by government officials and national and local peasant leaders. Then, once the LMA had taken hold and inaugurated the neoliberal era, the INA and the agrarian reform structures in general had allied with big capital—with Miguel Facussé at the helm—to convince the cooperatives to sell and thus leading to the current situation of pervasive poverty. (Altiok 1998, 8)

After these official presentations, it was time for the members of the cooperatives to speak. I will not dwell on the speeches here: it is enough to say that it was a moment for finger-pointing, as blame was directed at the INA for the way the agrarian reform had been deployed, at the businessmen and companies that were profiting from the sales, and at the male leadership of the cooperatives that had been corrupted and had sold the cooperatives' assets. It was also a moment for women like Eugenia to remind the participants that the sales had been a male deed and that "women would not have sold."[2] At the same time, it was a moment to propose the need for a "new" agrarian reform to improve the lives of those living in the Aguán.

At the close of the forum, it was the turn of Aníbal Delgado Fiallos to take the stage and present his position as the new director of the INA. Early into his speech, the INA's executive director noted that "it is important to propel a deep process of agrarian reform.... Logically, one thing is what is ethically desirable and another thing what is historically possible. That is why we at the INA have relaunched an idea of the agrarian reform that would be possible under the political, social and economic conditions of Honduras and within the frames of the standing legal norms" (Altiok 1998, 15).

What did this historically viable agrarian reform look like? It began with a broad land titling program, as well as the promotion of the access to land of Indigenous groups; second, a process of *reconversión empresarial* (business restructuring), which meant turning the peasant enterprises into profitable businesses; and third, the institutional strengthening of the INA, to make it more efficient and transparent, to avoid repeating "the errors of the past" and exclude those who had sold land from any future participation in agrarian reform projects. As we can see, undoing the agrarian counterreform process or embarking on a broad redistributive program was not to be part of this "new" agrarian reform.

Despite Delgado Fiallos's lukewarm proposal, the forum ended with an atmosphere of optimism and hope. At least he had come to the Aguán and had winked at the peasant movement, and the idea of relaunching the agrarian reform could become a reality. However, a couple of months after the forum, Hurricane Mitch crashed into the impoverished north coast of Honduras, and this new hope became mixed with despair, salting old wounds, creating new ones and above all, revealing the deep set of contradictions that had brought the Aguán into being. Further, the aftermath of the hurricane revealed the very unstable equilibria of political forces that were created by the imposition of the neoliberal project in the country since the 1980s.

While the previous chapter focused on the process of primitive accumulation that took place in the Aguán, this one explores instead the so-called transition to democracy and how it mixed violently and spectacularly with nature, in the form of Hurricane Mitch, to produce not only a new wave of dispossession but also the beginnings of a new wave of popular mobilization.

### The Democratic Transition as a Neoliberal Class Project

In Central America, the imposition of the neoliberal project was not only an economic process but also a geopolitical one. The decade of the 1980s was one of turmoil and unease for the United States, with the victory of the Frente Sandinista de Liberación Nacional (FSLN) in Nicaragua in 1979 and the escalating military conflict in El Salvador between the guerilla and the army. In this context, Honduras played a crucial dual role: on the one hand, it was the corridor through which military support flowed between the Sandinistas in Nicaragua and the insurgent FMLN in El Salvador. On the other, it became the base of operation for the U.S. attempts at destroying the guerillas in El Salvador and undermining the Sandinista government in Nicaragua. Thus, for the United States, assuring the political and military stability of, and control over, Honduras was fundamental.

This geopolitical importance translated into a massive transfer of financial aid that helped keep the country's economy relatively afloat. However, this was not the only step taken. Already in 1978, under intense international pressure, the Honduran military government announced its intentions of beginning the transition toward a civilian government, through organizing democratic elections and a constituent assembly. Notwithstanding the U.S. pressure, it was clear that the armed forces were entering this process from a position of strength. Despite the country's political and economic crisis, the military was not being forced out of office by an insurgent group (as in the case of Nicaragua); nor did they need to negotiate their exit with one such organization (as in the case of El Salvador). Instead, they were the central piece of the regional U.S. anti-insurgent strategy and a key factor in terms of the dynamics of domination within the country.

As we saw before, the military's rise to power was the result of the inability of the traditional political elite, organized in the two-party electoral system, to come to basic agreements regarding how to distribute power and interact with the subaltern groups other than through repression. As their reformist project began to modernize the state, the military itself began to grow roots in the institutional framework. From controlling critical economic and political posts in the government, eventually, the armed forces began to control pieces of the economy directly, for instance the telecommunications sector (Sieder 1995). Through this process, they also created connections with members of the country's economic elites, which allowed many generals to become businessmen. Thus, by the 1980s, any process of democratization had to be necessarily negotiated with the military and take its chokehold on the state into consideration.

As such, the new constitution of 1982 and the call for democratic election for November of that year were the result of negotiations between the armed forces and the country's traditional political elites, under the tutelage of the United States (Irías and Sosa 2009; Pirker and Núñez 2010). In this pact, the military agreed to "return to the barracks" in exchange for maintaining, and even increasing, the levels of U.S. military aid and retaining high levels of autonomy in relation to the civilian government. Politically, the pact and the new constitution came to formalize and strengthen the traditional two-party system, organized around the interexchange in power between the National and Liberal parties. The result was an electoral system with acceptable formal levels of transparency and mechanisms of representation; that did not translate into substantive changes in terms of the forms of government, political representation, or the protection of civil rights and liberties.

Honduras of the 1980s was dominated by the war against communism and the doctrine of national security, characterized by tight military control and high levels of state and parastatal violence, which took the form of disappearances, tortures, and summary executions of those suspected by the armed forces of being "communists" or "subversive" (Barahona 2005). We can also see just how invested the United States was in this transition, with the appointment of John Negroponte, one of Reagan's most trusted agents, as ambassador in Honduras between 1981 and 1985 (Kinzer 2001).

If the 1980s was the decade of democracy under military tutelage, the 1990s would be a decade of political opening under civilian control. With the end of the Cold War and the subsequent changes in U.S. foreign policy, pressure was put on the military and the national elites, by both the regional hegemon and the country's civil society, to promote an actual opening, particularly in terms of civil rights and liberties. As a result, starting roughly in 1993, Honduran society began a process of formal demilitarization. That year, the department of criminal investigation was removed from military control and placed under the public prosecutor's office. The following year, a set of crucial institutions that so far had been under military control, due to "national security" reasons, began to return to civilian authority. These included the Honduran Company of Telecommunications (HONDUTEL), the merchant seafarer, the General Directorate of Migratory Policy, the National Geographic Institute, and the civil aviation authority. Also, between 1994 and 1995, due to the mobilization of human rights organizations, the constitution was reformed to eliminate compulsory military service. Finally, in 1998 a new police law was approved, separating it from military control. That same year the figure of the supreme leader of the armed forces was suppressed, making the elected president the head of the military, at least formally. This final step in the subordination of the military to civilian control was the result of heavy pressure by the U.S. embassy and occurred after an amnesty was granted to officers persecuted for human rights violations in the 1980s (Cruz 2011).

Although there had already been attempts to promote the commercial liberalization of the country during the 1980s, it had been close to impossible to attract foreign investment and promote significant institutional changes at the time, due to the regional armed conflicts as well as the leeway given to the state by U.S. financial aid. It would not be until the pacification of the region through the peace accords in the 1990s and the increased leverage provided by the national debt discipline imposed by the IFIs that neoliberal tenets would become hegemonic.

This transition must be read in tandem with the domestic balance of power. During the 1980s, the elites closer to the government and traditional economic interests such as cattle ranching and timber extraction were able to block, or at least slow down, the imposition of the neoliberal project. However, with the changes mentioned above in the regional geopolitical context, the new transnational elite, organized around APROH, was able to push their project forward (Robinson 2003).

However, unlike what happened in other countries in the region, where the new economic groups were able to create their own new political parties (for example, the National Republican Alliance, or ARENA, in the Salvadoran case), in Honduras they were forced to join politics by infiltrating the two-party system both formally—as members of both parties and presenting themselves as candidates for both congress and the presidency—and, above all, informally, by making significant donations to both parties and trying to influence policies. The advance of the neoliberal project in Honduras took the form of an articulation between traditional forms of political organization and the political and economic disputes between the old and new economic power groups. For example, within these parties, the tug of war between the different political and economic projects mixed with the traditional system of competition between various strongmen (caudillos) representing different internal political trends. Thus, the traditional form of doing politics came to represent new interests.

The reason why the "new" elites could not create a new party or immediately take control of the traditional ones has to do both with the Honduran process of state formation and the country's racist political culture. As we saw in the previous chapter, by the 1980s the new entrepreneurial elite, dominated by Palestinians, was already the most important economic group in the country. However, their economic hegemony did not translate politically. For both Darío Euraque (2009) and Rodolfo Pastor (1985, 28), this "lack of correspondence between the political system and the social structure" was the result both of the level of entrenchment of the traditional elites in the government and of the ingrained and extensive racism against "The Turks."

This contradictory articulation between formal democracy, virulent anticommunism, and neoliberal instauration was neither new nor particular to the Honduran case. It was instead a somewhat familiar combination in the Central and Latin American context of the 1980s and 1990s. Further, according to William Robinson (1996), it responded to the main objective of U.S. foreign policy in the Central American region: sustaining a certain level of political stability that would allow the United States to maintain its hegemonic position. During the Cold War, this stability was better served by strong regimes that enjoyed significant military presence and followed the national security doctrine, whether they were formally democratic or not. However, with the fall of the Berlin Wall and the supposed transition toward a unipolar world, the militarized regimes of national security became not only unnecessary politically but also very expensive and detrimental to the ascendant neoliberal project and its mantra of economic freedom and increasing transnational articulation.

It is in this context that Robinson (1996) tracks the rise within U.S. academia of "transitology," which then spread across the developing world: the academic discussion regarding the steps that nondemocratic and undeveloped countries needed to take to transition toward modern, democratic regimes. According to Robinson, the emergence of "transitology" was actively promoted by the U.S. government in the form of grants, fellowships, publications, and sponsored meetings. Further, this was not only part of an academic movement but also of a broader shift in U.S. foreign policy, away from supporting dictatorships and other forms of authoritarian governments and toward favoring "polyarchy": a minimal definition of democracy, based on empirical and institutional terms and basic procedures, particularly the recurrent organization of formal and representative elections, and the alternation of power between various constituencies (Dahl 1973).

As such, the histories of countries such as Honduras from the 1980s onward tend to be understood and explained as truncated versions of the infallible theory of democratic transition, with no regard for the actual shape that this "transition" took in the context of the regional geopolitical dynamics and the dispute between dominant and subaltern groups. However, toward the end of the 1990s, in the aftermath of Hurricane Mitch, all the different contradictions riddling the Honduran "transition to democracy" came together in explosive and unexpected ways. Events on the ground demonstrated not only the analytical deficiencies of the transitology framework but also that democracy, understood and imposed in these terms, was in no way a resolution to the structural tensions and conflicts that had been at the heart of the historical process of state formation and passive revolution that I have been analyzing so far.

## Hurricane Mitch and Disaster Capitalism

Hurricane Mitch hit the Central American Caribbean coast on October 26–27, 1998. One of the strongest storms in the history of the Atlantic Basin, it struck Honduras the hardest, leaving a trail of destruction in its wake. Mitch was not your typical hurricane. From the twenty-eighth of October until early on the thirtieth, it hovered over the sea and then very slowly—between the thirtieth and thirty-first— began to move inland, first as a hurricane and then as a tropical storm that ended up covering most of the country. Due to this erratic behavior, it was initially thought that it would not be too destructive and that its effects would be limited to the north coast.

The country was ill-prepared to deal with what was about to happen. More than the winds themselves, it was the rains that did most of the damage. In some regions, the amount of rainfall over a few days was the same as the yearly average (Olson et al. 2001), and it was estimated by some farmers to have had the effect of ten years of rain (Holt-Giménez 2002). In the end, over 5,000 Hondurans died, more than 8,000 disappeared, and around 285,000 people lost their homes. Approximately 60 percent of the nation's infrastructure was severely damaged, and about 70 percent of the crops were lost, including coffee, bananas, and pineapples, which represented a loss of over US$800 million in the agrarian sector alone. This meant that around 38 percent of the Honduran population was directly affected by the hurricane, which caused total damages equivalent to 72 percent of the gross national product (FAO 2010). For all practical purposes, at the end of 1998, Honduras was surviving off the foreign aid that began to roll in once the level of destruction became evident.[3]

However, if Mitch, the hurricane, was a natural event that took place toward the end of 1998, Mitch the disaster was many years in the making. For example, according to a study by the FAO (2010, 2), the massive destruction left in its wake was the result of "a century of environmental degradation, poverty, unequal access and distribution of the land and military conflicts, together with almost eight months of droughts due to the El Niño phenomenon in 1997–98 ... causing floods of a greater intensity that should have been expected from a storm with these characteristics." This heavy rainfall fell on hills and mountains severely eroded from years of slash and burn migratory agriculture and turned into mudslides that rolled down into plains and valleys dominated by monocultures such as sugar cane and oil palms.[4]

Conversely, Mitch, the political-economic disaster, began a few weeks after the rains had stopped. According to Naomi Klein (2007, 395),

> In the two months after Mitch struck, with the country still knee-deep in rubble, corpses and mud, the Honduran congress passed laws allowing the privatization of airports, seaports and highways and fast-tracked plans to privatize the state telephone company, the national electric company and parts of the water sector. It overturned progressive land-reform laws, making it far easier for foreigners to buy and sell property, and rammed through a radically pro-business mining law (drafted by industry) that lowered environmental standards and made it easier to evict people from homes that stood in the way of new mines.

For the Canadian author, what happened in Honduras was a prime example of what she calls "disaster capitalism": a political strategy to push forward unpopular transformations that would probably fail in other contexts by exploiting the window of opportunity that opens when a society goes into shock and is in survival mode. In the Honduran case, disaster capitalism took two paths. On the one hand, the encrusted government elites moved forward with a set of privatizations and attempts to decrease public spending, particularly by lowering wages and laying off workers (Sosa 2016). On the other hand, they pushed for a set of policies aimed at deepening the neoliberal land regime. As such, during the process of reconstruction, the conditions for a broad process of dispossession were created.

It is important to point out that one of the global hallmarks of the neoliberal project, despite the narrative of state retreat, has been a proliferation of new laws and institutional frameworks designed to define how to govern the new commodities and subjects produced by the dual process of market liberalization and democratization. Thus, topics such as environmental and cultural rights began to be protected by international conventions and their related national policies (Anderson 2012; Graham 2009; Loperena 2017), at the same time that economic sectors such as mining or tourism demanded novel frameworks to facilitate the articulation between particular sites and the imperatives of capital accumulation on a global scale (Brondo 2013; Middeldorp 2014; Shipley 2013). The result was the proliferation of social conflicts all over the country around various topics and landscapes, such as land grabbing, mining, and hydroelectric projects.[5] One such landscape was the oil palm covered valley of the Aguán, where the battle drums of the agrarian reform began to sound loudly.

### The Rekindling of the Peasant Movement in the Aguán

Probably the most lucid voice regarding what was happening in the Aguán toward the end of the 1990s was that of Peter Marchetti, the then-Jesuit priest and coordinator of the PS. According to Marchetti,

> Standard Fruit [Company], Facussé and Morales are not citizens in the Bajo Aguán, but of the globalized world, and know very well how to pillage the local resources to enrich themselves and take advantage of the local traditionalism to increase their modern excesses. The companies operate without caring about regional development, just like the banana companies did at the beginning of the 20th century. With the [agrarian] counter-reform, the levels of economic activity in the valley plummeted because the three companies import most of their supplies and service structures. They are modern enclaves in a sea of misery (1998, 8).

In his reading, before the 1980s a sort of virtuous circle existed between the cooperatives, understood as need economies, and the regional market in which they spent most of their money. After the land sales, a few investors came to control the industry and the surpluses created were pumped out of the region. This control was achieved not only through the concentration of land and labor power that I described in the last chapter but also through what is known in critical agrarian studies as a "control grab": here, certain actors can control land and resources, such as water, without actually owning them, due to their strategic position within the value chain (Alonso-Fradejas 2012; Borras Jr. et al. 2012; Huggins 2014; León Araya 2019b). In our case, palm oil production is very susceptible to vertical integration and monopsonistic concentration of power, particularly in the phases of processing and commercialization. The bigger processing mills—particularly those owned by Facussé and Morales and, to a lesser extent, COAPALMA—could control the prices and large shares of the market, even without owning all the land covered with oil palms. This not only concentrated considerable power in a few hands but also increasingly placed palm oil monoculture at the center of life in the Aguán region.

Shifting from the valley to the hills, the situation was significantly worse. Not only were there fewer wage labor and commercialization opportunities available, but there was also less access to basic services such as education, health, or electricity. Moreover, after ten years of slash and burn agriculture, the hills were deeply eroded. This was also an indirect effect of the agrarian counterreform, since peasant families were forced to move to the hills in search of land or to escape the exploitative relations in the valley. Hurricane Mitch came then to reveal the effects of the way in which the Aguán's landscape had been produced. The patterns of destruction left by Mitch and the patterns of dispossession left by the agrarian counterreform overlapped with the expansion of the oil palm monoculture. The rains produced by the hurricane washed down the eroded hills, creating mudslides and river overflows toward the valley, and in the aftermath of the disaster, famished and homeless peasants followed the same path looking for refuge.

However, the mud, debris, water, and displaced peasants did not converge onto a homogeneous space. Around three decades of dead labor had produced a landscape shaped by the oil palm plantations and its contradictions. Levees created to protect the palm trees from the Aguán River's constant flooding also protected them from Mitch, reorienting and magnifying much of the damage toward the neighboring communities, many inhabited by former cooperative members (Casolo 2004; 2009).

From the beginning, the Catholic Church, and particularly the PS, took the lead in relief efforts. Besides the use of its buildings as shelters, the PS employed its cars in the rescue effort and helped organize the collection of food, drinking water, and medicines. Further, due to both the lack of logistical capacities shown by the state and the generalized suspicion by both Hondurans and foreigners regarding the levels of corruption in most public institutions, by November 1998 much of the reconstruction effort and resources were transferred directly to NGOs and the church (Falla 1998; Jeffrey 2002). This was further consolidated in May 1999, during a meeting in Stockholm between the Central American governments, five European governments, the IMF, and the World Bank. On this occasion, while the conditions for the reconstruction aid were being negotiated, NGOs and some grassroots organizations lobbied to make sure that a commitment to increase local participation was included in the process. Thus, "by signing the Stockholm Accords each Central American government committed itself to decentralization, citizen participation, transparency, environmental protection and the promotion of gender and ethnic rights" (Casolo 2004, 43). As a result, the contradictions between neoliberal reform and democratic opening became more apparent.

For the Jesuits, the disaster became a way of advancing their social transformation agenda in the Aguán. In 1999 the PS began a massive program of work for food, bankrolled by the USAID and supported by Catholic Relief Services. In the end, the PS came to channel around US$7 million worth of food aid to over 678 affected villages and neighborhoods (Casolo 2004).

At the same time, this period was one of intense peasant organization and struggle. In general terms, we can speak of two main types of peasant movements arising out of this context in the late 1990s in the Aguán: movements in the hills and in the valleys. On the one hand, hills peasant movements were created in the aftermath of Hurricane Mitch by landless peasant families from the hills surrounding the Aguán Valley. They had little to no organizational experience and very little knowledge of the oil palm monoculture. They tended to target for recuperation lowlands estates on the left bank of the Aguán River that, in most cases, were not covered by oil palms. Thus, initially, they dedicated their effort to reenacting the sort of agriculture that they knew best, namely, slash and burn production of staple crops. However, eventually, the attraction of monoculture became very strong, forcing these movements to seek paths toward the palm oil industry, mostly as sellers of labor power, but ideally as producers of the raw material.

The valley peasant movements, on the other hand, were created by former cooperative members and a younger generation claiming to be the sons and daughters of those who had sold. Born into and molded by the oil palm monoculture, these movements organized around the narrative that their lands had been taken away illegally in the early 1990s. They targeted former cooperative lands, on both banks of the river, that were cultivated with oil palms in full production. Unlike hills movements, their objective was to be a part of the oil palm monoculture but as raw material sustaining need economies and as a way of keeping for themselves a more significant cut of the surplus they produce. In what follows, I briefly present the history of two movements: the Peasant Movement of the Aguán (MCA), the quintessential hills peasant movement, and MUCA, one of the first valley peasant movements. Through their stories, we will glimpse the shape that disaster capitalism took on the ground and the attempts by these groups of organized peasants to wrest away the control of the palm barons over the plantation economy.

### The MCA and the Relaunching of the Peasant Movement in the Aguán

In September 2000 the Guatemalan Jesuit priest and anthropologist Ricardo Falla (2000) wrote an essay titled "Land Occupation Opens the way for Agrarian Reform," which begins with the following short description:

Around midnight on May 14, 700 landless peasants [families] of the Aguán, on Honduras's northern coast, occupied lands that belonged to the now dismantled Regional Military Training Center (CREM) and that are currently claimed by local cattle ranchers and farmers ... but the occupation continues and is proving to be a transcendental event.

For Falla this land occupation was "transcendental" on three accounts: (1) historically, due to the role played by the CREM during the 1980s as the place where the United States trained the Salvadoran army and Nicaraguan Contras; (2) socioeconomically, since "this occupation seems to be rekindling the much-needed idea of agrarian reform and could lead to the launching of a new, effective agrarian reform model to fight rural poverty"; and finally, (3) geopolitically, because "the CREM lands in the department of Colón's Caribbean coast area act as a corridor for drug-trafficking activities."

The families that participated in this land recuperation came mostly from the surrounding hills and neighboring departments of Olancho, Yoro, and Atlántida and had not been part of the cooperatives sold in the 1990s. Most had a direct or indirect relationship with the church, either as Delegates of the Word, lay workers, or through kinship ties with these groups. As such, if we had to locate a starting point for the MCA, it would probably be the forum "Together Let's Strengthen the Agrarian Reform" with which I opened this chapter, not because the MCA took shape at that moment, but because the central elements were starting to come together in an embryonic form. Here, the oral history of the region played an important role, as these groups began meeting in late 1998 and learned and discussed the history of the lands of the CREM and the peasant movement in the Aguán, the importance of collective work, and the need for a new agrarian reform, thus galvanizing a collective memory.

Hurricane Mitch was a catalyst on several different levels. First, due to the particularly devastating impact that it had on the hills surrounding the valleys of the Aguán, Lean, and Sula, a whole layer of rural poverty that had been hiding in clear view came down the hills into the major lowland towns and cities searching for refuge. These people had lost their homes and crops in the disaster, making the housing question a fundamental and urgent need. Second, the large amounts of aid money that were funneled to the country and the central role that the church had in the distribution, allocation, and use of these funds gave the church the material tools to advance in such a project. Third, even before Mitch crashed into the Honduran north coast, there were talks by the national peasant federations of coming together and relaunching the movement.

Finally, there was already in the region a place where the project could be carried out in accord with the legal limitations set by the LMA.

What eventually became the home of the MCA had been a U.S. military base known as the Regional Center of Military Training (Centro Regional de Entrenamiento Militar, CREM). The history behind this piece of land begins in 1972, when the INA gave around six thousand hectares of uncultivated land that had belonged to the Truxillo Railroad Company to Fausto Fortín Inestroza. This was an illegal transaction, since national land could only be used for agrarian reform purposes and could not be sold. However, sometime between 1975 and 1977, Temístocles Ramírez, a U.S. citizen of Puerto Rican origin, bought a bit over fifty-seven hundred hectares for less than US$80,000. This added another layer of illegality since, according to article 107 of the Honduran constitution at that time, foreigners could not own land near the country's coasts or international borders.

In 1983, at the express request of the U.S. government, the Honduran state expropriated Ramírez's lands to build the military training base. However, in 1987, Ramírez appealed to the U.S. government, demanding compensation for the lands he had lost. This, in turn, led the U.S. Congress to freeze US$20 million of financial aid until the Honduran government agreed to compensate Ramírez. On June 28, 1990, the Callejas government responded with Executive Decree no. 010-90, approving a payment of US$7.8 million for the agreed compensation, a price many times higher than Ramírez had initially paid (FIDH 2011, 35).

In the early 1990s, as the military conflicts in the Central American region waned, the United States "returned" the lands to the Honduran state. This meant that these territories could and should have been used for agrarian reform purposes, as they were national "fiscal" lands. However, the newly approved municipalities law (article 68) allowed local governments to sell and title national and ejido (municipal) lands in their jurisdictions. This reform, which was reversed just three months later, did not include "fiscal" or national lands such as the CREM. Nonetheless, between January and May 1991, the Trujillo municipality sold them to local cattle ranchers, retired colonels, and politicians for a total of less than US$50,000, less than Ramírez paid for them, and certainly less than what the state spent just one year before. Two years later, in 1993, the Honduran congress requested the attorney general's office to transfer the lands to the INA, to be distributed among landless peasants. However, in practice, the lands remained underused and occupied by the illegal claimants until 2000, when the MCA was created by occupying these lands.

## THE BIRTH OF THE GUADALUPE CARNEY

It was raining cats and dogs on the night of May 14, 2000, when the organized families made the trip to the former CREM in around fifty trucks, buses, and cars. They recalled later that they had been assured there would not be any problems entering; however, this was not the case. As they approached the former base, bursts of AK-47 gunfire cut through the sound of the rain, as the cattle ranchers' guards shot into the air trying to intimidate them. This was all for show and the guards at the gates put up a token resistance for a few minutes before being overwhelmed by the crowd of landless peasants.

Once the first truck went past the gates, the rest followed and began unloading. There were no shelters from the rain, and the families were forced to do the best that they could to put up nylon tents or rustic lean-tos covered with wild palm fronds. This was the end of the journey, but it was just the beginning of their struggles.

In a general assembly that took place on May 18—just four days after they entered the lands—the topic of how to name the new community came up. There was a debate between two alternatives: San Isidro, patron saint of the farm workers (*santo patrono de los labradores*), whose name day is May 15; and Guadalupe Carney, in honor of the U.S.-born Jesuit priest who dedicated his life to the peasant struggle and was disappeared by the Honduran military in 1983.[6] After a close vote the latter name won out and two days later, on May 20, during another assembly, the discussion turned to how the peasant movement should be known. After a lengthy discussion in which different possibilities were presented, those gathered decided to name their movement the Peasant Movement of the Aguán (MCA).

During the early months, the atmosphere combined effervescence, fear, and hope. Everybody knew that entering the lands of the CREM did not immediately translate into actual control over the fifty-seven hundred hectares that they were disputing. To consolidate their position, the peasants erected a roadblock in front of their new home, which just happened to be on the highway that connects the rest of the Aguán Valley with the international port of Puerto Castillo, stopping the flow of banana exports and pressuring the government into regularizing their tenure over the recuperated land. They also organized what they called "occupation tours," in which all but a few of the men and women left behind to protect the main camp and the children would march together to one of the many properties into which the original lands of the CREM had been chopped up during the 1990s sale, take control over the plot, leave some people to defend it, and move to the next one. These practices had two main effects. Internally, the tours helped galvanize the social and political bonds between the members. Externally, they created animosity and hate in the local elites and the neighboring communities, who saw the MCA as "invaders."

This aura of danger and rejection surrounding the newly created peasant community was heightened by the clashes between the MCA, the hired guards by the region's terratenientes and the police. For example, on July 27, 2000, there was a fierce clash with the guards of Henry Osorto, a former army colonel. In a gunfire exchange between the two groups, Diógenes Osorto, Henry's brother, was shot dead. Henry, a prominent figure in Trujillo, whose home stood as an affront on a hill in the middle of the lands claimed by the MCA, swore revenge, and tensions in the region rose to the point that the word in Tegucigalpa was that "civil war" had broken out in the Aguán (Falla 2000). In the end, the situation was brought somewhat under control with the intervention of a high-level commission named by President Carlos Flores Facussé himself, but as we will see later, this blood feud was far from over.

As the members of the MCA struggled to carve out a living space on the former lands of the CREM, they entered a set of relations with other institutions to stabilize their position in the zone and improve their living conditions. The staging of roadblocks was accompanied by efforts to legally formalize their tenure over the land as quickly as possible. On October 12 this strategy began to bear fruit, as President Carlos Flores Facussé visited the community to distribute the first nine definitive land titles and to commit to signing a decree to compensate the former "owners" for the land they lost.

As I mentioned earlier, the former CREM lands had been chopped up and divided into individual and private plots in the 1991 sale. This meant that each one of these plots had a legal deed; in total, there were around fifty plots. Receiving title to nine of these was, of course, an important event. As one former member of the MCA's board of directors in this period reported, "With this we now felt that we had really settled down on the land." Compensation for the former owners was a much thornier topic. According to Honduran agrarian law, since these were "fiscal" lands, the state did not need to pay for them. However, it did have to pay for the "improvements" made on the land (any sort of investment: trees planted, levees, buildings, or other infrastructure constructed).

Once the president left the community, he seemed to have forgotten his commitment to signing the executive decree, and the year 2001 began with the MCA roadblocking again to remind the president of his commitments. These new blockades lasted around nine days and involved a few clashes with the police, leading the president to sign Executive Decree no. 92-2001, which allocated nearly US$2 million to compensate the former owners. However, according to members of the MCA's board of directors of the period, half of that money was used by the INA to pay "institutional costs," and only twenty-three properties were legally transferred to the MCA. The remaining eighteen titles would have to wait until 2007, when Manuel Zelaya's administration made the transfer.

On a more quotidian level, the role of the church was crucial. At the same time as the MCA struggled to legalize their situation on the lands, they also began creating the community of Guadalupe Carney, and much of the work was bankrolled by foreign aid channeled through the church. The PS created two foundations (San Alonso Rodríguez in 1999 and Popol Nah Tun in 2003) to distribute and allocate the funds that initially came as part of the post-Mitch reconstruction process, but later also for various communal development projects. In this way, between 2000 and 2006, the Guadalupe Carney community received a significant amount of funds in the form of productive projects such as chicken farms and tilapia ponds (Cano 2010). However, in most cases, these projects failed, as they did not consider the local social and ecological conditions.

Once the external funding began to dwindle in 2005, the MCA as a political project, and Guadalupe Carney as a community, began to move in different directions. From the beginning, the board of directors and the MCA's structures—as the working commissions are known—were financed directly through external funds; members did not have to pay dues. Once the funds stopped coming in, various commissions—such as arts and sports—stopped functioning, and the board of directors had a harder time getting its work done. The situation worsened in 2008, when on the early morning of August 3, a group of Henry Osorto's armed guards fired upon a group of MCA peasants and detained a thirteen-year-old girl from Guadalupe Carney for around thirty minutes. The community responded first by calling the police, who told them that they could not intervene, and later by taking manners into their own hands. Roughly three hundred people surrounded Osorto's home, which, to recall, sat in the middle of the former CREM lands. The guards responded by firing into the crowd, killing at least one peasant, which in turn led the peasants to fire back and close in on the house. It is not yet clear how, but the house went up in flames, with a final death toll of eleven, including Henry Osorto himself and most of the people in the house.

After the "Casa Quemada" (burnt house) incident, as it is commonly known, the levels of repression and persecution by the local police forces and armed guards of the MCA increased. Arrest warrants were issued against the leaders of the organization, despite many of them not being present at the shootout, which forced eighteen of them to escape to Nicaragua for a few months until the tension subsided. This in effect decapitated the MCA as an organization, leaving most of the decisions to be taken by the local representatives of the national peasant federations.

Economically, things were not working out any better. The fact that most of the productive projects financed with cooperation funds had failed meant that in the end the families were left with limited options. Life became a complex combination of different sorts of activities, such as growing meager milpas (due to the poor quality of the soil), some form of meat or milk husbandry, or selling grazing grass as animal feed. Other community members worked as day laborers on the oil palm plantations close to the community, owned by Miguel Facussé and René Morales. Their fates seemed to be inextricably entangled with that of the oil palm monoculture. For yet others, the response was to migrate toward the United States in search of the American Dream. Nowadays, the landscape of the community bears the mark of this exodus, as cinderblock houses, with designs mimicking U.S. suburbia and built with remittances, pop up among the more traditional regional architecture of adobe houses. Also, most of the older people, those who took part in the original occupation, complain that many "outsiders" are moving into the community, buying the lands of those who either leave or are so impoverished as to not have an alternative.

According to agrarian law, these sales are illegal. However, as the case of the MCA clearly shows, the line between legal and illegal in this part of Honduras is defined by force. Some of the buyers of these lands are alleged narcos interested in laundering money, hiding weapons and drugs and having a foothold in the community. This is certainly a very different present from the future of hope that people like Ricardo Falla, Peter Marchetti, and the hundreds of peasants who came under the flag of the MCA imagined in the early 2000s.

The members of Tocoa's PS had seen in the MCA and the Guadalupe Carney community a chance for rekindling the agrarian reform in the region. However, as much as they tried, they were unable to manufacture an alternative to the oil palm monoculture. In practice, by following the organizational blueprint of the state and the agrarian reform—with its heavily disciplined collective enterprises—they reenacted the process of labor capture experienced by those families that arrived in the region in the 1970s and 1980s as part of the BAP.

## MUCA: The Sons and Daughters of the Agrarian Reform

While the history of the hills' movements began with Mitch, that of the valley movements is connected to the agrarian counterreform of the early 1990s. For the founding members of MUCA, it all started with the illegal sale of the cooperatives El Despertar, San Esteban, and La Trinidad, all of them oil palm producers located on the Aguán River's left bank. According to the oral account of former members, In the case of El Despertar, on March 5, 1994, the board of directors authorized the president of the cooperative to negotiate and sell 636 hectares of oil palm lands to the company Oleo Palmas de Centroamérica, whose majority partner was René Morales. Just as in most cases, there was no clear consensus within the cooperative as to whether to sell or not, but in a process like the one that I described in the previous chapter, in the end the sale was enforced from within by death threats against those who opposed it. However, unlike the case of Marino and Eugenia's cooperative, here those opposing the sale managed to organize against it.

According to Marcelo, whom we met before, and who is one of MUCA's founders, the peasants began to mobilize after they found out that the totality of El Despertar's land had been sold, and not a portion as had been initially decided. Marcelo immediately took off to Trujillo to try to ascertain what had occurred. A local lawyer told him that he should go to Tegucigalpa to figure out the whole process better. He slowly but surely managed to follow the paper trail back to a note dated March 5, 1994, in which the cooperative's board of directors authorized the president the sale. After his inquiry, it became apparent to him that there was a clear connection between businessmen such as Morales and the local governments and that he would not find any support at the regional level. Besides, it was evident that the sale had been illegal. Although the AML allowed the sale of agrarian reform lands, it had two requirements: first, the sale had to be approved by the cooperative's general assembly; and second, the deal had to be sanctioned by the INA. Neither of these conditions was fulfilled in this case: the note that authorized the sale of the El Despertar cooperative was signed only by the members of the board of directors—not the whole general assembly—and there was no documentation suggesting that the INA had ratified it.

Armed with this information, Marcelo gathered a group of former cooperative members and approached a lawyer who assured them that their case was as good as won and that they did not even have to pay him, because Morales would have to pay once he lost the case. Things, however, did not pan out that way. A few months after the peasants presented the legal claim, their lawyer told them it had been rejected. Hypothesizing that he had been paid off, the former cooperative members moved on, found another lawyer, and started the process anew. This pattern repeated itself several times. Each time they would hire a lawyer and pay his fees, only to find out later that their legal demands had been either canceled or forever stalled. However, far from deterring them, these developments gave them a sense of purpose and unity. They became increasingly convinced that they needed to become stronger by increasing their numbers. This was not particularly difficult, as the region in the late 1990s and early 2000s was awash with grievances and poverty.

We find a good example in the case of Marielos, whose interpretation of the coup I presented in the introduction. Born in the small municipality of Bonito Oriental—south of Trujillo and east of Tocoa—she was the granddaughter of a Salvadoran immigrant who had arrived in the region probably in the 1950s. Mother of four, she moved to Tocoa in her early twenties following her then-partner and father of her first child. However, in the late 1990s, she decided to leave the city for a nearby village to escape a situation of domestic violence. There Marielos began working in one of the few sources of employment available in the community: Dinant Corporation's oil palm plantation. She did various odd jobs there, starting with picking up the fruits of oil palm that fall from the bunches that men cut and fertilizing the palm trees. Later, when the company built an extraction plant nearby, she packaged vegetable shortening.

It was around this time that her estranged father began to visit her. Although he had never been involved with any of the agrarian reform cooperatives, in 1998 he had joined one of the groups that would eventually become MUCA. During these visits, he would insist that she joins the organization. She remembers him saying, "The land is necessarily the livelihood of the peasantry. Do you think it is fair that someone like Facussé should have all of it while people like us die of hunger?" By 2000 she began attending the meetings of one of the many similar groups scattered all over the Aguán Valley. Just as in the case of the MCA, the region's oral history was crucial. Marielos remembers how they would talk and discuss the agrarian reform legal framework, what happened to the cooperatives, how Facussé, René Morales, and other "foreign" terratenientes had been able to steal so much land, and why their struggle was both just and legal.

The meetings also provided space for young people like her, in her midtwenties, to meet former members of the agrarian reform cooperatives in their forties, fifties, and sixties, who shared with them the region's history: how the Aguán had been produced by them and how life then, without the terratenientes, had been better; that once they got rid of them, everything would be better again. As a result, different grievances, operating in different timelines, were articulated, enunciating an identity and a political narrative that wove together the aged dreams of the agrarian reform with the desperate hopes of a disenchanted generation that had been born with nothing.

In November 2005 a total of twenty-eight such groups came together to create officially the Unified Peasant Movement of the Aguán, changing the social composition of the movement in the process. While the founders—like Marcelo—were all former members of the lost cooperatives, most of the newcomers, like Marielos, were younger; some were children of former cooperative members, while others had been living on the margins of the oil palm monoculture. They had little to no experience working the land, and many of them had worked before in construction or as schoolteachers. As such, the creation of MUCA clearly reflected a region that combined a population strangled by poverty with massive riches produced and amassed around the oil palm monoculture. In both cases, the target of their frustrations was the same: the "foreign" palm men who controlled most of the monoculture and had enriched themselves at the expense of the people's misery.

This combination of different generations and backgrounds under one single roof came to inform MUCA's political strategies. If up to 2005 they had been content with trying to recover their lands through legal means, with the influx of more and new people, many with experience in other forms of popular mobilization, their strategy shifted toward direct action. The first such action, one that is well remembered as a foundational moment, came on February 7, 2006, with the "March of the 5000 Machetes" that I described in the introduction. Their demands were simple: the return of the lands that had been "stolen" in the 1990s (the older group), and the distribution of "new" land for the landless (the younger group). They remained on the bridge for four days, until a commission was sent from Tegucigalpa by the newly elected president Manuel Zelaya to negotiate, resulting in a set of agreements. This was the first time that MUCA used popular mobilization to force the government to negotiate directly. However, it came with a new lesson: what was agreed by the government under pressure would be forgotten once the pressure was lifted. The government never honored these initial agreements and MUCA was forced to take to the streets again.

MUCA's leadership decided that the way to move forward would be to combine legal processes with the traditional show of strength of the Honduran peasant movement: the recuperation of disputed lands. On January 7, 2007, they attempted to recuperate the disputed lands of La Concepción cooperative on the right bank. They reasoned that since this was one of the more advanced legal cases, a little nudge in the right direction would produce success. But this was a miscalculation, and they were evicted after five days on the land. As we will see in the next chapter, this was part of a more generalized upcycle of subaltern mobilization that led, in part, to Zelaya's infamous "turn to the Left" and his eventual demise.

On June 6, 2009, less than a month before the coup, MUCA decided to raise the stakes and go directly for the central axis of capital accumulation in the region: the extracting mills. Early in the morning that day, they entered and occupied the Exportadora del Atlántico extracting mill—property of Miguel Facussé and where Marielos used to work—in Quebrada de Arena, on the river's right bank, and remained in control for a few hours before they were evicted. This time the strategy had a significant effect, one clearly shaped by the moment.

The year 2008 in general saw a significant escalation of the conflicts between cattle and palm men, on the one hand, and peasant organizations, on the other. The conflict approached disturbing levels, and, once again, the chatter reaching Tegucigalpa and President Manuel Zelaya was that there might be the beginnings of a "civil war." Less than ten days after the extracting mill occupation, on June 17, Zelaya himself traveled to Tocoa to meet with the leadership of MUCA and sign a set of agreements. More importantly, a special commission made up of representatives of MUCA, the executive branch, and the Agriculture and Livestock Secretariat (SAG) was created to pursue a negotiated solution to the conflict. This seemed to appease the members of MUCA, who had already seen Zelaya's efforts to resolve the country's agrarian disputes, particularly those of the Aguán, and, allegedly, was offering to resolve the agrarian conflict in exchange for the peasant organization's support of the Cuarta Urna. All these processes came crumbling down less than two weeks later when Zelaya was ousted by the military and flown in his pajamas to Costa Rica.

In summary, the process of the imposition of the neoliberal project that began in the early 1990s with the signing of the SAPs picked up steam in the aftermath of Mitch and the wave of disaster capitalism. At the same time, in places like the Aguán, this cycle of dispossession was accompanied by a new cycle of subaltern organization around the idea of rekindling the agrarian reform. As the 2000s went by, this cycle continued to escalate; eventually, it would start to connect with protests and experiences of organization in other parts of the country, just as Manuel Zelaya was ascended to the presidential seat.

CHAPTER 5

# The Failed Assault on State Power

On Sunday, June 28, 2009, around 12:30 p.m., the Honduran congress convened to continue the ordinary session that had begun three days before on the 25th. Led by the then-president of Congress, the Liberal Roberto Micheletti Baín, the session was attended by all the members of Congress, except for those Liberals close to Manuel Zelaya and those from the UD. The first order of business was a report prepared by the special committee commissioned by Micheletti on the twenty-fifth to analyze the "administrative conduct" of President Zelaya.

Among other things, the report argued that "the president of the Republic, José Manuel Zelaya Rosales, has generated a climate of uncertainty, confrontation and division in the Honduran society." Further, it stated that "the Executive Power has taken unfortunate actions, defying the constituted authorities and the fulfillment of the constitutional and legal duties that in one way or another, impact on the normal development of the nation's life" (CVR 2011, 145).[1] Included in the evidence presented by the report, we find legal elements such as Zelaya's decision to not send to Congress the 2009 national budget, the sentence of the contentious administrative court of Tegucigalpa that declared the Cuarta Urna to be illegal, and the president's executive decree (PCM-20-2009) giving the order for the opinion poll to take place on the twenty-eighth. However, the report also proposes political arguments, such as the alleged lack of attention given by the government to the outbreak of the H1N1 flu, the country's economic crisis, and the increasing levels of insecurity.

Next on the order of business was reviewing the Congress's mail. The secretary, José Alfredo Saavedra, presented a letter, supposedly written and signed by José Manuel Zelaya Rosales and dated June 25, in which he resigned from his post as president due to the country's "polarized political situation" and his own alleged "health problems." The letter ended stating that with my resignation, I hope to contribute to heal the wounds of the national political environment" (CVR 2011, 146). Thereupon, Zelaya's resignation was unanimously accepted, and Micheletti appointed a new special commission to compose the corresponding decree draft and declared a half hour break. Meanwhile, in Costa Rica and still in his pajamas, Zelaya proclaimed that he had not written any such letter. When Congress reconvened after the recess, things became even more bizarre.

Probably informed by the absurdity of presenting a resignation letter signed three days before by a person who had been expelled from the country by the military and who had publicly stated that the note was false, the Congress had a change of heart. The draft of the decree regarding Zelaya's "resignation" was never presented, discussed, or approved by Congress. Instead, the legislators went back to the first special commission's report—the one on the president's "administrative conduct"—and proceeded to read a decree draft that concluded as follows:

> The irregular conduct of the president is manifest by repeatedly violating the fidelity of the republic and the country's judiciary, putting in imminent danger the rule of law and the system of democratic government that the Honduran people, by its sovereign will, has chosen and therefore, the National Congress is called upon to observe and enforce ... In conformity with article 242 of the Republic's Constitution, and the absolute absence of the president and Vice-President[2] of the Republic, the Executive Power will be exercised by the president of the National Congress. (CVR 2011, 147)

Before voting was held on the proposed decree, the floor was given to some of the members of Congress to speak their minds about what was happening. A few excerpts from their discourse are illuminating. For example, Juan Ángel Rivera Tábora of the Liberal Party declared, "In defense of the fatherland [la patria], we are all the Armed Forces. The Liberal Party abhors a coup d'état ... [but] the decisions being made now are to make this Constitution even more the Constitution of the Republic, so that no one pretends to ignore her."(CVR 2011, 149).[3] He was followed by José Toribio Aguilera, of the Unity and Innovation Party, who said the following:

> I would like to respectfully, but very seriously, call on the Ambassador of the United States in Honduras. He says, "Let him [Zelaya] get to the constituent [assembly]." Do you know what would happen if we let this movement that has the support of Venezuela, Cuba, Bolivia, and Ecuador continue? A bloody

confrontation ... The message that we need to send to the nation is that this coup d'état does not respond to personal issues. Instead, it is to correct and anticipate the [political Hurricane] Mitch that was taking shape here. (CVR 2011, 148–49)[4]

Finally, Juan Orlando Hernández, of the National Party and soon to become president of Congress and then of the republic in 2014, clearly more mindful of what was going on, stated,

> Today the secretary read a letter of resignation by the President of the Republic, and I want to emphasize, to let the Hondurans and the world know, that this National Congress when faced with the absence of the President of the Republic, cannot leave the Nation adrift ... I want to correct something also, to let the world know, that what transpired here was not a coup d'état, this is how the rule of law functions. (CVR 2011, 149)

After these discourses about coups that did not happen, and U.S. ambassadors who tried to stop them, Micheletti was sworn in as president until the expected elections of November 2009. Afterward, the national anthem was sung and Gilliam Guifarro Montes de Oca, of the National Party, brought the session to a close by leading a prayer.

Soon afterward the news traveled around the world, and the ousting of Zelaya was condemned by most media outlets, governments, and international organizations. Despite this inauspicious start, Micheletti's government—and the controversial Porfirio Lobo administration that followed—would manage to weather the diplomatic and political storm and bring some legitimacy back to the regime, with the tacit support of the U.S. government (Chayes 2017; Frank 2018).[5] Domestically, however, the coup split the country into three broad camps: those against the coup and who would eventually come to be known as the Resistance; those in favor of the "good coup" or "constitutional succession," as it was euphemistically called (Di Iorio 2010; Martínez 2010); and, finally, those who did not have a clear position concerning the crisis but were stuck in the middle nevertheless.

In this chapter I focus on the events that took place just before and around the coup to explore its connections with the process of formation of the Honduran state that we have been examining so far. I begin by going back to the late 1990s and follow the wave of subaltern organization and protests that began in the aftermath of Mitch and confronted Zelaya's government as a national uprising against the imposition of the neoliberal project. Next, I assess the 2005 election and the particularities of both this moment and Zelaya as a traditional political candidate. Third, I briefly examine Zelaya's left turn, from "above" and from "below," showing how it forged an unlikely alliance between traditional caudillo politics and subaltern mobilization. Finally, I present the last mile of the military ousting of Manuel Zelaya Rosales, to shed some light on the limits of the alliance created around the Cuarta Urna.

### From Mitch to Zelaya: The Rise of the *Resistencia*

As we saw before, the banana strike of 1954 signaled the rise of a robust peasant movement and a set of large labor unions. However, by the late 1970s, these organizations began to weaken due to internal fractioning and infighting, the country's economic crisis, and the government's efforts to shrink the public sector. Further, although Honduras had historically experienced lower levels of violence and political persecution than its neighbors, in the 1980s the implementation of the national security doctrine, wherein political disagreement was equated with sedition and the military and police forces were given free rein to respond to opposition with extreme violence, the peasant and labor movements' ability to carry out organizing work in their traditional manner was significantly stunted (Barahona 2005).

Around this same time, the Honduran Communist Party split over the issue of how the popular movement should respond to the increasing levels of state violence. Some, influenced by the Sandinista experience in Nicaragua and the guerrilla campaign in El Salvador and believing an armed response was warranted, moved ahead to create various revolutionary military organizations, of which the most prominent were the Cinchonero Popular Liberation Movement and the People's Revolutionary Union. These organizations carried out various daring operations, most of them in support of the guerrillas in El Salvador. Nonetheless, they were not particularly successful and quickly succumbed to the army's persecution, which included the assassination and disappearance of several of their leaders (Canizales 2008). By the 1990s, with the Sandinista electoral defeat in Nicaragua and the end of the Cold War, the Honduran guerilla experience as such was over. However, many of the former militants continued their political life as leaders and organizers of many regional and local social movements organized around topics such as ethnic rights, gender identity and sexual orientation, and protection of the environment.

Among some of the better known of these popular organizations we find the Council of Honduran Indigenous Peoples (COPINH)and the Honduran Black Fraternal Organization (OFRANEH), as well as the Bloque Popular (the

Popular Bloc, based in Tegucigalpa and closer to the labor movement), the Environmentalist Movement of Olancho (MAO), which mobilized against the destruction of the forest in the department of Olancho due to the government's predatory forestry policies, and the Aguán's own Popular Organizations Network of the Aguán (COPA), to whose story we will return briefly. Many of the activists concerned were also involved in the creation of the first national human rights organizations in the 1980s and 1990s (Committee of Relatives of the Disappeared in Honduras, COFADEH, 1982, and the Human Rights Research and Promotion Center, CIPRODEH, 1989), which began to pressure the government to improve the country's situation in terms of civil rights and liberties.

As shown by various studies focusing on the particular experiences of several of these organizations, what changed in the 1990s were not so much the grievances and objectives of the subaltern organizations but their political tactics and the discourses that they used to speak about these grievances (Graham 2009; Middeldorp 2014; Sosa and Ortega 2008). With the increasing levels of repression unleashed against anything that seemed even remotely communist, and the incorporation by the state and international institutions of new legal and discursive frameworks based on the language and logic of human rights, many organizations opted to take advantage of the recent openings and push forward their historical agendas through these channels. As such, what we find in this period is a silent multiplication of popular organizations within particular regional and local histories, with little to no articulation on the national scale but with apparent affinities due in part to the shared militancy of many of their leaders during the previous decades in various leftist movements and the identification of the neoliberal project and the transnational elites as their common foe.

In the case of the Aguán, the new forms of regional popular organization reflected the local political dynamics. As mentioned in previous chapters, one of the central tensions in the region was between the surrounding hills, inhabited by scattered communities of unorganized peasants, and the valley, the seat of the cooperatives and the oil palm plantations. By the 1980s different popular organizations based throughout the Aguán attempted to articulate their actions, in the context of the economic crisis of the cooperatives, the imposition of the neoliberal project, and the Jesuits' efforts to organize and improve the living conditions of the populations in the hills.

Probably the most paradigmatic of these attempts came in 1988 when the PS and the National Rural Workers Central (CNTC) invited the members of every popular group or association in the region—big or small—to come together under an umbrella organization called the Permanent Assembly of Popular Organizations of the Aguán (APOPA). This effort was carried out in conversation with leftist popular leaders from Tegucigalpa who were trying to create a broad national movement that could eventually capitalize electorally, an effort that ultimately resulted in the UD. Due to these factors, APOPA's objectives, strategies, and leadership ended up being controlled by the organizations of the valley, particularly the labor unions. Further, once the implicit electoral agenda behind the creation of the organization became evident, the CNTC and the PS clashed over strategy; eventually, APOPA dissolved in bitter infighting in the early 1990s.

A few years later, in 1996, and under a similar name, the Popular Organizations Network of the Aguán was created to coordinate the different regional efforts. However, just as in the case of APOPA, COPA was an expression of the social and political reality of the valley. In general, its membership still mainly came from the regional unions and particularly from state functionaries, such as INA's workers' union. As such, they had close affinities with the labor organizations and sectors of the more traditional Left, making them closer to national politics and natural allies of the National Coordination of Popular Resistance (CNRP) (on which more shortly). However, due to the region's social composition and the increasing unrest around land issues, COPA also supported and took into account the concerns of the organized peasantry, particularly those of MUCA, which, as we saw in the previous chapter, combined an older generation of peasant organizers with a new one of younger activists not necessarily of peasant extraction.

By the first half of the 2000s, the different efforts of local and regional organization began to coalesce at the national level, as a new cycle of protests began to pick up steam against the imposition of the neoliberal project, the destruction of the environment, and particularly the negotiation, and eventual approval in 2006, of the Free Trade Agreement with the United States (CAFTA) (Hernández Coto 2019). For example, in July 2003, as protests raged all over the country against a bill that introduced the privatization of water, various social organizations presented to Congress an alternative law draft that proposed, among other things, the definition of drinking water as a public good. However, while the proposal was formally received by Porfirio Lobo, the then-president of Congress, it was never discussed; instead, the original privatizing proposal was approved, drawing the ire of the popular organizations. This was followed by massive new mobilizations all over the country.

Finally, on August 26, 2003, a massive "march for dignity and resistance" paralyzed the city of Tegucigalpa. This was the first concerted action by the

CNRP, a broad alliance of very diverse labor, peasant, teacher, student, environmental, feminist, and Indigenous organizations that came together under the mantle of the fight against neoliberalism. Among their demands were the repeal of the new water law, as well as the suspension of the different extractive projects in the country (mining permits and hydroelectric dams) until the promulgation of a clear set of environmental protections. The march's participants also demanded better salaries for teachers and other public workers and the introduction of price controls over basic foodstuffs. Moreover, they opposed the new letter of intention signed with the IMF and demanded the return home of the troops sent to the Iraq War (Pirker and Núñez 2010; Hernández Coto 2019).

While the government savagely repressed these protests, and almost none of the demands described above were considered, the march for dignity and resistance signaled a significant change in the Honduran political dynamics, in particular the relations between dominant and subaltern groups. The birth of the CNRP showed the capacity of the different regional and local subaltern organizations for coming together and carrying out joint actions. Also, the sheer vastness of their demands, ranging from environmental protection and Indigenous rights all the way to labor conditions, foreign, and economic policy and access to land demonstrated the limits that the imposition of the neoliberal project had in terms of producing consent and "ideological and moral leadership" (Gramsci 1971). It is in this context that the national elections of 2005 took place.

### *"Urge Mel, Viene Mel"*: The 2005 Election

The year 2005 marked a continuation of the political and economic crisis that began in the aftermath of Hurricane Mitch.[6] During the 2000s the debt noose became tighter, as Honduras entered the UN's Heavily Indebted Poor Countries Initiative (HIPC) to help in the process of reconstruction. This program pardoned part of the country's foreign debt if the freed funds were used in the fight against poverty. The catch was that the government had to keep up to date in its commitments with the IFIs. This meant that the government had certain financial leeway to promote social policy but had very little control over the economic one.

In terms of economic performance, Honduras presented a mixed picture. On the one hand, the country's economic growth (6 percent) was the highest since 1993; on the other hand, it was only due to the steep increase of the family remittances coming mainly from the United States that both the commercial and currency deficits were not higher (ECLAC 2007).[7] Further, according to the UNPD (2006) Honduras's performance on the human development index had stagnated, and although there were some macroeconomic achievements (due mainly to increasing foreign investment in maquilas and the transport and telecommunication sectors), these had not translated into the improvement of living conditions, since the problems of poverty, inequality, and social exclusion remained. In this sense, Honduras not only continued to be one of the poorest countries in the hemisphere (over 62 percent of the households under the poverty line for 2006, and over 30 percent underemployment) but also one of the most unequal ones—with the top decile receiving more than half of the total income, as against the 2.5 percent received by the bottom one (Cordero 2009). This dramatic situation made outmigration one of the few alternatives for many Hondurans poor, both urban and rural. As a result, this historical moment was also marked by higher levels of social confrontation that took at least two forms. On the one hand, there were increasing levels of social protest all over the country and ranging over many topics, with a new set of regional political platforms operating as a distribution belt between local grievances and national mobilization levels that had not been seen in the country since the 1970s (Hernández Coto 2019; Shipley 2016). On the other hand, the country experienced escalating levels of civil insecurity, with a wave of kidnappings as the most visible manifestation.

As we can imagine, in this context, the electoral campaign was dominated by concerns over civil insecurity and violence, and corruption and transparency (Taylor-Robinson 2006). In the end, José Manuel Zelaya was elected president by a minimal margin, 49.9 percent of the vote against the National Party's Porfirio Lobo Sosa's 46.2 percent, in a process that was mired by accusations of fraud, as the Supreme Electoral Court declared the winner with less than 3 percent of the more than five thousand voting tables counted.

From the beginning, Zelaya's government was a weak one. Not only had he been elected by a minimal margin, but it took about a month for his victory to become official, as Porfirio Lobo and the National Party continued to reject the result and it would take the mediation of the U.S. embassy for the parties to come to an agreement (Martínez 2010; Meza 2015). Zelaya also had very little control over his party. He barely came out of the Liberal Party's convention as the presidential candidate, and very few members from his faction were elected to Congress. This was, in part, the result of his atypical political career.

Mel was born to a traditional cattle ranching and logging family from the Department of Olancho. His father, José Manuel Zelaya Sr., was a well-established and infamous figure in the country, who, as mentioned earlier, was involved in the Horcones Massacre of 1975. According to Juan Ramón Martínez (2010), Zelaya Sr. had shifted the family's political allegiance from the National to the Liberal Party in 1954 due to the influence of Modesto Rodas Alvarado. (To recall from chapter 2, Alvarado's designation as the Liberal Party's candidate was one of reasons behind the military coup of 1963.)

Thus, not only was Mel a newcomer, but he came from the more traditional landowning elites and not from the newer and more transnationalized sectors that held increasing political clout within the Liberal Party, represented by figures such as Miguel Facussé's nephew Carlos Flores Facussé, or Jaime Rosenthal, of Romanian-Jewish descent, whom Zelaya had just edged in the party's internal elections and whose son Yanni Rosenthal was appointed as minister of the presidency and would run as a presidential candidate for the Liberal Party in 2021.

Also, unlike most presidential candidates, Zelaya had slowly climbed up the party's ranks working in different government posts. He was first elected as a member of Congress in 1985 and was reelected in 1989 and 1993, but his real break came during his last term when the then-president Carlos Roberto Reina (1994–98), whose daughter was married to Mel's brother, named him minister of the Honduran Social Investment Fund, which oversaw the country's antipoverty strategy. Later, during Carlos Flores Facussé's government (1998–2002), he became a presidential adviser and helped design the government's reconstruction strategy in the aftermath of Hurricane Mitch. During this process, he met various social and community organizations as he toured the country. Probably because of this experience, he based his electoral campaign on a platform of *poder ciudadano*, literally "citizen power," understood as the expansion of public participation in political issues. His first act as president was to sanction the Civic Participation Law that had been presented in Congress by the Liberal Party just a day before.

Nonetheless, there was little that could be called radical in Mel's first years as president. While he declared that public participation would be the backbone of his administration, he publicly stressed the importance CAFTA would have for the country's development. Also, initially, there was not much difference between Zelaya's government and his predecessor Ricardo Maduro's (2002–6) in terms of economic policy or approach to the demands of subaltern groups. For example, he signed agreements with both the World Bank and the IDB containing the same privatization agenda as the previous agreements and promoting the construction of touristic megaprojects in the Bay of Tela, as well as ports and hotels in the Bay Islands. Additionally, he provided incentives to attract foreign investments in the form of maquilas and took the first steps toward the construction of various large hydroelectric dams in the western part of the country. These actions quickly placed him on a collision course with various social movements, notably the COPINH, a predominantly Lenca organization based in the western highlands, and OFRANEH, a Garifuna organization on the north coast (Brondo 2013; CV 2012; Graham 2009).

Further, in his first few months as president, Mel had to deal with a ten-day strike by the teachers' unions demanding a salary raise. Initially, the government responded with repression, to later sign an agreement with the Federation of Teacher Unions of Honduras (FOMH), probably the largest labor organization in the country at the time. Apparently, Zelaya financed the raise granted to the teachers with part of the money freed for the battle against poverty by the HIPC (Hunt 2015), inaugurating a tendency throughout his administration of giving concessions to certain subaltern groups without necessarily making any structural changes to the country's economy. However, if we are to track his infamous "turn to the Left," we must start with the controversy regarding energy and the prices of fossil fuels.

## "¿Qué será lo que tiene Mel que los imperialistas no pueden con él?": Zelaya's Left Turn from Above

Four days after being sworn into office, José Manuel Zelaya declared a state of "energy emergency" in response to the National Electrical Energy Company's (ENEE) imminent bankruptcy (reported losses of roughly US$160 million in 2006) and its incapacity to cover the country's electricity demands.[8] Since the Honduran energy matrix is dependent on burning fossil fuels, a significant part of the ENEE's financial problems reflected the fluctuations of the international prices of crude oil. As such, Zelaya's first action was to approve an emergency fund of US $15.8 million to subsidize fuel imports and slow down the rising prices while a definitive solution was found (Cunha Filho, Coelho, and Pérez Flores 2013).

The biggest problem faced by the Honduran energy sector was the chokehold that Esso, Texaco, and Shell and their national counterparts had over the import of hydrocarbons and their derivatives, which translated into high prices and the inability of the state to intervene. This was not something new. Already during Ricardo Maduro's government, an experts' committee (*comisión de notables*) was formed to explore the problem and propose solutions. One such proposal was to break the existing draconian contracts and call a competing international tender to hire a new company and secure a better deal. However, when Zelaya's government moved in this direction, it ran into the ferocious resistance from not only the importing companies and local partners, who decided to boycott the tender by not participating, but also from the U.S. ambassador, Chad Ford, who declared that this measure was a very sudden change in the "rules of the game" for foreign investment and would set a terrible precedent. This opinion was shared by a part of the country's corporate sector, which considered that the companies were within their rights to sue the state for their losses in the commercial courts created in the framework of CAFTA (Pirker and Núñez 2010).

Nonetheless, the government moved ahead with the process, and the U.S.-based company ConocoPhillips was awarded the new contract. Next, the government ordered the transfer of the port and fuel storage tanks to the new company. However, the initiative was short-lived, and the government was forced to backpedal, as the company in control of the fuel storage tanks refused to hand them over and the U.S. embassy presented a formal complaint (Cunha Filho, Coelho, and Pérez Flores 2013). It was in this moment that we could locate the start of Zelaya's swift turn to the Left.

In July of that same year (2007), Mel visited Nicaragua for the celebration of the twenty-eighth anniversary of the Sandinista Revolution, a decision criticized by the Honduran Right and the U.S. embassy. By December Zelaya had made the official announcement that Honduras would be joining the Venezuela-led program of Petrocaribe, which would allow the country to access fuels at a much lower rate and pay for part of the bill with agriculture exports.[9] On June 22, 2008, a month after the first Venezuelan fuel shipment arrived in Honduras, Zelaya announced his intention of joining the Hugo Chávez-led regional integration project of the Bolivarian Alternative. Two months later, on August 25, with the votes of the Liberal Party and with Hugo Chávez and Bolivia's Evo Morales at his side, Mel informed the public that Honduras had officially joined the ALBA.[10]

Zelaya followed this sudden turn of events with a strident anti-imperialist public discourse, as well as a set of unorthodox policies. For example, toward the end of 2008, the government unilaterally raised the minimum wage by 60 percent. Other policies included promoting lower interest rates to expand the access to credit (which cut down on the profits of the financial sector); creating a state-owned radio and TV station to combat the traditional elite's control over mass media; building a commercial airport at the location of the military base of Palmerola; and strengthening state companies, such as the ENEE, which went against the neoliberal dogma of market liberalization. Unsurprisingly, all these policies met with resistance by the local economic and political elites, as a result of which Mel and his government found themselves embroiled in increasing conflicts with both dominant political parties.

Observers have identified several factors to explain Zelaya's turn to the Left. First, as already mentioned, Mel's electoral campaign was based on the promise of expanding public participation, an idea that was not only his but also a requirement of the HIPC agreement that the Maduro government had signed in 2005 (Cunha Filho, Coelho, and Pérez Flores 2013). Also, due to his role in previous governments as the officer in charge of the state's strategy against poverty, Zelaya had toured the country and met with leaders and members of many social organizations and had learned how effective certain types of social policies could be to garner support from subaltern groups. The funds liberated by the HIPC to finance antipoverty policies further made the left turn possible, as Zelaya used the HIPC funds to promote social policies that would garner widespread support, without having to make changes to the country's political and economic structure.

Another argument advanced to explain this left turn was the episode with the energy sector that I characterized earlier. One of Mel's central electoral promises was to lower the prices of both fuels and electricity. However, he quickly found himself stuck between the social protests pushing for him to keep his word and the inability to change the fuel importing formula. In this context, joining Petrocaribe was a desirable alternative and a pragmatic response. Allegedly, the initial negotiations and the channel of communication between Zelaya and Chávez were facilitated by members of the Honduran president's close circle, particularly Patricia Rodas Baca, the then-foreign minister and daughter of the aforementioned Modesto Rodas Alvarado (Pirker and Núñez 2010). This close circle was formed by a younger generation of Liberal militants who had ties with both the Honduran and Latin American Left and who, according to some analysts, had been trying to move up the party's ranks and "return" the party to its social democratic origins. They found in Zelaya an excellent opportunity to get closer to power and used the energy debacle to come through for the president and cement their position in the government (Martínez 2010; Meza 2015), facilitating his turn to the Left in the process.

Still, while these explanations are plausible, they make little sense unless we consider the geopolitical context in which they became possible. Zelaya came into power in a position of relative weakness: he had gone from barely winning his party's convention to barely winning a highly controversial national election, which compounded the low levels of legitimacy that the political system already had. Further, his grip on his own party was frail to say the least.

Not only did he have very few loyal members in Congress but he was also embroiled in an internal power struggle due to the decision to designate Rodas Baca as president of the Liberal Party, despite her lack of experience and leftist orientations. Also, as the fuel imports episode showed quite clearly, even his less radical policies were met with vicious resistance from the country's economic and political elites, as well as the U.S. embassy. In this context of relative isolation from the traditional partnerships of power, Zelaya's government moved to those closer to his positions: domestically, the popular movements; internationally, Chávez's fuel-funded geopolitical project.

This meant both a political opening and a closing that took the form of three dynamics. First, thanks to the financial and political support of Venezuela and the other "pink tide" governments of the region, Mel was able to develop an unusually autonomous political line, particularly in relation to U.S. foreign policy toward Central America. Second, since his domestic support came from "below," not from "above," the places and the forms of doing politics shifted away from the traditional elite negotiations behind closed doors. Finally, thanks to both of these factors, Zelaya's government found itself on a collision course against all the traditional powers in the country and their virulent anticommunism, which was fed continuously by Zelaya's strident anti-imperialist, and thus anti-American, rhetoric and the fear that he would turn Honduras into a new Venezuela or Cuba.

### "*Mel, amigo, el pueblo está contigo*": Zelaya's Left Turn from Below

Most analyses of the coup leave their argument on the government's left turn at that: as a process from above in which Zelaya's decision to join first Petrocaribe and then the ALBA, as well as his increasing political affinity with Chávez, made clear his intentions of turning Honduras into a socialist country and remaining in power.[11] However, what this narrative leaves out is the role that the escalating levels of subaltern political organization and mobilization had in pushing Zelaya toward a transformation of the Honduran political system that probably went way beyond what he had imagined.

From the perspective of the subaltern sectors, Zelaya's presidency was greeted with reserve. Not only did he have the typical background of a traditional politician but his first policies did not differ significantly from politics as usual in Honduras (Hernández Coto 2019; Sosa 2016). However, unlike previous governments, where the grievances of subaltern groups were always ignored, Mel and his officials were (selectively) open to creating spaces of dialogue.

It is important to emphasize that this was a monumental change. Hegemony in Honduras, as it came to be formalized in the 1980s pact that resulted in the new constitution and the "transition to democracy," was based on the idea that political power would be shared and divided between the elites, within the framework of the two-party electoral system (Barahona 2018). Further, any dispute or disagreement needed to be solved through pacts and negotiations taking place behind closed doors. The military's role was to safeguard the constitution, or rather specific interpretations of it, and to ensure the general status quo. The relationship between dominant and subaltern groups played out in a combination of consent and coercion, where the former was manufactured through an ironclad control over mass media by the elites and the ever-increasing influence of the different religious denominations present in the country, particularly Pentecostal churches (Girard 2013); coercion, meanwhile, operated through the repression of anyone who fell out of line. What could not be allowed was the interjection of independent subaltern actors into this discussion.

This tension between a formally representative political system, structured around the exclusion of most of its members from the dynamics of government, is the inherent contradiction of liberal democracy that Marx (2009, 66) identified in the Eighteenth Brumaire of Louis Bonaparte: "The parliamentary regime leaves everything to the decision of majorities; how shall the great majorities outside parliament not want to decide? When you play the fiddle at the top of the state, what else is to be expected but that those down below dance?"

What Zelaya did was play the fiddle of public participation at the top of the state, and those below began to dance. As a result, certain disputes that emerged in the aftermath of Mitch were profoundly transformed during Mel's administration. We find a prime example in the passing of Decree no. 18-2008, related to the land conflict in the Aguán.

This decree was the result of the pressure applied by peasant movements on the ground, particularly those in the Aguán (Ríos 2014). In the previous chapter we saw how, by 2008, the region had become an agrarian conflict hotspot. However, events in the region were not isolated from discussions that were taking place elsewhere. Already in August 2006, Vía Campesina Honduras had organized the National Forum for Agrarian Reform and Rural Development, in which the country's peasant organizations demanded not only the relaunching of the agrarian reform but also the creation of alternative commercial alliances with initiatives such as the ALBA. Less than a year later, in May 2007, the CNTC occupied INA's central offices in Tegucigalpa to demand lands and justice for their fallen comrades. That same year, the Coordinating Council of Honduran Peasant Organizations (COCOCH) protested in front of the INA and the presidential house to demand a stop to the country's neoliberal agrarian policy (Hernández Coto 2019). These actions forced the hand of Zelaya's government, which opened a channel of communication and negotiation with the peasant movement, eventually crystallizing in Decree no. 18-2008.

According to various people I interviewed, both in the Aguán and in Tegucigalpa, the contents of the decree were greatly influenced by the peasant leaders of the Aguán, who saw it as a first step in recovering the lands that were lost during the agrarian counterreform of the 1990s. Among the most relevant aspects of the decree were: creating an inventory of agrarian law cases (de facto occupations, without legal clarity) that had been pending for at least two years in the INA, the National Agrarian Council (CNA), or the Supreme Court; acquiring those lands that were not the subjects of pending agrarian law cases but had been occupied by peasant families for a certain number of years; issuing close to US$36 million in agrarian debt bonds to compensate owners for these lands; and allowing the INA to expropriate in those cases in which the disputed property was proven to be national land. The decree also created a special commission to provide follow-up and enforcement of the decree, which would have allegedly resolved around 426 open cases, titling around 40,000 hectares and benefiting approximately 20,000 families, including those of the MCA.

Clearly, far from bringing about any integral agrarian reform, the objective of the decree was to resolve a set of specific conflicts, many of them in the Aguán, and bring to a stop the more general cycle of peasant mobilization. Allegedly, the idea was that, once political passions had cooled and Zelaya's power had been consolidated, the problem of land idleness and landlessness would be approached by a new "integral" agrarian reform. However, the reaction by the large landowners was of total rejection, both legally—with the Honduran National Federation of Farmers and Cattlemen (FENAGH) questioning the decree's constitutionality in the Supreme Court—and politically, with a steep increase in the levels of violence against peasant communities. For example, in the Aguán, the epicenter of much of the conflict in this period, we find various such cases, of which I will mention just two: first, the already-discussed harassment by Henry Osorto of the MCA, which eventually led to the Casa Quemada incident in August 2008, and second, the gunning down of the MCA leader Irene Ramírez, on June 11, just one day after he spoke on a local radio station in Trujillo in favor of the Cuarta Urna.

FENAGH'S case before the supreme court was based on ten points, of which four are most relevant here. First, the suit alleged that the created commission violated the principle of equality, as the landowners only had one representative, while the peasant sector had at least three votes. Also, according to the FENAGH, the fact that in many cases the peasants were "usurpers" of land would make them a "privileged class" within the commission. Second, the decree violated various constitutional principles, including the right to property and the right to legal equality and security. Third, the creation of a commission with the power to expropriate private lands went against the current agrarian law (the AML). Fourth, due to these factors, the decree contradicted international trade agreements, such as CAFTA, particularly concerning legal security and the protection of private property.

While the decree was presented in the media as a controversial policy that opened the doors for state-led expropriation and promoted a new wave of land "invasions" to the detriment of private investment on agriculture (Önder 2018), it fueled the dreams of many peasant communities and activists that saw in it the possibility of, at last, receiving legal access to lands for which they had been struggling for several decades. It also came to seal a political alliance between Zelaya's government and the peasant movement, which reflected a growing sentimental bond between those families involved in the movement and the figure of Zelaya. This was of course not only the result of Decree no. 18-2008 but also had to do with a set of populist policies that reshuffled much of the patronage system in the country and improved the living conditions of the poorest in very concrete ways. For example, when the country entered the ALBA, the Venezuelan government donated trucks and agricultural machinery that was distributed among the peasant movements, as I witnessed during my time in the Aguán (see figure 4).

We find in the example of Decree no. 18-2008 a pattern that would repeat itself during Zelaya's late presidency: processes of subaltern political organization and mobilization that predated Mel's presidency by more than a decade found in his government an opening to push forward their demands. This opening did not exactly come out of Zelaya's kind heart but rather emerged from a combination of the government's isolation and the high levels of popular mobilization, both by specific organizations and the CNRP. However, it promised a future in which policies being proposed and pushed from below could lead to a profound transformation of the Honduran legal and political framework and would necessarily include the active participation of subaltern groups. At the same time, as the FENAGH's legal challenge clearly illustrates, any of these transformations meant going against and dismantling the legal

Peasant besides a truck donated to Honduras by the ALBA, Bajo Aguán region, 2013. The brand, Veniran, is a joint venture between Iranian and Venezuelan companies. Photo by the author.

and political levees and trenches that had been raised around the neoliberal project and taken the shape of the rule of law.

### The Fourth Ballot Box and the Path to the Coup

On June 28, 2009, the Honduran Executive Power called for a popular ballot, a sort of referendum, on whether a fourth ballot box should be included in the upcoming November elections, allowing Hondurans to decide whether a new constitutional assembly should be convened to draft a new constitution. This call lit up all the alarm signals of those sectors opposed to Zelaya, who saw it as an attempt to follow in the steps of his pink tide "friends"—Hugo Chávez above all—and perpetuate himself in power by making presidential reelection possible in the new constitution. Most of the Left saw this instead as an excellent opportunity to achieve effective participation in the country's decision-making process, reverse some of the policies imposed since the 1990s and, in a sense, "refound" (*refundar*) the state.[12] The differentiation between the two sides was so cliché that if it were not for all that was in play, it would be comical. On the one hand, against the Cuarta Urna we find the National Congress, the judiciary, the Supreme Court, the domestic economic elites, the U.S. embassy, the leadership of both traditional parties (PN and PL), the Catholic and the major Pentecostal churches, the mainstream media, and broad sectors of the middle class. On the other hand, in favor of the Cuarta Urna we find the Executive Power, a minority party (Unificación Democrática; UD), the CNRP, the organized labor and peasant movements, a few Catholic priests and dioceses and some local media, particularly the not-so-small sector of community radios.

This is not the place for a fully fleshed-out account of what happened between March 23, when the consultation was first announced, and June 28, when Zelaya was ousted. It is enough to mention that both sides mobilized all the resources available to them. In the case of the "NO" position (against), the consultation was declared illegal by different courts and unconstitutional by the Supreme Court; it was opposed by both traditional parties and viciously attacked by the mainstream media. Mel and those in favor of the "YES" vote responded to each challenge by politically maneuvering on the very edges of legality, using popular mobilization in the streets to secure the consultation.

For example, on June 25, the date of Mel's alleged resignation letter, the Superior Electoral Tribunal ordered that the electoral material for the Cuarta Urna be withdrawn, as the consultation was illegal. Zelaya rejected the ruling and asked his followers to join him on a "mission." Accompanied by a multitude of people and a caravan of vehicles, Mel drove to the Hernán Acosta Mejía airbase in Tegucigalpa, where the military was holding the confiscated electoral material for the referendum. After a tense confrontation with the soldiers guarding the electoral material, Mel and his followers took it to the presidential house, from where it was distributed all over the country. By then, the die had already been cast. Although there were some attempts by both sides to reach a rapprochement and negotiate a peaceful solution to the crisis, at the end of the day the political wagers and the level of social and political polarization were too high for "politics as usual" to be enough, and Zelaya's kidnapping and the coup that it entailed became a logical (albeit not the only possible) resolution to the crisis.

Zelaya's attempts to move forward with his proposal against the resistance of all the national formal political institutions and traditional ways of doing politics placed him and his government outside of the "rule of law" and showed the subaltern groups ever more blatantly that there was nothing apolitical or neutral about the state. As such, the dispute over the Cuarta Urna was the straw that broke the camel's back, making of the coup a necessary evil to protect the "dominant but dead" Honduran neoliberal state form (Smith 2008). Let me develop this idea some more.

As we have seen in this chapter, Zelaya followed a trajectory from traditional oligarch politician following the line of the IFIs and the local elites; to the *comandante vaquero*, the "cowboy commander," as he was also colloquially called due to his ubiquitous Stetson hat, allied with Hugo Chávez and the ALBA. This transition was the result of the articulation of at least four factors: (1) Zelaya's own political experience, his left-leaning inner circle, and his focus on public participation; (2) the high levels of organization, mobilization, and pressure that the popular movements were able to place on the government; (3) Venezuela's geopolitical project; and (4) the relative weakness of the executive office in Honduras, which pushed him toward his only allies.

It is important to add, however, that there was nothing simple or straightforward either about this alliance or about the push for a constituent assembly. Initially, when Zelaya first hinted at his plan for a new constitution, many actors among the traditional elites, allegedly including Porfirio Lobo, supported the idea. However, as it became evident that Mel's plan also included the active participation of the national social movements, the elite positions shifted against it. In other words, the problem was not necessarily with reforming the constitution in and of itself, but with who would be involved in the process (Meza 2015).

At the same time, there is no consensus regarding where exactly the idea came from. For many, it was an attempt by Zelaya, influenced by the experiences of the pink-tide governments in the region, to remain in power beyond 2009. According to other commentators, instead, it was an effort by Zelaya to use his popularity to drive a wedge between the traditional parties and become a new political force to be reckoned with, in the context of the future constituent assembly (Martínez 2010; Meza 2015). However, this argument takes for granted the stability and strength of Zelaya's alliance with the popular movement. It is important to remember most of the popular movements approached this alliance with suspicion, and it was in the streets, through their actions, that they made the government respond to their demands.

For example, on February 1, 2008, the CNRP celebrated the first Workers, Peasants, Teachers, Community, and Popular Movements Forum, which took place in San Pedro Sula. This meeting resulted in a call for a national civic strike on April 17 and the presentation of a twelve-point unified plan of popular struggle against the neoliberal project.[13] The national strike of April was massive, with roadblocks staged all over the country, but it was also brutally repressed by the police and armed forces. Nonetheless, the members of the CNRP called for a second day of national protests on May 14. This time, not only were the protests not repressed by the police but they coincided with the final day of the thirty-eight-day hunger strike by a group of state prosecutors protesting the corruption in the judiciary system. This mounting pressure forced Zelaya's hand, and the government negotiated with the popular organizations. According to interviews undertaken by René Mauricio Hernández Coto (2019) with activists who took part of these negotiations, Mel agreed to resolve some of the demands presented in the twelve-point plan;[14] at the same time, he argued that many of them were beyond his power, due to his weak position in Congress. For others, he explained, the constitution needed to be amended. Zelaya and the leadership of the CNRP found common ground around the ideas of the constituent assembly and of refounding the country, cementing a conjunctural alliance in their defiance of the powers that be in Honduras and the neoliberal project.

This was an odd alliance. On the one hand, Mel, even after being reborn to the Left, continued to be the clear embodiment of the traditional Honduran caudillo politics, whose rebellion was read by many as an attempt to craft his own political movement. On the other hand, the CNRP was a highly diverse platform of social movements and organizations, with different ethnic, social, historical, and geographical backgrounds, which had few, but crucial points in common. Besides the crucial consensus on the need to fight against neoliberalism, these actors could not see eye-to-eye on many topics. The result was a combination of political strategies and tactics accompanied by important conversations regarding what Honduras's future should look like. In this sense, behind the tendency to focus only on Zelaya, his actions, and his loudmouth approach to doing politics, it is important to look into the experiments of political transformation, policy formation, and discussions of disagreements that were taking place in the background, which link events taking place on the national scale, like the Cuarta Urna, with very concrete actions like the March of 5000 Machetes. It was against these efforts, and the future that they envisioned, embodied, and foreshadowed, that the 2009 coup was directed.

### The Never-Ending Militarization of Honduras

While it is hard to say that Honduras was in a good place in 2009, it is also clear that everything began to go from bad to worse from that point forward. Economically, the aftermath of the coup came with a tendency toward the overexploitation of labor and the increasing concentration of wealth in a few pockets (Johnston and Lefebvre 2013; Waxenecker 2019). Thus, according to data from the World Bank, in 2018, the income shares of the lowest 20 percent was 3 percent, while that of the highest 20 percent was 56 percent of the country's income, making of Honduras one of the most unequal countries in Latin America.

Politically, the arrival to the presidency first of Roberto Micheletti and then of Porfirio Lobo brought about a political devolution that initially aimed at stopping the increasing activity of subaltern groups and their alliance with Zelaya's government. However, with the arrival of Juan Orlando Hernández to the presidential chair in 2013, this political devolution turned into a fully-fledged "revanchist" (Smith 2008) class project, where the interests and rule of the dominant groups came to be preserved by blood and fire.

The fifteenth of seventeen brothers and sisters, JOH, as Hernández is commonly known, was born in 1968 in the Department of Lempira, close to the border with El Salvador. While not a soldier himself, he graduated from the Military Northern High School in San Pedro Sula, where he also received the military rank of second lieutenant of infantry. He then moved to Tegucigalpa and studied law at the National Autonomous University of Honduras (UNAH), where he also became president of the student government. During this period, he met his future wife, Ana Rosalinda García Carías. As if to prove that everything in Honduras moves in cycles, her great uncle was none other than Tiburcio Carías Andino (Mercado 2014).

Later, Alvarado received a master's in public management from the State University of New York in Albany. After his return to Honduras, in 1997 he was elected to Congress from the National Party, where he remained during four consecutive terms. His political breakthrough came in 2010, in the aftermath of the coup, when he was elected as president of Congress. During this period (2010–13), the Honduran Congress took advantage of the lack of members of the opposition to approve a set of controversial policies aimed at dismantling most of the changes implemented by Zelaya's government, as well as pushing forward a new political agenda of militarized economic liberalization, which would become consolidated during Alvarado's two presidential terms (2013–22).

In terms of militarization, JOH created a new tax to finance the security forces, as well as the five-thousand-member Military Police for Public Order (PMOP), which quickly became the government's shock troops against any form of protest. Also, in 2012 he pushed forward the creation of a controversial police unit with military training to fight against organized crime and those organizations identified as "terrorists."

As a result, if in 2009 the country's defense budget represented 3.79 percent of the government's total budget, by 2016 it had reached 6.19 percent (Donadio and Tibiletti 2010, 232). These numbers are more impressive when seen in absolute terms: if in 2008 the total defense budget was over US$121 million, in 2016 it was well over $330 million. Also, in terms of military personnel, the number nearly doubled, going from just above nine thousand in 2008 to over fifteen thousand in 2016 (Donadio and Kussrow 2016, 175).

Further, JOH's government oversaw the return of members, or former members, of the military to high government posts. This was something unseen since the early 1990s and pushed against the process of demilitarization of political life that Honduras had experienced during that period. For example, his minister of defense, Julián Pacheco Tinoco, was a former general who had previously headed the country's intelligence agency, and who has been allegedly connected to drug trafficking (Dudley 2016), as we will see in the next chapter.

This process of militarization accompanied, or rather enforced, the opening of new spaces for capital accumulation. Under JOH, Congress approved a new bill to attract foreign investment and created a commission to promote public-private alliances to manage public works and services, which in practice became a way for private companies to profit from public contracts (Chayes 2017). It was also during this period that the infamous law for the creation of Special Development and Employment Zones (ZEDES) was proposed. The ZEDES are special economic zones that enjoy legal, administrative, and financial freedoms; they have the prerogative to establish their own legislative, judicial, and taxation systems. Based on U.S. economist Paul Romer's ideas on "charter cities," the ZEDES law had been originally presented as intending to set up Special Development Regions (RED) and declared unconstitutional in 2012, to later be reworked and approved in 2013 (Geglia 2016).

For this to be possible, Congress, in a late-night session under the control of JOH, removed the four (out of five) magistrates of the Constitutional Chamber of the Supreme Court who had declared the RED law unconstitutional. Incidentally, this change in the composition of the constitutional court would become crucial in April 2015, when article 239 of the constitution was interpreted as unconstitutional, paving the way for JOH's subsequent reelection in 2017.

Much more can be said about JOH's trajectory since the ousting of Zelaya. For example, we could mention that it was during his first administration that the first maximum security prisons were built in the country, or that in 2015 it was proven that he had received money from the plunder of the Honduran Institute of Social Security (IHSS) for his 2013 presidential campaign. Or that in 2016, Bertha Cáceres, a Lenca Indigenous leader, was murdered due to her opposition to the construction of the Agua Zarca Hydroelectric Project in the country's western highlands, and that the plot to kill her involved former members of the military, included one who studied in the United States, as well as allegedly members of the Atala Zablah family of the country's transnational elite (Mackey and Eisner 2019; Lakhani 2020). Or that Global Witness released a report in 2017 singling out Honduras as the world's "most dangerous place to defend the planet" (Global Witness 2017).

In sum, unable and unwilling to produce any sort of consent around their project of plunder, the dominant bloc turned its eyes to a strong figure that could impose its will, just as it did in the 1930s with Tiburcio Carías. "The tradition of all past generations weighs like an alp upon the brain of the living," who, Marx tells us, "anxiously conjure up into their service the spirits of the past, assume their names, their battle cries, their costumes to enact new historic scenes . . ." (2009, 1).

Juan Orlando Hernández, the second coming of the dictator, married to his great niece, attempted to reenact his spirit. To Tiburcio Carías Andino's slogan of "order and peace" JOH raises his own: "*Voy a hacer lo que tenga que hacer para recuperar la paz del pueblo hondureño*" (I will do what needs to be done to recover the peace of the Honduran people), a phrase that he has constantly repeated. Both dictators embody the conviction that peace can only be imposed through order, and that order only flows through the barrel of the gun. And while Carías Andino and the UFCO—The Octopus or the "White Fleet" as it was also known—were two sides of the same coin, JOH hitched his fate to another nefarious economic activity: drug trafficking.

CHAPTER 6

# Militarization, Rent Capture, and the State-Narco Relations

On October 3, 1963, Ramón Villeda Morales was captured by the Honduran military at the break of dawn and flown to Costa Rica. While the coup ended Villeda's government, it was well known that one of its main objectives was to stop the certain victory of the Liberal Party's candidate Modesto Rodas Alvarado in the upcoming elections and prevent the ascension to power of his strident antimilitary and anti-National Party positions. The other more implicit objective was to arrest the wave of popular mobilization and subaltern organization that began with the 1954 banana strike. The result was the militarization of the country and the rise of the armed forces to the heights of government, which would begin to loosen its grip only in the 1990s.

"Hegel says somewhere that great historic facts and personages recur twice. He forgot to add: 'Once as tragedy, and again as farce.'" (Marx 2009, 1). Forty-five years, eight months, and twenty-five days after the ousting of Morales, on June 28, 2009, Juan Manuel Zelaya Rosales was captured by the Honduran military at the break of dawn and flown to Costa Rica. The coup plotters sought to stop in its tracks Zelaya's left turn and his alliance with Chávez and the ALBA, as well as to stymie his alleged intentions of staying in power beyond 2009. One of the principal architects of the government's left turn was Patricia Rodas Baca, Modesto's daughter. The other, less explicit, objective was to arrest the wave of popular mobilization and subaltern organization that began in the aftermath of Hurricane Mitch. The result was a process of militarization of the country and the rise of the armed forces to the heights of government, in a way not seen since the 1980s.

Zelaya Rosales for Villeda Morales, Rodas Baca for Rodas Alvarado, Romeo Vásquez Velásquez for Oswaldo López Arellano, Dinant Corporation for the UFCO, Barack Obama for John F. Kennedy... The conditions under which the second coup took place also caricature the context of the first.[1] In both cases, formal political power, military power, geopolitics, and the strategies of capital accumulation came together to produce a particular matrix of domination, in which different actors, in similar positions, showed themselves willing to go all the way to preserve and expand the privileges that come with them.

We have explored so far how the dynamics of capital accumulation shaped, and were shaped by, the disputes between dominant and subaltern groups in the process of formation of the Honduran state through the particular history of the Aguán. We have also examined how, in the aftermath of Mitch, the increasing levels of subaltern mobilization, combined with the particular conjuncture of Zelaya's government (his personal political project, the government's relative weakness, his leftist inner circle, and the Chávez geopolitical project), led to a collision with the traditional structures of power: the armed forces, the traditional economic and political elites, and the U.S. embassy—a collision that in turn produced the conditions of possibility for the coup. In this chapter, we will connect the conjuncture of 2009 with that of the coup of 1963 and explore some continuities along the thread of the relationship between power and land.

In chapter 1, I noted the historical political marriages that were born during Carías's regime between the Liberal Party and the labor and peasant movement on the one hand, and between the National Party and the armed forces on the other. For Villeda and others, the viability of a Liberal government depended on concessions and avoiding any confrontation with the armed forces. The result emboldened López Arellano, leading eventually to Villeda's demise. Apparently, Zelaya never got the memo. During his term, Mel gave various concessions to the armed forces, including an increase of the country's military budget,[2] as well as trying to secure the loyalty of Romeo Vásquez Velásquez, chair of the military's Joint Chiefs of Staff, by extending in January 2008 his post beyond what was stipulated by the constitutive act of the armed forces. However, due to Vásquez Velásquez's reluctance to support the Cuarta Urna, Zelaya removed him from his post on June 24. One day later, he was reinstated by the Supreme Court under the pretext that the president did not have such power. It would be under his authority that Mel was captured, and it was the Joint Chiefs of Staff who allegedly decided to send Zelaya to Costa Rica to avoid bloodshed (CVR 2011). Here, geopolitics and history are also important. It is impossible to imagine that this decision was not informed by what had happened in the failed coup of 2002 in Venezuela, where popular mobilization, as well as the actions by the presidential guard, freed Hugo Chávez from captivity, thwarting the attempt against him by the country's Right and a sector of the armed forces.

There is a thread to follow between both Honduran coups. With the constitution of 1957 and the coup of 1963, the Honduran armed forces began a process of political ascension and control over the state structures. As I mentioned before, this allowed many of them to become businessmen, but this was not the only way in which they benefited economically. As much as the Honduran economy has changed over time, it continues to rest on capturing rents: palm oil, tourism, maquila, remittances, and drug trafficking have replaced, or rather, combined with, banana and sugar exports and mining. Within this, the crucial component of rent capturing is the control of space. Crops must grow somewhere; hotels must be built somewhere nice; and drugs and migrants must traverse space, and the money accrued from overcoming the frictions of the traversal—remittances and dirty money—must either be moved or transformed (laundered) to fulfill its purpose. If we add the military's control over the borders, their supposed monopoly over violence, their logistic capabilities permitting an active presence in any location on the country's territory, their control of key state institutions in different moments of the Honduran history (such as economic planning, merchant shipping, and criminal investigation), and their crucial role within the U.S. geopolitical project, we find a key cog within the Honduran rent capturing machine. This is the beginning of the state-narco relations, more commonly known as the "narco-state."[3]

### Of Land, Narcos, and Power

The story of the deepening of the state-narco relations in Honduras runs parallel to the production of the conditions of possibility of the 2009 coup d'état. What we find at the crux of both histories is the process of militarization and concentration of power around a small, albeit varied, elite that has treated the country as its own private estate, in a context of neoliberal modernization under the tutelage of U.S. geopolitical interests.

Regarding this last point, while the discourse and official objectives of U.S. geopolitical interests have changed over time, they have been incredibly consistent in terms of their practices. Particularly glaring has been the unwavering support by the Pentagon and the State Department of the Central American armed forces as their main regional allies, even in the face of their atrocious record in terms of human rights and involvement with organized crime (Robinson 1996; Gill 2004; Holden 2004). The result has been a constant state of war since at least the 1960s: first against the "red menace" of communism, then against the "white menace" of cocaine. Further, the U.S. strategy during the Cold War period in many ways shaped the need for a war against drugs later.

As various authors have argued, there is an uncanny correlation between the neoliberal project, extraction economies (such as monocultures and logging), and the consolidation of state-narco relations and illicit economies in Latin America (Ballvé 2020; Devine et al. 2020; McSweeney 2020).

On the one hand, the logic of regulatory liberalization and free transit of commodities, including the construction of infrastructure and the renegotiation of nation-state limits, has facilitated the processes of contraband and money laundering that provide the spatial framework for drug trafficking enterprises to flourish. On the other hand, the devastating social and economic effects of neoliberal policies, in terms of inequality, poverty, and what Cindi Katz (2008) has called the "scoured landscape of social reproduction," have created a sense of hopelessness and despair that are exploited by both rapacious capitalist elites and traditional criminal organizations able to take advantage of the new conjuncture. For example, the corridors used to move drugs nowadays through Central America and Mexico repeat the routes used by the smugglers of old to move contraband as varied as cattle, stolen cars, guns, and even dairy products (Anderson 1983; Dudley 2016; Moreno 2015; Maldonado 2010). Further, what are often seen as disparate flows, like migration and drug trafficking, have tended to conflate.

In an aptly titled article, Nicaraguan sociologist José Luis Rocha (2011) refers to drug traffickers as "the First Horsemen of Neoliberalism," who have "changed Central America's 'dessert economies' into increasingly more profitable and globalized 'vice economies.'" However, what we find today rather is a combination between desserts (i.e., coffee, sugar, and bananas) and vices (cocaine), with rent capturing at the center.

For geographer Tim Hall (2013), there is a general tendency within the literature on illicit economies to ignore the relationships between economic flows and the spaces they traverse. For example, while ample attention is paid to the organization of illicit commodity chains and the impact that they have on the areas where they land, very little is said about the spaces that they pass. He concludes that "illicit (and licit) trade routes then engender their own political, as well as economic and social, geographies which, in an increasingly interconnected world, are worthy of greater attention by geographers" (380).

Kendra McSweeney and her colleagues (2018, 124) follow this cue to argue that, unlike other commodities, "the value of an illicit good such as cocaine accrues steadily not with its refinement as a good but with its geographical position—its *place* relative to the global grid of (border) regulation and interception." Further, they point that what happens in places like the Honduran Moskitia, where their work is centered, articulates licit and illicit practices that occur in different places. For example, money attained illicitly through drug trafficking can be invested into licit activities such as cattle ranching, which in turn leads to other types of dynamics, such as land grabbing and deforestation (see also Ballvé 2020; Devine et al. 2020).

Add oil palm plantations and mining projects to cattle ranching, and you find yourself in the Aguán. Here the historical process of formation of the region that I have described was combined in the 1990s with the opportunities opened up by the parallel projects of neoliberalism and "drug war capitalism" (Paley 2014), to produce an alliance between members of the military, the regional political and economic elites, and drug traffickers.

### "But at Least the *Narcos* Share": Generals, Congressmen, and Drug Lords

In June 1978 the bodies of Mario and Mary Ferrari, two middle-class cocaine and emerald traffickers, were found in a winch well in the outskirts of Tegucigalpa. This was a big scandal at the time, not only because they had disappeared six months earlier but because their murders appeared to be linked to Ramón Matta Ballesteros, the infamous Honduran drug lord who had helped create the trafficking connections between the Colombian and Mexican drug cartels in the 1970s and would also be involved in the 1980s in transporting military supplies sent by the United States to the Nicaraguan Contras, through his airline SETCO (Dudley 2016).[4]

In the aftermath of the finding of the corpses, *El Tiempo* and *La Prensa*, two of the most important Honduran papers at the time, began reporting that the murders of the Ferraris were connected to a broader process of military collusion in drug trafficking that went all the way up to the top of the hierarchy, including the head of the military intelligence services Colonel Leónidas Torres Arias, former student of the School of the Americas (Gill 2004), the chief of Interpol Lt. Juan Ángel Barahona, and Colonel Armando Calidonio Sr., member of the National Investigative Unit (DIN) and father of Armando Calidonio Jr., the former mayor of San Pedro Sula and former member of Congress with the National Party. However, none of the military alleged coconspirators in the murders, or in drug trafficking in general, were convicted.

According to Peter D. Scott and Jonathan Marshall (1991), it was Melgar Castro's inability to suppress such damning information that would cost him his job as head of state. The result of this "cocaine coup," allegedly financed by Matta Ballesteros himself, was the rise to power of General Policarpio Paz García, a figure closer to the drug lord's interests.

What this event revealed was the extent to which Honduras had become a strategic point in the drug trafficking routes between South American production and the U.S. market. Also, it demonstrated that there was a clear connection between the Honduran military, local drug lords and businessmen, such as Matta Ballesteros, and the transnational drug trafficking business—all of this with the United States' blessing, or at least their complacence, as "Jimmy Carter's administration chose to overlook its knowledge of Matta's role, perhaps because Paz, unlike Melgar, supported Somoza in his struggle against the Sandinistas" (Marshall and Scott 1991, 55).

Eventually, in 1988, Matta Ballesteros was detained by U.S. marshals on Honduran soil, in an act that contradicted the country's constitution, which at the time prohibited the extradition of Honduran citizens. In response, a massive popular manifestation took place in Tegucigalpa, resulting in the partial burning of the U.S. embassy, an event that showed both how popular Matta Ballesteros was in Honduras and the level of entrenchment that his operation had in the government, as he roamed free despite all the proofs against him. As Thomas Zepeda, a DEA agent posted in Honduras in the early 1980s decried, "It was difficult to conduct an investigation and expect the Honduras authorities to assist in arrests when it was them we were trying to investigate" (Marshall and Scott 1991, 56; U.S. Senate Committee on Foreign Relations 1988). The case of Matta Ballesteros also shows how the U.S. geopolitical imperatives, the fight against communism in this case, took precedence over everything else, including, for example, the unintentional creation of the infrastructure for their next great nebulous war: the "war on drugs."[5]

In the 1990s, as the Cold War faded, the war on drugs became the new game in town in Latin America. Military intervention and resources were justified under the effort of curtailing drug traffic, particularly of cocaine, into the United States. However, in places such as Honduras, where the state-narco relations ran deeply through the armed forces, this meant giving resources to fight drug trafficking to those who were apparently directly involved in it.

As we well know, far from stopping the drug trade, these policies have created a trail of blood and drug money that traverses the entire Central American region (ten Velde 2012; McSweeney 2020; Paley 2018), and Latin America more generally. However, the emergence of the policy did mean that traffickers needed to carry out their business much more discreetly than Matta Ballesteros ever did. As a result, the trafficking networks dug even deeper into the government structure and the territorial dynamics of the spaces shaped by their contraband. In the Aguán, this is exemplified in the figure of Óscar Ramón Nájera López.

A native of the Department of Colón, Nájera had roots in Olancho, the country's largest department and hometown to both Manuel Zelaya and Porfirio Lobo. Born to a large cattle ranching family, Nájera studied agronomical engineering in Honduras and Costa Rica and worked during the 1970s in the INA on the creation of the cooperatives in the Aguán. Later, in the 1990s he became a member of Congress with the National Party, where he remained in office during six consecutive terms, making his one of the longer, albeit not the longest, tenures in Congress (Barahona 2018). He also owns various oil palm plantations in the region and his family's name appears recurrently in the testimonies that I collected in the Aguán. They are remembered as part of the regional landowning elites present before the arrival of the BAP and as a family that managed to maintain most of their landholding throughout the agrarian reform period; there is at least one school named after Nájera in the region.

In the 1990s, as a member of Congress, Nájera was vital to the approval of the Agrarian Modernization Law. This was no coincidence. One of the great winners of the agrarian counterreform in the Aguán was the late Reynaldo Canales, owner of Aceydesa, one of the largest palm oil companies in the region, Nájera's close friend and one of the more significant financial backers of his political career.

According to a report by the Honduran digital news outlet Contracorriente (2017), it was precisely during the decade of the 1990s that Nájera consolidated his landowning empire in the Aguán. This period coincides with the regional economic and social crisis that followed Hurricane Mitch, the unraveling of the agrarian reform, and the rise in importance of Central America as a trafficking route due to the anti-drug crackdown in both Colombia and Mexico (McSweeney and Pearson 2013; Paley 2018). This created ripe conditions for trafficking organizations to proliferate in the region, as the political vacuum left by the weakened agrarian reform cooperatives was filled by regional strongmen such as Nájera. Indeed, this was a region where the working positions destroyed by the agrarian counterreform left most people, particularly young men, with the choice between working for a pittance on the palm oil plantations, migrating to the United States, or working for a criminal organization.

One such organization was Los Cachiros band, which operated mainly in the departments of Colón and Olancho. This organization, led by the Rivera Maradiaga brothers, started operating in the early 1990s, as the band shifted to drug trafficking from the family's tradition of cattle rustling that went back to at least the 1970s (Moreno 2015). By the mid-2000s they had become the country's largest drug transporting organization, to the point that, in 2013 a press release by the U.S. Department of Treasury claimed that the group controlled 90 percent of the clandestine airstrips in the Honduras (InSight Crime 2017; United States Department of Treasury 2013).

In January 2015 Juan Gómez Meléndez, a former governor of the department of Colón and allegedly Los Cachiros's main political operator and money launderer, was murdered in broad daylight in the city of Tocoa. This prompted various members of the family-run enterprise to turn themselves over to the DEA and start talking. Their testimonies began to reveal a broad and deep network articulating their transportation empire with many central players of the Honduran elite, including, for example, high-level members of the military, such as Julián Pacheco Tinoco, the former general and JOH's minister of security, who was the head of the military battalion in the Department of Colón in the early 2000s, when Los Cachiros were rising to prominence, and who had a very close relationship with Juan Gómez Meléndez (Dudley 2016).

Also, according to Devis Leonel Rivera Maradiaga's testimony, high-ranking politicians such as Nájera had accepted bribes in exchange for political protection and assuring the free transit of their contraband through the department of Colón. As a result, in December 2019 U.S. Secretary of State Michael Pompeo released a statement declaring that Nájera and his immediate family members were ineligible for entry into the United States, "due to his involvement in significant corruption. In his official capacity, Mr. Najera engaged in and benefitted from public corruption related to the Honduran drug trafficking organization Los Cachiros" (U.S. Embassy in Honduras 2019).

Notably, at the time when Rivera Maradiaga mentioned him as involved in drug trafficking, Nájera was on a business trip to Indonesia, the largest producer of palm oil in the world. When he returned to Honduras, he was asked about his thoughts about this matter, to which he famously answered, "*me la pela*," "I couldn't care less."

The political influence of Los Cachiros did not stop at the regional scale. The testimonies presented by the Rivera Maradiaga brothers also implicated Fabio Lobo, Porfirio Lobo's son, and Antonio "Tony" Hernández, the brother of the current president, Juan Orlando Hernández. Both have been found guilty of being involved in drug tracking by U.S. courts. Along the many accusations laid against Tony Hernández is receiving US$1 million from El Chapo Guzmán, the infamous Mexican drug lord, to help finance his brother Juan Orlando Hérnandez's presidential campaign.

Greasing the political and military gears of the drug trafficking machine was not the only destination of the money accrued through trafficking. Receiving payment ("dirty money") for moving the goods is just the first step in the business, as it still needs to be turned into expendable money ("laundering"). According to Teo Ballvé (2019, 218), "since narco-capitalists operate with such a wide initial profit margin, they are willing to engage in this second-step of expanded commodity production almost indiscriminately—even at a loss. Why? Because they are willing to make an investment in which they earn a mere 70 cents on the dollar in, say, an oil palm project as long as those 70 cents are now freely spendable."

In the case of Los Cachiros, their business portfolio extended from hardware stores, cattle ranches, oil palm plantations, mining concessions, and a zoo all the way to a construction company that won various public tenders to build roads (Dudley 2016; Moreno 2015). Crucial in this respect was their relationship with the powerful Rosenthal family and their Continental Group, which provided loans to finance many of these enterprises. The most damming evidence of their relationship came in July 2017, when Yani Rosenthal, the aforementioned minister of the presidency during Zelaya's government, plead guilty in a U.S. court to laundering drug money for Los Cachiros and was handed a three-year prison term (Dudley 2019). Let us remember that he was also the Liberal Party's presidential candidate in the 2021 elections.

Finally, according to the Honduran media, the value of assets seized from Los Cachiros exceeds well over US$800 million (Nolasco 2013). Further, according to the calculations of Steven Dudley (2016, 14) and the team of InSight Crime, the transporting market alone is valued at between USD $600 and $750 million per year, representing around 3 to 4 percent of the country's GDP, or about half of the money generated by Honduras's top export, coffee. While most of this money goes into bribes, conspicuous consumption, and sustaining the laundering machine, a substantial portion also goes into cementing the traffickers' position in society and garnering popular support. Just as Matta Ballesteros was known for supporting the poor of Tegucigalpa, Los Cachiros were known for their support to the communities of Colón. During the time that I lived in Tocoa, I heard stories of neighborhoods being electrified or having their roads fixed by "*los primos*"—the cousins—as they were commonly known in the region. Further, they also created licit jobs in their different enterprises and were well-known for taking care of those who worked for them, something very uncommon in the region.

Bringing social order was another of Los Cachiros's functions. When I first arrived in Tocoa, I was struck by the fact that most storefronts were very lightly barred, or not barred at all, which contradicted the discourses regarding just how dangerous the region was supposed to be. I soon learned the reason. One day I was in the barber shop that I frequented to learn the town's gossip, and someone mentioned that a body had been found floating in the Aguán River. When I asked if anyone knew how he had died, the barber speculated that in the last few nights a few stores in the town had been broken in to and robbed and that "los primos don't like it when they come to make a mess in their town."

It should come as no surprise that, on September 2013, when the Obama administration named the Rivera Maradiaga family as head of Los Cachiros drug trafficking cartel and the Honduran government confiscated various of their properties, thousands of people took to the streets of Tocoa to protest and demand the return of the assets and the public recognition of all the social good that Los Cachiros's businesses did in the region (Moreno 2015). I was in Tocoa that day and was struck by the combination of fear, love, and respect that most protestors professed, both verbally and in their signs, for the Rivera Maradiaga. I mentioned to a friend, an old leftist militant who at the time worked for a human rights NGO, with whom I was standing by on a corner of the central park of Tocoa, that the mobilization did not look staged to me. He responded, "Definitely not! It reminds me a lot of the 1980s when the gringos took Matta Ballesteros and we burned the embassy. People know that in Honduras the government is more corrupt than the narcos. Both steal, but at least the narcos share!"

While no embassies were burned in 2013, this is a good example of the level of social, political, and economic entrenchment that such groups have in the region's social fabric. This is an entrenchment that is the result of both spectacular demonstrations of violence, such as floating bodies in the river, and of filling in for the failed promises of development made in the name of the state.

Beyond the chilling picture that these criminal cases paint, I am interested in bringing attention to the articulation between the deepening of the state-narco relations and the time-space dynamics of the regions the drug trafficking routes traverse and reshape. In the case of places like the Aguán, Olancho, or the Moskitia, the articulation between their relative historic isolation from the rest of the country—particularly the limited presence of state institutions other than the armed forces—and the liberalization logic of capital accumulation of the neoliberal project created the perfect conditions for organizations like Los Cachiros to flourish, in tandem with politicians like Nájera (Barahona 2018).

At the same time, it is important to point out that these state-narco relations were built upon the foundations of the process of state formation that precedes them by quite a few decades. The figure of the military strongmen that represented, or embodied, the state in the country's different regional spaces was created by Carías in the 1930s. Further, the peaceful coexistence and articulation between organized crime, the regional cattle ranching elites, and their military counterparts in the Aguán dates to at least the 1980s and the creation of the first agrarian reform cooperatives. Thus, figures like Nájera, Pacheco Tinoco, or the Maradiaga brothers occupied positions that already existed. However, at the turn of the century, the landscapes upon which these relations were being produced were covered by a profitable business in the shape of the palm oil plantations created by the agrarian reform and the impoverished labor that it preyed upon.

### "*¿Quién dijo miedo detrás de una palmera?*": The Palm Oil Plantation Economy and State-Narco Relations

It is an open secret that the oil palm plantations make an excellent front for illicit activities: they are an expensive year-long operation with a high entry cost that both requires constant investments and creates a continual cash flow.[6] The plantations cover vast amounts of land that, under the sacrosanct institution of private property, make it hard to know, let alone control, what happens inside. This has led to a historical connection by most people in the region of the Aguán between the palm trees, *las palmeras*, as the plantations are commonly referred to, and activities outside of the law. Throughout history, the palm trees are a place where robbed goods are hidden, through which fugitives escape from the law, but also where furtive loves are consummated, bodies are dropped, and women are raped.

After the 1990s, with the sale of the cooperatives and the beginnings of the drug trafficking economy, the connection between the plantations and the illicit became much more sinister. The palm trees came to be connected to the region's rising body count, related to both the new wave of agrarian conflict that I characterized in the previous chapter and the increasing presence of organized crime. Besides the activity of organizations such as Los Cachiros, the Aguán became home to various roaming armed bands of young men for hire, many of whom had been deported from the United States or had had some basic military training in the Honduran armed forces, and who carry out odd jobs, including protecting drug transshipments and landings and robbing fruit from the palm oil plantations to sell it for pennies on the dollar in the various extraction mills present in the region.

In this context, the historical image of the Aguán as a wild land beyond the control of the state became even stronger, as it combined with images of the "colombianization" of the region. That is, a discourse emerged that presents drug trafficking as an invasion by foreign drug cartels that needed to be controlled before they managed to destabilize the region (Ballvé and McSweeney 2020). As a result, starting in 2011 the Honduran government sent a special military task force, dubbed Fuerza de Tarea Xatruch to pacify the Department of Colón,[7] declaring a state of exception, prohibiting civilians from carrying firearms, installing permanent check points in various parts of the region, controlling and restricting people's mobility and patrolling the different private palm oil plantations in the region.

In the case of the Aguán, based on the particular articulation of political, military, and economic power that I have drawn, the militarization of the region came to strengthen the state-narco relations. By being placed under the de facto control of the military, the Aguán became a huge grey area in which it is hard to differentiate the illicit from the licit and truth from myth, resulting in a generalized context of impunity (HRW 2014; Global Witness 2017). This has made the job of organized crime and their allies easier, and that of subaltern and human rights organizations harder.

The Jesuit priest and psychologist Igancio Martín-Baró (2003) used to describe the situation in El Salvador of the 1980s as one of "organized disorder": where, due to the indiscriminate and high levels of violence, there was a sense that danger and death could come from anywhere, and that it was extremely difficult to differentiate the "good guys" from the "bad" ones. As a result, questions regarding who should be blamed for the ensuing chaos and who should be responsible of solving it become extremely muddled. In short, in contexts such as the Aguán, or the border between the United States and Mexico (Wright 2006), impunity should not be understood as a lack of presence of the state, but rather as a set of practices and discourses that enable the reproduction of illegal and/or unjust situations.

For example, in the midst of the conflict between MUCA and the palm oil barons, the media ran various stories claiming that members of the Colombian FARC's were training "guerrilla cells" in the region under the cover of the peasant organizations (La Prensa 2010). Also, MUCA and other organizations began to report that Colombian former paramilitaries were being hired as private guards by people like Facussé (Bird 2013), and that the peasant movements were being infiltrated by paramilitaries (Olson 2021). As a result, due to the general lack of information regarding the history and political economy of the region, it became very difficult to know whom to believe and what exactly was going on, let alone figure out who were the "good" and the "bad" guys. All of this enabled the continued and systematic exploitation of peasant labor and the dynamics of dispossession we have described so far. A specific example will be useful here.

According to a cable of the U.S. embassy in Tegucigalpa (2004) released by Wikileaks, on March 14, 2004, a plane full of cocaine landed on a property owned by Miguel Facussé. About thirty heavily armed men unloaded its cargo and burned and buried the plane afterwards. When the authorities came to investigate, Facussé claimed that he did not know anything about the situation. However, according to the leaked telegram,

> Facusse's property is heavily guarded and the prospect that individuals were able to access the property and, without authorization, use the airstrip is questionable. In addition, Facusse's report obviously contradicts other information received from the law enforcement source... The source also claimed that Facusse was present on the property at the time of the incident.
>
> Of additional interest is that this incident marks the third time in the last fifteen months that drug traffickers have been linked to this property owned by Mr. Facusse. In July 2003, a go-fast boat crashed into a sea wall on the same property and engaged in a firefight with National Police forces. Two known drug traffickers were arrested in this incident and 420 kilos of cocaine were recovered. Earlier in the year, another air track terminated at the same property and appeared to have used the same airstrip.

Less than a year after the 2009 coup, this apparent connection between Facussé and drug trafficking became more macabre. On April 6, 2010, 210 families of the MCA decided to recuperate 510 hectares of El Tumbador, an oil palm plantation controlled by Miguel Facussé but which had been part of the original 5,700 hectares of the CREM. According to different testimonies, there was an initial agreement with the plantation's security team that if the families remained within those 510 hectares, there would be no problem. Most of the families involved in this recuperation came from those groups of the MCA that had had particularly bad luck with the allocation of the lands, and either had too little or too poor land. El Tumbador was covered in peak producing oil palms and thus became an important source of income for these families.

Just four months later, in August, a second group of families decided to occupy the remaining lands of El Tumbador, which were not included in the original CREM. While this led to the eviction of both groups by the military and Facussé's security forces, the situation did not end there. On November 15, 2010, around 120 to 180 people arrived in the early morning at the gates of El Tumbador in an attempt to recuperate these lands once more. However, this time, they were quickly ambushed and hunted down as they reached the gates of the plantation, resulting in the killing of five peasants; four others were gravely injured. According to people who took part in the failed occupation attempt, the massacre was perpetrated by an armed group composed of private security guards and supported by a unit from the Fifteenth Special Forces Battalion of the armed forces based in Río Claro, Trujillo. In the end, although Miguel Facussé went on TV the next day and all but admitted that his hired armed guards were behind the murders (Torres Funes 2016), he was never charged.[8]

Allegedly, the reason Facussé was so zealous of this property is its strategic location, controlling a bay that was often visited by speed boats at night. We can, of course, draw our own conclusions. However, whether Facussé or those close to him were involved in drug trafficking is beyond the point I am trying to make. El Tumbador massacre was just one example of a long tradition of produced impunity in the Aguán that allowed people like Facussé to be above the law and literally get away with murder (HRW 2014).

The El Tumbador massacre had a significant political effect in the region. Besides showing what appears to be an evident collusion between the armed forces and figures such as Facussé, it also demonstrated to what lengths the palm oil barons were willing to go to protect their property and the price that could be paid in the struggle for land. The massacre also stopped for more than a decade the attempts by members of the MCA to recover the remaining lands of the CREM.[9]

Finally, this example shows just how hard it is to prove the involvement of people such as Facussé with organized crime. According to the testimony of Devis Leonel Rivera Maradiaga, in 2013 Fabio Lobo asked for his help to introduce a shipment of cocaine coming from Venezuela into the country. Allegedly, the drug traffickers used a landing strip found on one of Facussé's properties. When asked about it by the team of InSight Crime, Roger Pineda, the spokesperson of Dinant Corporation, responded by letter denying the accusations and arguing that "unfortunately, as it happens to many others in rural areas, we have been victims of drug traffickers who have use our properties illegally, and without our consent, cooperation or permission, to transport their contraband around the country without being detected" (Clavel 2017).

Since the connection between landowners and businessmen and their estates has not really been explored or proven by the Honduran authorities, Pineda's argument is plausible, and thus it becomes that much harder to determine whether Corporación Dinant is culprit or victim. Something similar takes place in the case of the El Tumbador massacre. On the one hand, Facussé claimed that his guards were in their right to use force to defend his private property, and with its silence, the justice system agreed. On the other hand, since the Honduran authorities never took into account the claims made by the families of the victims and various human rights organizations regarding the involvement of the armed forces (Ponce 2020), the case was left at that. This is how impunity is produced: the discourse of the Aguán as an unlawful and chaotic frontier amid a war justifies the use of force to impose order, and the lack of research by the state regarding the relations between licit and illicit activities creates a context in which everything is permitted.

As long as the relationships between palm oil plantations, their owners, and drug traffickers are not disentangled, and as long as the perpetrators of crimes such as the El Tumbador massacre continue to run free, it is impossible to imagine that the stranglehold that criminal organizations and the palm oil companies have over the region will be broken, even after the death of Miguel Facussé and the capture of the Maradiaga brothers. As such, it is evident that the palm oil plantation economy and the drug trafficking economy are two sides of the same coin.

### The Aguán after June 28, 2009

"If they are going to kill us anyway, we might as well die in our lands." It was with these words, and a shrug of the shoulders, that a leader MUCA explained to me why he and around other six hundred peasant families had decided to occupy over twenty thousand hectares of oil palm plantations on December 9, 2009. Less than six months after the military coup that ousted President Manuel Zelaya, this decision signaled a shift by MUCA away from FNRP strategy of peaceful demonstrations, mostly in the capital Tegucigalpa, in their efforts to bring down the de facto government of Micheletti and return Zelaya to power. The same questions of legitimacy and justice were at the crux of the lands being occupied.

Expanding over twenty estates on both banks of the Aguán River, the peasant recuperation targeted plantations covered in oil palms, legally owned by Miguel Facussé and René Morales, the two main palm oil barons of the region. In response, several attempts were made to evict them, but once the news of the occupations reached the ears of the many landless families scattered around the Aguán and other places, many flocked to join them. According to MUCA, their membership increased overnight to over three thousand families (MUCA 2010). This increase in the size of the movement made it almost impossible to evict them all, especially since they knew the terrain better than the police and military, vanishing at times from one lot just to appear afterward on another.

The occupants managed to force the hand of the government and, in February 2010, negotiations began between MUCA and Porfirio Lobo's administration. MUCA's demands were straightforward: twenty thousand hectares of cultivated lands (oil palms), as well as the reinstitution of the commission that Zelaya had created just before being deposed to organize the process of redistribution of the lands possessed by Facussé, Morales, and Canales. The government's counteroffer was very limited: a much smaller amount of land, close to three thousand hectares, which the peasants would have to pay for in their totality to the current owners, as well as the establishing a set of "co-investment" agreements—basically a form of contract farming—with Facussé's Dinant Corporation and Morales's Agropalma. The end result was somewhere in between these two proposals. The government agreed to purchase three thousand hectares of oil palm lands and another three thousand hectares of uncultivated lands in the first three months, with another thousand cultivated and four thousand uncultivated hectares one year later, for a total of eleven thousand hectares. An arbitrated price of over US$6,000 per hectare was determined by specialists.[10] The money would be paid in its entirety to the landowners by the state, which would then collect the payments from MUCA at a low rate of interest. The government also committed to providing twenty-five hundred families with health services, as well as schools and the construction of two hundred houses in two years.

In mid-April 2010, the agreement was signed at gunpoint, as on April 7, the government deployed over seven thousand soldiers and policemen in the region, which led to higher levels of repression and the murder, under mysterious circumstances, of four members of MUCA. Nonetheless, MUCA viewed the agreement as a victory since it was the first time that they had managed to pry anything away from Facussé. Their members were relocated into six settlements on the right bank: La Aurora, La Concepción, La Confianza, La Isla, and El Marañón. In the end, MUCA had received around half of the land promised and only a few posts for teachers. Once again, the state's promises lasted as long as the peasant organizations' pressure remained on the ground.

Consequently, MUCA was left with very little space—less than five hectares per family—in relation to the number of mouths that they had to feed. As a result, many single women and older men began to be pressured to leave the organization, and thus improve the family-to-land ratio. We can identify a cycle in which peasant movements tend to attract new members in the moment of direct struggle for land—when they need strength in numbers—only to try to downsize once they are in control of the land (Rangel Loera 2010).

The agreement also split MUCA down the middle. The members of the former cooperatives El Despertar, La Trinidad, and San Esteban, located on the left bank, and San Isidro, located on the right bank, refused to sign the agreement. According to them, they did not have to pay for the land, because they had not sold it; they therefore decided to continue with their legal claims, thus giving birth to the Authentic Reclaiming Peasant Movement of the Aguán (MARCA).

The members of MARCA continued with their struggle, combining presence in the disputed lands through occupations with lawsuits in court. Nevertheless, they changed their legal strategy. Initially, they had denounced the illegality of the sales to Morales and Facussé; now, instead, they sued the former boards of directors that had sanctioned the sales. In the case of El Despertar, reflecting similar situations in the other cooperatives, the then-president of the board of directors accepted that he had acted illegally, and that the sale agreement should be nullified.

The legal process dragged on for almost two more years, during which the members of MARCA would occupy one or two of the claimed estates for as long as they could, before being evicted by the police and the military. These occupations would last between a few hours and a few months, and it was a harsh period for their families. They were harassed and several members were killed—both in clashes with the security forces and in targeted assassinations—while identified MARCA members were placed on a blacklist and unable to work on the oil palm plantations in the region. They survived thanks to the solidarity of their neighbors, the palm fruit that they could cut during their occupations, and the remittances that their sons and daughters would send from the United States to support the movement.

Eventually, on June 29, 2012, three full years after the coup, the Honduran Supreme Court ruled in favor of MARCA, giving them full control over the El Despertar, La Trinidad, and San Isidro cooperatives (they had gained control of San Esteban in May 2011). This was, of course, received with great joy by the members of the movement. They remember how on that day they went over to the plantations with members of the police to carry out the eviction order against Agropalma. They would tell me with great pride how they used to be the ones evicted by the police and the private security guards, but now it was their turn to evict the palm men.

This joy, however, was short-lived. On September 22 of that same year, Antonio Trejo, the lawyer who had led the final legal offensive, was shot dead by unknown gunmen in Tegucigalpa while he was attending a wedding. The news brought great grief to the members of MARCA, who began to fear the beginning of a new cycle of evictions. They were right. In September 2013 the San Isidro cooperative was evicted, followed by evictions in El Despertar and La Trinidad in May 2014. These evictions represented an actual reversal of decisions of the Supreme Court and illustrate unmistakably the ease with which powerful interests in Honduras can bend the law.

For many members of MARCA, this was the end of the road. Without money or work in the cooperatives, the Aguán became an inhospitable place. The region continued to be militarized under the double argument of making sure that no more occupations took place and curbing the escalating violence related to drug trafficking. Moving around the region became much harder and more dangerous, limiting even more the possibilities of finding work for most young men, many of whom now turn to the various criminal organizations in the region as an alternative. The outlooks are even worse for young women, whose prospects are to get married and become at-home mothers, take the worst-paid jobs in the oil palm plantations, or leave the region in search of work or study opportunities.

Although migrations to the United States from the Aguán have been occurring for at least three decades (León Araya and Salazar Araya 2016), the last few years have seen a significant increase in the amounts of people leaving the country. The result has been a morbid combination and overlapping of the criminal networks dedicated to the trafficking of narcotics and people (Salazar Araya 2019). The fact that the two networks share the same routes and many of the same technologies and actors makes them part of the same logics of rent capturing that I mentioned before.

As a result, certain communities in the Aguán are becoming ghost towns. For example, in February 2019 I made a short visit to the small village in which Eugenia and her husband Marino live. Before the evictions of MARCA, this was quite a vibrant place, with the street full of young men who worked in the cooperatives' plantations, riding the motorcycles that they had bought on credit. Children would be running around and the MARCA-owned *consumo*, a midsize utility and foodstuff store, would be filled with young women buying food and chatting with their friends.

This time around, not only were the streets mainly empty, but everyone I talked to spoke of how it was now dangerous to hang out in the streets. Not only were there various criminal bands roaming the place but the military patrols tended to harass the people they found. For young men, this meant having their shirts lifted to check if they had any incriminating tattoos; for women, being molested or goaded.

Moreover, after the cooperatives were evicted, there was much less work in the now-private plantations and the salaries were much lower than they had been under MARCA. As a result, most young men and women were forced to leave the region in search of better living conditions, or simply to save their lives, as was the case of many of the peasant organizers and human rights activists I had met just a few years earlier. What I did find were older people such as Eugenia or Marcelo, who were now taking care of their infant grandchildren, left behind by their fleeing fathers and mothers.

We began our story with the flight of people like Eugenia and Marcelo toward the Aguán in search of a better future. In the process, their lives became intertwined with the process of formation of the Honduran state. They produced the cooperatives and the palm oil plantations of the agrarian reform in the Aguán and in the process transformed themselves into a market-oriented, palm oil-versed working force. Later, they suffered and fought against the imposition of the neoliberal project in the country, through the structural adjustment projects of the 1980s and 90s and the wave of disaster capitalism in the aftermath of Hurricane Mitch. In the process, they forged a coalition with a vast and varied set of organizations in different parts of the country that shared many of their grievances. As a result of their collective struggle with these other forces, they managed to force the hand of Mel Zelaya and enact an alliance that changed the political landscape of the country, and in the process that, of the Aguán. For example, it is not coincidence that on the morning of June 28, 2009, as the military were kidnapping Zelaya in Tegucigalpa, the community of Guadalupe Carney, home of the MCA, was surrounded and occupied by the Honduran armed forces.

The conflict that followed, and which has been much more extensively covered by scholars and activists (FIDH 2011; Kerssen 2012; Bird 2013; Önder 2018), is just the latest chapter of this messy and bloody story. When the narco cartels of South and North America began searching for alternative routes to keep their booming business going, they found in the Aguán the perfect mixture of despair and political articulation between armed forces, political figures, and organized crime for them to thrive. In the process, the ability of people like Facussé and his Corporación Dinant to assert control over the regional space also increased, and with it, their stranglehold over the region. It was now the time for the sons and daughters of the Eugenias and Marcelos of the Aguán to follow on the footsteps of their mothers and fathers and take flight in search of a better future.

## CHAPTER 7

# Honduras, the Neoliberal Workshop or the End of a Cycle?

On May 22, 2011, the then-Colombian president Juan Manuel Santos and a representative of the Venezuelan president Hugo Chávez signed what came to be known as the Cartagena Accords. In exchange for Venezuela's backing of Honduras's readmission into the OAS, the Honduran government agreed to allow Zelaya to reenter the country and dismiss all legal proceedings against him, as well as to recognize any attempt by the National Front of Popular Resistance, the broad alliance of sectors that came together in the aftermath of the coup, to become a formal political party (Gordon and Webber 2013). These accords, which were supposed to bring to a formal close the crisis created by the coup, were apparently negotiated by Zelaya and those close to him behind the back of the rest of the leadership of the FNRP, opening up an inner rift between three main camps (Frank 2018): first, a group of former members of the Liberal Party who followed Zelaya in the aftermath of his ousting and were very interested in participating electorally; second, a loose group of leftist political organizations, mainly from the labor and peasant movements, who had gravitated toward the UD and were critical of Zelaya but shared an interest in electoral participation; and, finally, what came to be known as the Refoundational Space (Espacio Refundacional), a mixed bag of grassroot movements, feminist organizations, LGBT activists, Indigenous and Afro organizations, and autonomist and radical youth organizations. The two better known and larger organizations within this camp were the COPINH and the OFRANEH, which had butted heads with Zelaya during his truncated administration.

The dispute among these groups played out in two general assemblies of the FNRP that took place during 2011 in Tegucigalpa. At the time of the first meeting, in February, Zelaya was still abroad and did not participate; the event was the result of more than six months of discussion between the different organizations regarding what the future of the Front, and the resistance

Motorcycle parked near Tocoa's Central Park, 2013. Notice the stickers in favor of both Xiomara Castro for president and Adán Fúnez as mayor of Tocoa. Photo by the author.

against the coup, should be. While consensus was hard to come by from such a varied combination of actors, the official decision that came out of this first assembly was to focus on grassroot and popular self-organization and avoid participating in the 2013 elections. The reasoning behind this decision was that since the political structures of the coup remained intact, the conditions for electoral participation simply did not exist (Gordon and Webber 2013). However, by June 26, when the second general assembly was held, it seemed that the situation had changed. With Zelaya now present and taking advantage of both his popularity among FNRP followers and the tendency toward bossism that has dominated Honduran politics for much of the country's history, the resolution of the first assembly of not participating electorally was reversed and the political party Libertad y Refundación (Liberty and Refoundation, or LIBRE) was created.

LIBRE has participated in the three elections that have taken place since the ousting of Manuel Zelaya. In 2013 it fielded Xiomara Castro de Zelaya, Mel's wife, as the presidential candidate; she came in a close second to JOH in an electoral process marred by allegations of fraud. LIBRE also gained 37 of 128 seats in Congress, just behind the 48 gained by the National Party. Also debuting in this electoral process was the Anticorruption Party (PAC), with eighteen seats in Congress and led by Salvador Nasralla, a well-known television personality and narrator of the national football team's matches who espoused a strong anticorruption but also anticommunist discourse.

In 2017 LIBRE and the Innovation and Social Democracy Union Party (PINU) came together to form the Alianza de Oposición Contra la Dictadura (Alliance against the Dictatorship), with Salvador Nasralla now running as their presidential candidate. This was a pragmatic alliance between two groups that did not see eye-to-eye on most topics—Nasralla being an avowed anticommunist and Xiomara Castro and LIBRE "democratic socialists"—that aimed at removing Juan Orlando Hernández from the presidential chair. It is important to remember that the Honduran constitution prohibits presidential reelection; however, in 2012 JOH and the National Party, through their control over Congress, imposed a new constitutional court, which, in turn, declared reelection legal. Thus, in the eyes of everyone other than the president and the governing party, his was an illegal candidacy and the consolidation of a dictatorship that began to emerge in 2009.

The 2017 presidential election was an extremely close and controversial affair. As it usually happens in Honduras, before the official results were communicated, both JOH and Nasralla had declared themselves winners. Later, the electoral tribunal announced preliminary results with 57 percent of the ballots counted, showing Nasralla with a 5 percent advantage over Hernández. However, after this first announcement, the webpage where the preliminary results had been published went offline for ten hours. When it finally came back online, the difference between the two frontrunners began to close and eventually JOH was declared the winner with the slightest of advantages (1.63 percent, just over fifty thousand votes).

The results were received with fury and disbelief by the followers of LIBRE and the Alliance against the Dictatorship, who claimed that the elections had been stolen from them and demanded that JOH resign as president and new elections be convened. Protests and riots ensued in different parts of the country for the rest of 2017 and early 2018, including a call by Zelaya for a general strike in December; the police and armed forces responded with force and martial law was declared. In the end, according to COFADEH, between November 26 and December 31, 2017, 30 people had been "executed," 232 had been injured and more than a thousand had been detained as a result of crackdowns on the protests against the fraud (COFADEH 2018).

These elections were also questioned internationally, as different governments called for a return to order and peace, and even Luis Almagro, the infamous general secretary of the OAS, released a statement claiming that the electoral process had been full of irregularities and deficiencies and proposing that the elections should be held again. This proposal was quickly rejected by the Honduran government, but Hernández did call for a "national dialogue" to "consolidate peace" and try to cool the tempers down. Nasralla and most of the traditional parties, but not LIBRE, agreed to participate in the process, which was mediated by the UN and took place between August 28 and December 11, 2018, with 169 agreements reached on topics such as human rights and electoral reforms. However, according to Manuel Zelaya and the leadership of LIBRE, since these agreements were not binding, they were very much useless. Further, from their point of view, since this dialogue organized by an illegitimate president, it was also illegitimate, its only function being to bring some legitimacy to a tarnished government. It became clear that, if the Cartagena Accords, the return of Zelaya to Honduras, and the creation of the legal conditions for LIBRE were aimed at bringing the political crisis of the 2009 coup to a close, they had failed miserably.

### The Three Honduran Coups

For Miriam Miranda, the coordinator of OFRANEH, the ousting of Zelaya in 2009 was the first in a series of three coups (Saravia 2021). The second one took place in 2012, with the changes imposed on the Constitutional Court by JOH and the passing of the ZEDES's law, which came to severely undermine the national constitution and sovereignty. The third coup took place during the 2017 elections, when not only did JOH openly violate the constitution with his reelection but the election itself was stolen from the opposition.

In the process, through these three coups, according to Miranda, Honduras had become a neoliberal workshop. First, the ousting of Zelaya initiated a cycle of coups that extended through Latin America during the next decade (Paraguay, 2012, Brazil, 2016, and Bolivia, 2019). Second, the ZEDES law proved an extractivist's dream, giving capital absolute control not only over resources and people but also over policy and the law. Third, the rise of power of JOH was the consolidation of a "narco-state" like no other, with the influence of drug traffickers reaching all the way to the top, destroying the country's already weak democratic institutions and making of Honduras a "failed state" (Saravia 2021).

Seen from this perspective, the 2021 elections were not only about deciding who would be the country's next president. Rather, they were a moment of judgement of the last twelve years of government by the National Party, which had led the country to a critical economic and social crisis, aggravated and laid bare by the COVID-19 pandemic,[1] with the migrant caravans toward the United States as the most visible effect. It should come as no wonder that we find the same levels of polarization and political tensions that framed the 2017 elections resurfacing around the 2021 process.

Early on, Juan Orlando Hernández declared that he would not be looking for another term, an announcement that was received with both hope and distrust by the opposition. On the one hand, since the National Party really did not have any strong or popular political figure that could substitute JOH, it opened the door for the opposition to win the election convincingly enough to limit the possibilities of a fraud. On the other hand, for many it was hard to imagine that JOH would leave power peacefully and renounce the immunity that came with the post, particularly in the context of continued prosecution by the U.S. judiciary of Honduran politicians involved with drug trafficking.

From the beginning of the electoral cycle there were attempts to create an alliance between the opposition parties; at the same time, the different political figures angled to make sure that they would be the ones in position to take advantage of the new political opening. Finally, on October 13, LIBRE, PINU and Nasralla's new party, the Partido Salvador de Honduras (the Savior of Honduras Party, PSH) signed a political agreement to "reestablish the democratic order and the rule of law in favor of the Honduran people" (Deutsche Welle 2021). Xiomara Castro became the presidential candidate, with Nasralla and Doris Gutiérrez of PINU as the first and second presidential designates, as vice presidents are known in Honduras.

This was, once again, a pragmatic alliance that aimed at getting JOH and the National Party out of power and bringing an end to the "dictatorship." After this, the election became a clear race between LIBRE and Xiomara Castro on the one hand and the National Party and Nasry Asrufa, the incumbent mayor of Tegucigalpa, who had on his side the party's electoral machine, including the ability to use public funds to buy votes, on the other. Watching the campaign from the outside was the Liberal Party, led by Yani Rosenthal, who had plead guilty to charges of money laundering for Los Cachiros in a U.S. court.

The electoral campaign was an extremely polarized affair: LIBRE claimed that if they won, they would dismantle the corrupt structures of the dictatorship, including repealing the ZEDES law. The National Party conducted an anticommunist campaign that focused on the alleged dangers that LIBRE would unleash against private property and family values. It was also a very bloody process, with at least thirty-one politically motivated murders, including of a candidate for mayor of the Liberal Party.

On Sunday, November 28, Hondurans went to the polls in an atmosphere thick with expectations. For much of the foreign press, one of the main questions was whether the complaints of fraud and ensuing violence of the 2017 election would repeat themselves. In case of the domestic media, particularly those that sympathized with the opposition, the message was simple: the higher the levels of voting, the harder it would be for the National Party to steal the elections. This assessment was accompanied by a call to vote early, to vote peacefully, and to remain vigilant to guard the results and protect every vote.

In the end the elections took place in a relatively peaceful manner, and more than 3.5 million Hondurans (above 68 percent of the rolls) participated, making these the elections with the highest popular participation in the country's history, as young people participated en masse and enthusiastically. Xiomara Castro became Honduras's first female president with over 50 percent of the votes. Asrufa and the National Party came in a far second, with just over 36 percent, and the Liberal Party, with the worst result in their recent history, did not reach 10 percent. However, this resounding victory did not translate into a significant control over Congress: LIBRE won 50 out of 128 seats, with the National Party coming in a close second with 44, the Liberal Party 22, and the PSH fourth with 10 seats. As such, the new government would have to negotiate to have enough votes to push its agenda. For example, simple majorities (sixty-five votes) are needed to approve new laws. However, constitutional reforms require a qualified majority (eighty-six votes).

In general terms, the new government came into power in a triple bind. First, most of the people who voted for LIBRE expected the government to transform the country's dire economic and political situation quickly. For example, one of the most common lines used during the electoral period by LIBRE's militants and candidates was that people would no longer need to migrate to have a better life. Second, besides LIBRE not having a dominant position within Congress, the new Honduran government inherited a set of international obligations that would constrain their ability to promote radically different economic and social policies.

Thirdly, as I have shown throughout this book, in Honduras, hegemony and the ability to govern depend on pacts and negotiations between different groups. Immediately after the elections, the alliance between Nasralla and the leadership of LIBRE came to agreements on certain topics, while showing increasing frictions on others. Further, while certain economic sectors showed some concerns regarding the new president's position on topics such as the ZEDES, people such as Eduardo Facussé, the president of the Industrial and Commercial Chamber of Cortés, one of the most important economic organizations in the country, claimed that the time had come for the government and the private sector to work hand in hand to improve the economic condition of the country. In this vein, it is worth mentioning that one of the first meetings that Castro had as elected president was with the COHEP, historical representatives of the Honduran business class involved in her husband's ousting in 2009 (Silva 2021).

After her win, various high-ranking officials of the U.S. government, including Vice President Kamala Harris, who traveled for the presidential inauguration, congratulated Xiomara Castro. Three topics have dominated these messages: improving economic conditions, solving the migration crisis, and combating corruption. While one should take these signals as the usual diplomatic response to the arrival of a new government, they also point to the fact that LIBRE and Xiomara Castro are not seen as a threat to the economic interests of the Honduran economic elite and U.S. geopolitical interests. Only time will tell how this will play out.

Taking all these elements into account, a few things should become clear. First, the arrival of LIBRE is far from the continuation of Mel Zelaya's government as it stood at the time of the 2009 coup. LIBRE's internal composition is very complex and far from homogenous. Further, the irruption of a new generation of militants and organizers has had an important impact on the Honduran political scene. The increasing role of women and feminist activists within the party is also an important deviation from Honduran politics as usual. Xiomara Castro becoming the first female president of a country with some of the worst levels of femicides and gender-based violence in Latin America should not be taken lightly (ECLAC 2021).

Furthermore, the disastrous economic, social, and political record of more than a decade of Nationalist governments has done much to erode the support for the more traditional structure of power, as well as diminish the influence of an anticommunist discourse that seems very much detached from the interests of a younger generation that did not live through the Cold War. For example, as I heard a young woman say on a radio program in the run up to the elections, "They say that we should be afraid of communism because it will take away our property. However, the few things that I had, I lost them to the corruption of this government. So, either they are the communists, or they are the ones that are afraid to lose what they have stolen."

At the same time, the Latin American geopolitical context changed drastically between 2009 and 2021. As I argued before, Zelaya's alliance with Chávez's Venezuela and the ALBA project had given his government a certain independence from the U.S. strategy for the region. By 2021, that was no longer an option. Castro would have to negotiate in a context dominated by increased U.S. attention to Central America, as well as China's increasing role in the region. As such, one of her electoral promises was to shift the country's alliance away from Taipei and toward Beijing, which risked some tensions with Washington. She would also have to deal with some legacies of JOH, such as the decision, encouraged by the Trump administration, of relocating Honduras's embassy in Israel from Tel Aviv to Jerusalem. Finally, her government would have to navigate a convulsive Central American conjuncture, with Nayib Bukele in El Salvador and Zelaya's historical ally Daniel Ortega in Nicaragua taking a more authoritarian line and attracting the ire of the imperial power to the north. For example, in December 2021 the Biden administration organized a "Summit for Democracy," to which neither JOH, Ortega, nor Bukele were invited to participate. While one should criticize Washington's hypocrisy, as Juan Guaidó, the self-proclaimed president of Venezuela, was invited, this slight gives us a clear sense of the new diplomatic line that the early Biden administration intended to follow on the isthmus.

### The End of the Two-Party System?

Since the 2013 election and the rise of LIBRE as one of the most important electoral forces in Honduras, observers have proclaimed the death of the Honduran two-party system. The 2021 elections, the arrival of Castro to the presidential chair, and the historical debacle of the Liberal Party all appear to point in this direction. However, when we move from the national to the regional scale, things are not so clear. Here I present the example of two political figures from the Aguán to show what I mean.

Let us begin with Óscar Nájera, whom we met in the previous chapters. He was first elected to Congress by the National Party in 1990, where he remained until the 2021 elections, when he failed to win one of the four seats allocated to the department of Colón. An iconic figure in the region, Nájera has spoken very openly about his lifelong friendship with the Rivera Maradiaga brothers, the now-imprisoned founders of Los Cachiros, and has been implicated in various of court cases against Honduran drug traffickers in the United States and is included in the Engel List.[2] At the same time, he has never been questioned regarding any of these accusations in Honduras. However, the loss of his parliamentary seat also meant the loss of his political immunity.

In an interview he gave just a few days after the 2021 election, Nájera argued that the National Party's defeat was the result of a punishment vote against Juan Orlando Hernández's acts of corruption and the high levels of impunity. He also claimed that he had nothing to hide and that this was the end of his political career (Dada 2021). What comes next for Nájera is yet to be seen, but his political defeat ended a cycle of political control that lasted more than three decades.

However, it may be premature to think that with this vote of punishment and the ousting from Congress of figures like Nájera the close relations between drug traffickers, politicians, and businessmen in the Aguán that I have described throughout this book came to an end. Rather, what we can see is a reconfiguration within the regional elites. Here, the case of Adán Fúnez, the presidentially elected governor of the Department of Colón, is a good example.

Other than the fact that he was born in 1950 in the mountains of the department of Colón, there is little we know about Fúnez's early life. His political career took off when, amid accusations of embezzlement, he abandoned a local transportation cooperative to establish his own company, Tranportes Mirna, in the early 2000s and began to cultivate a close relationship with Óscar Nájera, the former president Porfirio Lobo, his son Fabio, and Fredy Nájera, a former congressman of the Liberal Party. It is worth remembering that these last two are currently imprisoned in the United States for drug trafficking.

A militant of the Liberal Party, Adán Fúnez was an adamant defendant of the Cuarta Urna and a close associate of Manuel Zelaya in the region. During the 2009 electoral season he openly supported the FNRP, but later, as the November elections closed in, he returned to the Liberal Party and ran for mayor but lost. In 2011, when LIBRE was created, he once again left the Liberal Party to enroll in LIBRE, as part of the 28th of June Movement, comprising a group of former members of the Liberal Party. He was elected mayor of Tocoa in 2013 and reelected in 2017.

Fúnez's tenure as mayor was marred by controversy. In 2013 or 2014, a mining concession located within the borders of the Botaderos Mountain Carlos Escaleras National Park, allegedly granted originally to the Riviera Maradiaga, Los Cachiros, was transferred to Inversiones Los Pinares, a company owned by Lenir Pérez and his wife, Ana Isabel Facussé, daughter of Miguel Facussé. Ironically, this national park takes the name of Carlos Escaleras, a union leader, member of COPA and mayoral candidate for the UD, who was murdered in 1997 due to his resistance against the installation of a palm oil extraction plant in the Aguán by Miguel Facussé.[3]

In 2015 various communities and grassroots organizations from around the city of Tocoa, including the San Alonso Rodríguez Foundation, the Catholic Church, and COPA, came together under the name of the Comité Municipal de Defensa de los Bienes Comunes y Públicos de Tocoa (the Municipal Committee in Defense of the Common and Public Goods of Tocoa; CMDBCP) to protest against the mining project and the effects that it would have on the Guapinol, San Pedro, and Ceibita Rivers and watersheds, which supply water to tens of thousands of people.

They went to Fúnez to request for a *cabildo abierto*—an open town hall meeting—at which they intended to declare Tocoa a "mining free territory" and thus close the door for the mine. He refused the request, but in a public meeting that took place in 2016 was recorded saying to the audience, "I can't believe that all of you from the San Pedro area, being friends of Javier [Rivera Maradiaga] and the entire Rivera family, didn't know that he had requested those concessions, including the one above the lagoon. Didn't you know . . . that the EMCO [concession] belonged to your friend and mine, Javier Rivera?" (Ávila 2020)

That same year, Adan Fúnez and the municipal secretary Norma García, who was also a LIBRE candidate for Congress in the 2021 elections, had forged a municipal minute that claimed the community of La Ceibita knew about, and agreed with, the mining project. This was a crucial document for Inversiones Los Pinares's effort to gain an environmental license (Diario Colón 2021). Also, as a 2020 report has shown, Nucor Corporation, one of the largest steel producers in the United States, spent at least four years associated with this mining project (Ávila and Mackey 2020).

This did not stop the CMDBCP, which combined written requests for the cabildo abierto with roadblocks, occupying the municipality, and contesting the mine's constitutional legality. The peak moment of these protests came in August 2018. After the running water of the community of Guapinol began to run muddy and contaminated, the residents of the community and the CMDBCP staged an "Encampment in the Defense of Water and Life," blocking the road leading to the mine site. The blockade, maintained by around 140 people, lasted for 88 days, until October 27, when the protesters were evicted by a combined military and police force of more than 1000 officers. In the days following the eviction, the conflict extended to other communities, and in Ceibita, armed supporters of the mine burned down the houses of a family who opposed it, resulting in the death of one person.

In September 2018, before the encampment was evicted, the mining company presented a lawsuit against eighteen of the protesters for illegal encroachment, public and private property damage, and restricting the right to free passage. Of these, thirteen were prosecuted and the list of charges presented against them was extended to include illicit association, arson, and illegal detention. These were the first environmental activists accused of illicit association, which necessarily includes preventive detention (ACAFREMIN 2020).

Much more could be said regarding the Guapinol conflict. For my interests, I would like to point out two processes that intersect around the figure of Adán Fúnez and the pause that it should give us regarding the alleged change that could come with LIBRE. First, we can read the case of Guapinol as part of the longer arch of conflicts around mining that began in the aftermath of Hurricane Mitch in 1998 and the logic of "disaster capitalism" that I described in chapter 4. Thus, if the CNRP first, then the FNRP, and later LIBRE later, are all attempts to break away from the imposition of the neoliberal project in the country, Fúnez and his brand of politics is rather its continuation.

Further, the case of Fúnez points toward the complicated relationship that exists between the FNRP and LIBRE, and between the state and the subaltern organization that take part in the FNRP. It was one thing for organizations close to the FNRP to organize against a municipal government that was controlled by the National or Liberal Party, who were understood to be their opponents. It was quite another to try to organize against a local government controlled by a mayor from LIBRE, who was supposed to be their ally.

Funéz, who was reelected during the mining conflict, is not the only former member of the Liberal Party who shifted to LIBRE. In fact, as I have discussed elsewhere, in the 2013 elections most of the candidates LIBRE presented for Congress and municipalities came from the internal political fractions closer to Zelaya and of Liberal extraction, such as the 28th of June Movement (León Araya 2016). Seen from this perspective, the role of a political party such as LIBRE has more to do with co-opting or redirecting the political excitement that was generated by the coup among subaltern groups and that took the shape of the FNRP than with embarking on the radical project of political transformation and "refoundation" that organizations such as COPA or

COPINH had imagined. Thus, LIBRE, by shifting the terrain of political dispute from the "streets" to the "ballots," turned the promise of change into a "revolution without revolutionary change": in short, electoral politics emerged as a form of passive revolution (Abrahamsen 1997).

Second, in terms of the regional political dynamics of the Aguán, Adán Fúnez apparently fulfills a role similar to that of Óscar Nájera: connecting the illicit and the licit economies, the national with the regional, and articulating politicians, businessmen, and, as his public friendship with Los Cachiros shows, drug traffickers. This role is independent from party colors and speaks to the concrete correlation of forces in the Aguán region and its historical connections to processes taking place in other scales; be it palm oil exports, mining projects, or drug trafficking.

# CONCLUSION

*The Coup and the Palm Trees* has attempted to explain some of the conditions of possibility for the 2009 coup d'état and the Honduran conjuncture as it stood in 2022, through the telling of the double history of the processes of formation of the region of the Aguán on the one hand and of the Honduran state on the other. The central argument is that to understand how and why Manuel Zelaya was ousted from the presidential seat in 2009, why such a massive number of Hondurans are fleeing the country toward the United States, and why Honduras has become a quintessential "narco-state," we need to go back in history and explore how certain circumstances from the past continue to animate the country's present and set limits on what might be possible in the future. For example, we saw how the process of agrarian reform produced a set of differentiations within and between the cooperatives in the Aguán, which later informed the process of agrarian counterreform in the 1990s. The latter in turn sparked a wave of land conflicts in the aftermath of Hurricane Mitch that arrived at the doors of the 2009 coup and continue to be very much alive to this day.

In what follows, I would like to briefly characterize what I consider to be the three main threads along which the main arguments of this book emerge: (1) the coproduction of landscapes and subjects; (2) the militarized formation of the Honduran state; and (3) democracy as pacification.

## The Coproduction of Landscapes and Subjects

The Central American postcolonial period has been marked by a constant effort to develop a relationship with the global market that would allow the region to transform its supposed natural riches into modernity and progress. From coffee, bananas, and sugar to pineapples and palm oil, the agrarian history of the isthmus is one of attempts to develop a modern agriculture export sector that is diversified, efficient, and highly productive.

*The Coup and the Palm Trees* tells the story of one such effort, through the history of the production of the Bajo Agúan region. It narrates how it went from being seen as a set of "empty" or "idle" lands before the 1970s to becoming the centerpiece of the Honduran agrarian reform during the 1980s, the "capital of the agrarian counterreform" in the 1990s, an intense site of agrarian conflict around the time of the 2009 coup, and the home of Los Cachiros in the aftermath of the coup. This brief timeline should not be understood in simple linear terms; rather, it should be seen as a process of amalgamation or sedimentation, of different processes, taking place on different temporal and spatial scales.

Crucial to this story has been the Honduran agrarian reform. Dubbed the "fundamental task" in the process of modernization of the Honduran state during the second half of the twentieth century, the agrarian reform was supposed to improve the economic and social conditions of the country in at least two directions. First, by distributing land to poor landless peasants, it would allow them to enter the market as both producers of foodstuffs and exportable crops and consumers of an expanding domestic market. Second, by introducing new technologies, it would turn "idle" or low-yield lands into highly productive and industrialized fields that would become the engine of national development.

The agrarian reform was also tasked with transforming the highly unequal agrarian structure that Latin America in general had inherited from the colonial period. The idea was that if you redistributed land, you would break down the landowning elite's control over resources and labor, thereby also redistributing political power. Further, from the perspective of the incipient bourgeoisie, giving land to the poor peasantry was a way of cementing an alliance with them against their alleged common enemy: that same landowning elite. In the resulting process of "modernization from above," productivity was increased, new crops were introduced, but neither the unequal distribution of land nor the living conditions of most peasant households were truly transformed. However, this is not to say that significant changes did not take place.

The BAP, which I described in chapter 2, is a good example of what the agrarian reform imagined itself to be, and how in reality it ended up looking very different from the original intent. Technically designed with the help of the OAS, the BAP was presented as an all-encompassing project, one that would mix the labor of landless peasants brought from different parts of the country with foreign capital in the form of debt to transform a set of lands that, from the perspective of state and capital, were "empty" or "idle." Seeing the Aguán as a rich and open canvas, the officials of the Honduran government proposed the BAP as a way of inscribing development into the countryside and solving many of the problems that it was facing. First, by removing organized peasants from conflict-ridden areas in different parts of the country and bringing them to the Aguán, it would curb the wave of peasant organization that had begun with the banana strike of 1954 and had increased in the aftermath of Hurricane Fifí in 1974. Second, since these lands were understood as "empty" state-owned lands, the BAP would permit distribution to the landless without affecting the landowning elites or having to pay for confiscated lands. Third, by including export-oriented crops, the project would diversify and increase the country's export basket and thus create revenue for the state. At least notionally, it was a win-win situation.

In practice, everything was quite different: far from an empty territory, the Aguán was a rebellious space, in which both elites and subaltern groups resisted the imposed colonization by what they saw as external groups. However, as we saw in chapter 2, while the regional elites were able to negotiate an accommodation into the new framework and remain in a dominant position, the poor peasant, Indigenous, and Black families that had been living in the region before the BAP were forced to either join the peasant cooperatives or migrate toward the surrounding hills. In either case, this was experienced as a process of dispossession.

Also, far from docile and malleable, the peasant families that came from different parts of the country had particular histories of political organization and of understanding the world that clashed on many occasions with the grand ambitions of the state officials. For example, initially many of the cooperatives preferred to produce crops that they already knew, such as maize, instead of the citrus trees and oil palms that the INA wanted to introduce. It would take a hurricane, and the disciplining power of debt, to force these cooperatives to turn to planting oil palms. At the same time, many of the households that migrated into the BAP ended up preferring to abandon their cooperatives and move into the surrounding hills that were understood as spaces of independence.

Finally, while the Aguán was full of highly fertile lands, it also had a set of environmental conditions that needed to be circumvented: the heavy rains tended to make the Aguán River flood, which meant that infrastructure had to take this into account, from levees to protect the crops to high bridges that would not be constantly destroyed. Also, much of the valley was covered in thick bush (guaimil) that needed to be cut down for agricultural fields to be created.

*The Coup and the Palm Trees* also argues that the process of implementing the BAP took a significant amount of disciplining of both the unruly peasants and wild nature. Within the logic of the agrarian reform, distributing land was never enough. Peasants, if left to their impulses, were individualists who would prefer self-provisioning. Furthermore, due to their lack of education and basic lack of national values, they were hardly seen as ready to become productive citizens. Thus, granting land had to be accompanied by a pedagogical process in which they became more modern, law abiding, and market producing citizens.

In the case of the Aguán, this pedagogical process took the shape, for example, of the PROCCARA workshops, the housewives clubs, the radio literacy programs, and the requirement that to become a beneficiary of the agrarian reform one had to join a cooperative and work collectively. Debt also played an important disciplining role, as the cooperatives were forced to pay for their land and, thus, had to produce crops that would allow them to generate enough of a profit to keep up with their debts.

As I argued in chapters 2 and 3, this was also a deeply gendered process. The central subject of the agrarian reform was the heteropatriarchal household, where the father worked in the fields while the mother kept the house and took care of the children. Further, each household was supposed to have a single monetary income, provided by the male head, who would use it to buy the commodities needed to provision the whole family. The monetization of subsistence had two main effects: First, it curtailed the independence of women, as it all but eliminated their access to resources that were not mediated by their bread bringing male partners and family members. Second, it disincentivized the diversification of the production by the cooperatives, as more land dedicated to cash crops such as oil palms meant more money to pay debts and for spending. In the process, gender differentiation was inscribed spatially, as "female" places and "male" places became ever more separated.

By the 1990s, with the agrarian reform process all but dead, the Aguán Valley was a deeply transformed space. In much of the region guaimil had given way to fully producing palm oil plantations. Also, poor peasants from different parts of the country had been turned into poor cooperative members who were well versed in the (mono) culture of oil palms. Starting in 1992 with the passing of the Agrarian Modernization Law, a massive process of dispossession concentrated seven out of every ten hectares distributed in the Aguán during the agrarian reform period in the hands of a limited set of large Honduran landowners and transnational companies. In the process, the monoculturally versed peasantry was freed, just to end up working in the same plantations that they had formerly owned and produced. Further, with the accumulated lands came the dead labor of the former cooperative members, in the shape of the plantations, the levees, ditches, roads, and ports that they had constructed almost for free, as well as the millions of dollars invested by the Honduran government to finance the whole enterprise.

By the 2020s, the Honduran palm oil sector was worth more than US$320 million in exports each year. While there are more than eighteen thousand raw material producers, three companies—Dinant, JERAMAR, and ACEYDESA—controlled more than 60 percent of the exports (Rauda, Villagrán, and Sánchez 2017; León Araya 2019a). Not surprisingly, as we saw in chapter 3, these same three companies were involved in the process of agrarian counterreform in the Aguán. In other words, there is a very clear relationship between the raid of the 1990s in the Aguán of the state coffers and the labor of the cooperatives, and the current structure of the sector.

What this quick overview shows us is the importance of understanding the production of subjects and landscapes as part of one and the same process. First, as Tania Murray Li (2014; 2018; Li and Semedi 2021) has argued, narratives about "empty" or "idle" lands are always also narratives of "lazy" or "wasteful" natives who have let the land lie fallow. In the case of the Aguán, the idea of the valley as a fertile but empty space only made sense by presenting the local dwellers as backwards or erasing their existence all together. To be clear, this was not only a problem of misrepresentation: it also allowed the state to appropriate large expanses of lands without having to pay a dollar or recognize the claims of people who had been living in the region for decades. We find a similar situation in the 1990s, where the explanation given for the economic failure of the agrarian reform cooperatives in the Aguán was the lack of efficiency and laziness of the cooperative members, and not the lack of state support, the crippling debt, the devaluation of the lempira, and tumbling global palm oil prices.

Another way in which we can think about the relationship between subjects and landscapes has to do with the margins of maneuver for political action and change. In places like the Aguán, the presence and influence of plantations is massive: the regional landscape is dominated by rows upon rows of oil palms, and the distance between places is usually defined by how long it takes to go around the plantations that stand between you and your objective. They are the major source of salaried work and the primary source of the little money that circulates within the region. The plantations hire local contractors, pay for school parties, and sponsor soccer teams and the yearly float parade to celebrate the *cultura palmera*, the palm culture. Tocoa, the regional capital, is known as the "city of palms," and its emblems includes two large oil palms.

Also, oil palms have been constructed as the only viable crop in the region in economic (better price in the market) and environmental (flood resistant) terms. Never mind the fact that they occupied by force the most fertile lands of the region and that a whole set of levees and other infrastructure is oriented toward protecting them. At the same time, oil palm plantations are seen as both spaces of danger and violence and as an opportunity to leave poverty behind. They are presented as a dangerous monoculture that destroys ecological diversity at the same time that they are seen as the key for a better future for the local poor. The oil palm is the development wager of the state, even as it is understood as creating an unruly landscape in which illegal activities such as drug trafficking can flourish. All these contradictory elements live together, side by side, creating a situation in which the "naturalness" of the dominant position of the palm oil industry goes unquestioned, hiding also in the process the significant amount of violence required to keep everything together.

Further, this sense of the regional situation's naturalness creates a worldview in which it is very hard to think outside the plantation. In chapter 4 I discussed the differences between what I call valley and hills peasant movements. While the first one, organized by former members of the cooperatives, targeted peak producing palm oil plantations, the second one, mainly made up of people coming from the surrounding hills and with little experience with oil palms, targeted "abandoned" lands that they could use to produce milpa. However, as I showed in the case of the MCA, as time went by, the hills movements' everyday life became colonized by the logic of the plantation, with the attempts to recover the lands of El Tumbador as the greatest testimony to this tendency. From this perspective, it is important to point out that the central point of the agrarian conflict in the Aguán is not whether oil palms should be grown, but who should keep the value that is produced by the activity: need economies such as MUCA and MARCA, or large private companies such as Dinant.

Finally, it is very important that we understand the palm oil plantation economy and the drug trafficking activity in the Aguán are two sides of the same coin. This connection is not necessarily direct, (although as we have seen in the cases of Facussé, Nájera, or Fúnez, it just might be); rather, it points to the fact that they both thrive under the same conditions. The landscapes of the plantation economy tend toward the concentration of wealth, resources, and opportunities in a few hands, while being surrounded by a sea of poverty and despair, creating a situation in which young men in particular are forced to make the impossible choice between working as day workers on a plantation for a pittance, joining a criminal gang, trying their luck migrating toward the United States, or joining the military. For young women the prospects are even more limited, characterized by work on the plantation differentiated along gender lines that limits them to the worst paid jobs and migration and drug trafficking accompanied by different forms of gender violence.

I call the choices young people face in the region an impossible decision because, while it might seem that they have the option of making "good" or "bad" choices (the plantation or migration, as against the cartel), all options seem to lead down the same road of poverty and premature death (Gilmore 2007; 2017).

## The Militarized Formation of the Honduran State

Since their independence from the Spanish Empire, the different Central American societies have searched for ways of becoming viable national states; that is, as the regional elites understood it, becoming exporters of raw materials and foodstuffs that could circulate as commodities in the global market, to produce a surplus that could both enrich them and be reinvested into the modernization of their countries. In the process, the more traditional ways of controlling labor and nature also changed, as new subaltern groups (rural working class, landless peasants), incipient petit bourgeoisies, and their political organizations began to stake a claim on the fruits of their labor, the control over land, and a say in how their societies were and should be governed. Framed by the languages of nation, rights, and citizenship, the process of modernization and state formation became a dispute between subaltern and dominant groups, where the maneuvering space of each was deeply conditioned by the region's geopolitical context.

According to Peter Thomas (2006), Gramsci's notion of passive revolution "comes to signify the pacifying and incorporating nature assumed by bourgeois hegemony in the epoch of imperialism" and as such, "the concept has almost become synonymous with modernity" (73). For all Central America, with the exception maybe of Costa Rica, this form of modernization has rested much more on coercion than consent, which has placed violence workers (Seigel 2018), and particularly the armed forces, in a central position.

As I discussed in chapter 1, before the 1930s the Honduran military was basically a set of barely fitted and poorly trained bands of soldiers, loyal to specific strongmen. With the rise of Carías in that decade, this began to change, as control of the military became centralized, due to both internal and external dynamics. Internally, as subaltern groups became more unruly, the traditional elites became more willing to forego the formal control of the state and the rents that came with it, in exchange for remaining the dominant force in society. Internationally, after the inauguration of the Panama Canal in 1914, the political stability of the isthmus became an increasingly important security issue for the United States, which became more invested in modernizing the Central American armed forces and having a bigger influence over them.

However, it would be a mistake to think that this relationship was a unilateral one. As various authors have shown, Latin America has had an important role in the production of the United States as an empire (Grandin 2006; Schrader 2018). Further, events taking place in Central America have also had an important influence on U.S. foreign policy: from the creation of the Panama Canal to the two wars against Sandinistas (Acuña 2015; LeoGrande 1998). It is then more precise to speak about a process of co-formation of the U.S. empire and the Central American states, a co-formation that has been informed by what Lesley Gill (2004) has dubbed "imperial solidarity." By this we mean the networks of cooperation, complicity, and dependency between the Pentagon and the Central American armed forces that rest not only on material support but also on the construction of a shared worldview in which the capitalist order will lead to progress.

*The Coup and the Palm Trees* contributes to these more nuanced discussions regarding the nature of U.S. imperialism by presenting two cases in which we can see that, while the influence of the United States on the Central American armed forces was significant, it was neither absolute nor unilateral. As far as we know, in both the 1963 coup against Villeda Morales and the 2009 coup against Zelaya Rosales, the U.S. embassy was not necessarily in favor of the ousting and, in fact, tried to dissuade the military from going forward with their plans. In both cases, Washington ended up supporting the new de facto regimes for pragmatic regimes: in 1963, because Oswaldo López Arellano and the Honduran military were an important ally in the "war against communism," and in 2009, because of Zelaya's alignment with the Chávez-led ALBA project, as well as internal negotiations in the U.S. Congress (Johnston 2017). Thus, more important than having the support of the United States, what seems to be needed in Central America to get away with a coup is making sure that you are either seen as an important ally or as the lesser evil in the eyes of the imperial power to the north.

As a result, the Central American armed forces in general, and the Honduran ones specifically, have been able to gain significant independence from their national states, as their existence rests ever more on being part of these networks of imperial solidarity. At the same time, it has placed them historically in a position to exploit the isthmus's geopolitical position.

Because of Central America's position as a bridge between South and North America and a narrow strip of land between the Atlantic and Pacific Oceans, the historical formation and practice of political power on the isthmus has been organized around its traversal: from transoceanic canals to transcontinental routes, the control over by whom, what, and how it is crossed has become an important site of accumulation of political power and capital in the form of rent. The armed forces' mission of protecting national sovereignty, the inordinate number of resources that they control in relation to any other state institution, and their legal use of force and logistical presence in all of the national territory are all factors that place them in a particularly good position to mediate and broker exchanges between different geographical scales and actors.

In terms of mediating between scales, the Honduran armed forces have been a historical ally of the interests of the United States, not only in geopolitical and security terms but also in economic ones. For example, the Honduran military has always supported, at least formally, the different global "wars" waged by the United States, from the "war against communism" during the Cold War to the "war on drugs" of the last decade. At the same time, they have guarded the interests of transnational capital, from the United Fruit Company in the early twentieth century to the expansion of palm oil, tourism, and mining projects in the country in the aftermath of Hurricane Mitch.

The armed forces have also been crucial in mediating the relations between classes. Between the 1930s and the 1990s and starting again in the aftermath of the 2009 coup, the Honduran armed forces have played the role of arbitrators between the National and Liberal Parties, and between subaltern and dominant classes. Mainly, their function has been to break the stalemate between opposing groups, a function that has tended to take the form of what Antonio Gramsci called Caesarism, "in which the forces in conflict balance each other in a catastrophic manner ... that a continuation of the conflict can only terminate in their reciprocal destruction ... and then a third force C intervenes from outside, subjugating what is left of both A and B" (Gramsci 1971, 219).

According to Benedetto Fontana (2004, 178–79), this third force is always already an active factor in the conflict and "the subjugation is the unintended consequence of an intervention whose purpose is to freeze and to redirect the antagonism, certainly the open, political forms of it, in order to prevent the reciprocal destruction." For our case in point, this "third force," the Caesar, has always resulted from the articulation between U.S. geopolitical and geoeconomic interests in the region and authoritarian figures or political projects close to the Honduran armed forces.

In the 1930s it was Carías, in the 1970s Oswaldo Arellano and the military junta immediately after, and in the aftermath of the 2009 coup, it was JOH. In all these cases, the rise of the Caesars was preceded by periods of significant subaltern mobilization, for example the 1954 banana strike and the protests in the aftermath of Hurricane Mitch. In each of these cycles of political mobilization, the subaltern groups have first managed to include some of their demands in the ensuing reformist projects—Villeda Morales and Zelaya Rosales—just to be bloodily repressed in the aftermath of the subsequent military coups.

What should catch our attention regarding the continuation in terms of the relationship between subaltern and dominant classes is the different formal institutional environments in which they have taken place. Since 1981 Honduras has held elections every four years; in the 1990s the armed forces ceded much of their formal presence in government and policing was transferred to civilian control. Moreover, the country has an ombudsman office and a legal system for the protection of human rights. However, the levels of violence in the country are similar to, and even exceed, those of the preceding period.

It is misleading to pin this solely on the emergence of criminal organizations such as the *maras* and the drug traffickers, or on the supposed capture of the state by corrupt elites that, in any case, were already there. Class struggle is at the end of the day a better indicator. The armed forces, as all violence workers, secure their reproduction through the capture of rent: they are gatekeepers and enforcers who get paid for securing a certain order. History is, of course, full of exceptions, but in general terms, it is more cost-effective for the armed forces to side with the dominant groups that control capital and need to keep the frictions of its circulation to a limit. It is indicative that, in the case of the two coups examined here, administrations with high levels of popular support attempted to "buy" the support of the armed forces through public rents (funding) or giving them more political and economic autonomy. However, as we have seen, in both cases this was a lost gamble.

As such, another main conclusion of this book is that while institutional redesign might be necessary to clearly demarcate the role, obligations, and tasks of the military, it will never be sufficient by itself. As long as the Honduran elites can continue to count on the support of the armed forces to impose their will upon society, and as long as the U.S. government continues to enable this situation through its almost unwavering support of the Honduran military, the conditions for Caesarism will continue to exist and any attempt at truly democratizing the country will very likely fail.

## The Narrative of the Transition to Democracy

Discussions on the Central American current conjuncture are saturated by democracy: of the dangers posed to it by authoritarian figures such as Nayib Bukele, Daniel Ortega, or Juan Orlando Hernández; of how the wounds of corruption fester and kill the incipient democratic institutions; or of how people are losing their trust in democracy. As such, the solutions proposed are to double down on the process of "transition to democracy" that had begun in the 1990s with the peace accords: to carry out periodical elections, have alternation in power, and secure the independence of the judiciary and the separation between the different branches of government. In other words, using the language of "transitology," Hondurans are urged to develop a "mature" democracy like those allegedly found in the Global North, to achieve social peace, political stability, and economic development.

However, what is often forgotten in these discussions is that what was promised in the 1990s was a peace process in which formal democracy would be accompanied by a significant betterment in the living conditions of everyone, as well as the demilitarization of society. In other words, peace was supposed to go beyond ending the armed conflict. In practice, however, this latter was the only goal actually achieved.

Central America continues to be one of the most dangerous regions in the hemisphere, with murder rates that rival those of the 1970s and 1980s (Cruz 2011). Poverty continues to be rampant, as more than thirty million of the around fifty million people who live in the isthmus are under the poverty line (EFE 2021). Also, while open armed conflict between rival military foes has ended, this has not translated into a meaningful process of demilitarization. Within the language of transitology, one of the goals was to promote "democratic security," which, in brief, refers to separating civilian and "domestic" security, tasked to the police, from the "external" defense of the national borders and the sovereignty of the nation, entrusted to the armed forces. All of this, of course, was to be guided by the upmost respect of human rights and civil liberties. Various authors have pointed out the arbitrariness and general futility of separating external and internal security (Seigel 2018; Neocleous 2014; Schrader 2019). However, even if we accept it as a useful analytical distinction, the results of this process of demilitarization in Honduras have been meager to say the least (Argueta and Walter 2020a).

As we saw in chapter 4, in Honduras during the 1990s a significant number of institutions were passed from military to civilian control. At the same time, the size and budget of the armed forces decreased. However, starting with Zelaya, the process of formal demilitarization began to roll back. In his bid to secure their loyalty, Mel designated fifteen military men in key posts of the ENEE, extended Romeo Vásquez Velásquez's period as head of the military beyond his constitutional mandate, and increased the armed forces' budget. With JOH this devolution turned into a new cycle of militarization, not only of domestic security but of society as a whole. Beyond the creation of new branches of military police that I discussed in chapter 6, JOH began to involve the armed forces in areas as disparate as rural development and the effort against COVID-19 (Argueta and Walter 2020b).

Once again, these changes cannot be seen just from a domestic perspective. The end of the Cold War did not signal the end of U.S. involvement in the Central American security agenda: after 9/11 the "war against terrorism" translated in the isthmus mostly into the war against maras and youth gangs. Later, in the mid- and late 2000s, it morphed into the "war on drugs," which began with the squeeze on Colombian and Mexican cartels, whose effects we already discussed in chapter 6. Finally, since the Trump administration, and particularly as the migrant caravans began to increase in size and visibility in the late 2010s, American involvement in the region has been sold as a "war on illegal migration."

What all of these "wars" have in common is that they present as the cause of chaos what are really the symptoms of the imposition of the neoliberal project in the region, and always target poor people from disenfranchised communities. Gang members come from the poorest Central American urban neighborhoods and initially emerged as a result of the waves of refugees deported from the United States in the 1980s and 1990s. Drug traffickers and migrants are, more often than not, young people trying to escape the conditions of poverty, inequality, and despair left in the wake of the wave of dispossession that was unleashed on their communities during the 1990s, just as the bells of "peace" and "democracy" were being rung. Finally, in all these cases, these enemies of peace, order, and progress are presented as external to society and, as such, enemies of the state and thus viable targets for state violence. This is particularly salient in the case of drug trafficking, where the cartels are presented as an "invasion" from Mexico and Colombia, when, as we have seen, groups like Los Cachiros are very much the result of the conditions of possibility already in the country. In other words, far from a set of different and specific wars, it might be more accurate to speak about a continued "class war" (Neocleous 2013).

In summary, the narrative of the transition to democracy only makes sense in relation to the broader process of imposition of the neoliberal project that, far from redistributing wealth, was interested in achieving exactly the opposite: carrying out a massive plunder of resources and opportunities that had been outside of the reach of capital. It is then more useful to think about the transition to democracy as a way of legitimizing the liberalization of the markets, as part of the alleged movement toward freedom, democracy, and development (Dunkerley 1993; Robinson 1996).

The articulation of war, democracy, and capital accumulation that I am pointing at is, in a way, what the critical concept of "pacification" is trying to capture (Neocleous 2013). Very succinctly, pacification understood from this perspective is a process in which state power is used to fabricate a social order organized around wage labor: "Pacification dreams of an unruly world populated by disobedient subjects who refuse to go along with the state's vision for order. Pacification does not announce the end of hostilities, but the beginning of compliance-or-else" (Correia and Wall 2018, 91).

*The Coup and the Palm Trees* has presented a very concrete example of how pacification has played out in Honduras. In chapter 6 I noted that in 2011 the government set up the military task force Xatruch and enforced a state of exception in the department of Colón that prohibited civilians from carrying firearms and set up various check points over the region of the Aguán. The formal objective was to bring security to the region and stop the land occupations of palm oil plantations and to disrupt drug trafficking. In practice, what it did was pacify the region in favor of the interests of the plantation economy. The disarmament disproportionately affected peasant communities, whose members were left with nothing to defend themselves, while the security firms that provide security to the plantations can move around armed. Further, members of the Xatruch, together with members of other forces such as the military police, are usually involved in the evictions of land recuperations, as part of their task of protecting private property, but do little to stop the continuous murders and harassment of peasant organizers. As such, the role of the Xatruch force and the state of exception is to enforce the conditions under which the plantation economy thrives, while bringing the disobedient and unruly subjects under control.

In short, the process of pacification that is accompanied by the discourse of the transition to democracy tries to present Central America in general,

Young man works among oil palms, Bajo Aguán region, 2021. Photo by Jorge Cabrera/Contracorriente.

and Honduras in particular, as "open for business," as Porfirio Lobo's government titled the conference organized in May 2011 to attract foreign investment to the country. Honduras is marketed as a place with abundant and available natural resources and a docile and cheap labor force, as a place that is striving toward political stability and legal security and is therefore safe for investing. This is an image that, at the same time, obscures the great amount of violence that is needed to stop the whole thing from busting at the seams. However, those practices and actions that tend to be presented as the enemies of the democratic order might be seen, from an alternative perspective, as the actual bearers of what democracy could look like.

According to David Graeber (2020), there are two main ways in which we can approach and understand the notion of democracy. One is through the history of the word "democracy," from ancient Greece to the present-day regimes that call themselves democratic. The other way is through its practice, as a relatively open and egalitarian model of (community) government. For Graeber, there is a contradiction between these two approaches when applied to modern states. Basically, if the state is understood mainly as a way of organizing violence (the Weberian definition of the monopoly of legitimate violence), then it becomes impossible to reconcile democratic practices with the coercive institutions and mechanisms that protect the social order. Thus, the

British anthropologist concludes that academics tend to search for the origins of democracy in the places where they are least likely to be found: in the manifestations of the states, which tend to subjugate the local experiences of self-government and collective deliberation. Thus, instead of thinking about democratic states, Graeber invites us to think about the state against democracy.

Reversing that formula, Henri Lefebvre proclaims that "there is no democracy without a struggle against the democratic State itself, which tends to consolidate itself as a bloc, to affirm itself as a whole, to become monolithic and to smother the society out of which it develops" (2009, 61; see also Abensour 2011). From this perspective, then, democracy as practice is not to be found in the armored and institutionalized peace that has been produced in Central America since, at least, the 1930s. Nor is it the political regime, inscribed in a few stone tablets as commandments (thou shall vote and alternate in power!), that has accompanied the neoliberal pacification of the isthmus since the 1990s. Rather, we find it in the struggle by subaltern groups against the institutionalized forms of inequality, plunder, and violence that have defined the process of state formation in the region.

Paraphrasing Antonio Gramsci's (1971, 54–55) "methodological criteria" on the history of subaltern classes, the history of (popular) democracy in Honduras is necessarily fragmented and episodic. That is, it appears in flashes, such as the 1954 strike in which, according to historian Suyapa Portillo Villeda (2021, 270), for the first time "Hondurans stood up to capitalism and the US State Department alike, with nothing but their machetes for work, their pans and *hornillas* (stoves) for everyday sustenance, tortillas, their weathered hands and backs, and a lot of hope for change to get out from under the boot of a complicit dictator." It appeared also in the waves of popular mobilizations that led the administrations of Villeda Morales and Zelaya Rosales to put forward policies against the concentration of wealth and power by the country's elites and their transnational allies. However, as the Italian communist also reminds us, the political activity of the subaltern groups "is continually interrupted by the activity of the ruling groups," as demonstrated by the two bloody coups of 1963 and 2009.

*The Coup and the Palm Trees* has been an attempt to show how these struggles over power and democracy take shape on the ground. It is a history of the different ways in which peasants (organizations, households, and individuals), from different parts of the country, migrated toward the Aguán in search of land and autonomy. It is a narrative of their constant struggle to stake a claim on the landscapes and value that they produced in the form of the palm oil plantation economy and thus limit the concentration of power, resources, and opportunities by a limited set of companies and terratenientes. While this book has been a testament to the destruction and desolation left in the wake of the agrarian counterreform and the imposition of the neoliberal project, it has also shown how peasant struggles pose a different way of thinking about the recent history of the country and the seeds of what the future should look like.

# ACKNOWLEDGMENTS

Writing this book about the Bajo Aguán took a little bit of luck and much more support and help than I could fit into these pages. To make a long story short, while studying at the Graduate Center of the City University of New York (GC-CUNY), I got to know the amazing work that El Centro Inmigrante does with Mexican and Central American *jornaleros*, day workers, on Staten Island. There I met numerous Hondurans, many of whom came from the country's north coast, who were fleeing their country in the aftermath of the 2009 coup. It was through these conversations that I began to learn about the National Front of Popular Resistance (FNRP), the popular organization that grew in the aftermath of the military's ousting of Manuel Zelaya in June of 2009, and the plight of the Lenca, Garifuna, and peasant organizations struggling at the time against the hardly legal, and definitely illegitimate, government of Porfirio Pepe Lobo. Above everything else, I learned how little I knew about Central America and particularly about Honduras.

At the anthropology department at GC-CUNY I found a vibrant space to explore my interest in the intersection between agrarian studies and state formation. I am particularly grateful for the diverse and generous cast of mentors that I found there. Marc Edelman was an incessant source of knowledge, advice, and literature. To this day he continues to be a source of inspiration and I am proud to be able to call him friend. Katherine Verdery has had an enduring effect on my understanding of the state and taught me to always focus on relations, never on things. Kate Crehan introduced me to the work of Antonio Gramsci and fostered my interest in Marxism through long conversations and cups of coffee. Neil Smith, before his untimely death, was always a friend, quick to ask how I was doing, share old copies of his *Antipode* collection or his notes on Milton Santos, and invite me to dinner. Finally, I was also able to partake in some great discussions with a group of teachers who to this day continue to influence and inspire my own work: Ruthie Wilson Gilmore, Don Robotham, John Collins, Vinay Gidwani, Michael Blim, and the late Fernando Coronil and Leith Mullins.

At CUNY I also met a group of brilliant scholars whom I am happy to still be able to call friends. In no particular order: Emily Channell, Margarite Whitten, Martín Cobián, Neil Agarwal, Saygun Gokariksel, Ahmed Ibrahim, Rocío Gil, Andreina Torres, Julio Arias, Linsey Li, Jeremy Rayner, Megan Hicks, Ryan Mann-Hamilton, Lalit Batra, Ted Sammons, and Mark Drury.

I also received significant support from the Wenner-Gren Foundation, which first awarded me a Wadsworth International Fellowship to partially fund my coursework. Later, I also received a dissertation fieldwork grant that allowed me to carry out the first and longest part of the ethnographic and historical work upon which this book is based. Without their support and their trust in my work, I would not have been able to carry out my doctoral studies, nor complete the book that you have in front of you.

In Honduras I was lucky to find a group of people willing to open their doors to me and help me along the way. Before my arrival in the country, the historian Dario Euraque invited me over to his home for a weekend of conversations and discussions that helped me better frame my initial research project. In Tegucigalpa Gilda Rivera has always been a friend, providing a room and warm conversation. The people from FIAN-Honduras provided me with much logistical help and support. To Danielito, Nelly, and Claudia, thank you for your never-ending warmth. To Esteban, thank you for showing me the ropes when I first arrived in the Aguán and for letting me bunk in your home in San Pedro Sula. Finally, I owe a great debt of gratitude to Gilberto Ríos Sr., to whom this book is also dedicated, who showed great patience with my insistent questions regarding the agrarian history of Honduras. His stories about the struggle of the Honduran peasant movement always filled my imagination and if this book makes any contributions in that regard this is first and foremost because of his teachings.

In the Aguán, the list of people whom I would need to thank is both endless and, for security reasons, better kept short. In Tocoa, the Fundación San Alonso Rodríguez, and particularly its former director Juana Esquivel, were always highly supportive of my work and provided a haven to meet with people and organize workshops. Also, El Profe Tifre and El Chele were key informants, and good friends, who helped me navigate both the present and past of the region. I would also like to thank the members of the Permanent Observatory of Human Rights of the Aguán (OPDHA), who allowed me to accompany them around the region as they attempted to protect their communities from the constant attempts by the state and terratenientes to evict them. I will not name all of you, but I do not need to, you know who you are. Thank you, friends, this book is for you. The same goes to the people from the different communities and peasant organizations with which I worked all around the Bajo Aguán region.

I would also like to express my immense gratitude to Pedro Marchetti and Jennifer Casolo, whom I met in the Guadalupe Carney and who quickly invited me to their home in Guatemala. They granted me access to many important documents that cannot be found elsewhere, and their stories and thoughts on the region have guided much of my writing in the post-Hurricane Mitch (1998) period. I hope that you can see how much my work has been influenced by yours.

Many of the ideas you will find in this book greatly benefited from my participation in two parallel academic projects. First, since 2016 I have taken part in a set of conferences and a book (Mckay, Alonso-Fradejas, and Ezquerro-Cañete 2021) on the land question, land grabbing, and agrarian extractivism in the Americas. It has been an honor for me to be able to share and bounce ideas with such a talented group of scholars, including Ben McKay, Zoe Brent, Diana Ojeda, Jun Borras, Marc Edelman, and Alberto Alonso-Fradejas. I hope to be able to continue to learn from all of you. Second, since 2019 Preeti Sampat and I have working on a book project, on what we are calling an anthropology of land. Here I have been able to share my work and discuss it with an extremely talented set of scholars: Alejandro Camargo, Kregg Hetherington, Ahmed Ibrahim, Sohini Sengupta, Elan Abrell, Kai Bosworth, Soni Grant, Sarah Ruth Sippel, Ximena Martinez-Trabucco, A. R. Vasavi, and Stefan Dorondel.

The University of Costa Rica (UCR), where I have worked for more than a decade, provided a space to sharpen and develop my craft. Verónica Martínez and Génesis Guzmán have been both brilliant students and research assistants, helping in the transcription of various interviews and the recollection of information in different moments of writing this book. I have also found a group of kindred spirits with whom to think and conspire: Mario Zúñiga, Sergio Salazar, María José Guillén, Jorge Quesada, Adriana Sánchez, and Alonso Ramírez.

The fantastic photograph that garnishes the cover was provided by the talented Seth Berry; Contracorriente, the Honduran digital news outlet, gave me permission to use two of their pictures; and Paola Luna made the map of the Bajo Aguán region. I would also like to thank everyone at the University of Georgia Press for bringing this project to fruition: Mick Gusinde-Duffy for finding value in this project and his support throughout; the two anonymous reviewers, whose sharp and constructive comments improved massively the quality of this work; Lea Johnson who made sure that everything moved forward in an orderly manner and was always available to answer my questions, Matthew O'Neal, Irina du Quenoy, Kaelin Broaddus, Rebecca Norton, Candice Lawrence, Christina Cotter and the rest of the editorial and design team, who turned this book into a reality; and the series editors of Geographies of Justice and Social Transformation, Mat Coleman and Sapana Doshi, for including my book in such distinguished company.

Gratitude of the highest order goes to my family, and particularly my mom, who taught me that we are only as good as the relations we nurture and foster. Finally, I save my deepest and greatest gratitude and admiration for D. O., who has read more drafts of my work than anyone should have to, and whose brilliant ideas have made this book that much better. If that wasn't enough, she has also filled this time with more care and companionship than I could have imagined. While only one name appears in the front cover of this book, know that the only reason that it exists is because you were there for the journey. As such, and as they say, "*nadie nos quita lo bailado*."

# NOTES

### INTRODUCTION

1. According to Eduardo Baumeister (2013, 26), Honduras went from producing over 80 percent of its domestic staple crops needs in 1970 to less than 50 percent in 2009.
2. The most infamous case, of course, being that of the Hernández Alvarado brothers: Juan Antonio (better known as Toni Hérnandez), the younger brother, was found guilty of participating in the international trafficking of cocaine by a U.S court; and Juan Orlando (better known as JOH, the former Honduran president), is currently on trial for supporting drug trafficking in a U.S. prison.
3. I am deploying here rather loosely Theodor Adorno's approach to the notion of "constellation" in Negative Dialectics. According to the German philosopher, in a constellation, "the history locked in the object can only be delivered by a knowledge mindful of the historic positional value of the object in its relations to other objects—by the actualization and concentration of something which is already known and is transformed by that knowledge" (1973, 1:163). For a different take on the notion, and uses, of constellations within queer urban studies, see Gieseking (2020).

### CHAPTER 1. DICTATORSHIP AND REFORM

1. Unless stated differently, my account of the 1963 coup is based on Mario Argueta's (2009) excellent book on Ramon Villeda's political career.
2. Each one of these reforms tended to concentrate more power around the figure of the president. For example, in the constitution of 1936, the president was designated as *policía mayor*, literally, supreme policeman, which meant that he could take control over the national police. It also allowed the executive to expel people from the country and eliminated the age limit of sixty-five years of age to be president (Carías was to turn sixty that same year). In 1939 a series of other constitutional reforms was passed, including the designation of the municipal authorities directly by the president and not by popular election. According to Mario Argueta (2008, 103), this reform "only came to increase the concentration of power in the Executive. In this way, the last traces of popular expression by electoral means disappeared."
3. For example, it was a common practice by the regional middlemen to significantly overstate the number of soldiers that they had on their payroll, in order to increase the amount of money that they received from the government and pocket the difference (Holden 2004).

4. Although these companies did not leave much in terms of taxes, their weight within the local economy was significant. For example, in 1929, bananas accounted for 85 percent of all Honduran exports, a figure that decreased somewhat over time but in 1950 still accounted for 70 percent of total exports and 45 percent by 1960 (Del Cid 1988, 139).

5. According to Robert Holden (2004, 68), between 1824 and 1950 the Honduran executive branch changed hands 116 times, and only thirteen presidents held the office for four or more years.

6. The Communist Party of Honduras was originally created in 1922 in the north coast in the city of San Pedro Sula. However, by the 1940s, due mainly to the repression unleashed by the Carías regime, the party had stopped operating (Villars 2010). It would not be until April 10, 1954, that the "new" Communist Party would be formed in the city of San Pedro Sula (Barahona 1994).

7. I would like to thank one of the anonymous reviewers for pointing this out.

### CHAPTER 2. THE POLITICAL ECONOMY OF THE HONDURAN AGRARIAN REFORM

1. Most of my ideas on the disciplining of peasants come from conversations, shared panel sessions, and my reading of the excellent work of Maite Yie Garzón (2015) on the agrarian transformations of Colombia. In particular, her book Del patrón estado al estado patrón has been a continuous source of inspiration for thinking about the agrarian reform as a subject-making dispositif. I have also found Maureen Sioh's (2004) work on the relation between landscape and state making in Malaya very useful.

2. To be clear, and as the editors of the Selections from the Prison Notebooks remind us in the introduction to the section on Americanism and Fordism, Gramsci does not present a definite answer as to whether what was happening in the United States at the time was the sign of a new historical epoch or "merely a conjunction of events of no lasting significance" (Gramsci 1971, 277).

3. Inspired by the work of the French legal thinker León Duguit, the social function doctrine is based on the idea that property was not actually an individual right but rather a social function. Through a set of six lectures given in Buenos Aires in 1911 and published a year after, Duguit laid out an argument that subsequently had a paradigmatic influence in the Latin American legal and constitutional thought of the twentieth century (Ankersen and Ruppert 2006; Foster and Bonilla 2011; Mirow 2010). In synthesis, for Duguit, there was a problem with the classical liberal theory of property based on the abstract idea of an isolated individual that was ingrained into both the Declaration of the Rights of Man of 1789 and the Napoleonic Code. Here, under natural law, owners could do as they please with their property and both the state and other individuals should refrain from acting against this right, unless they broke any other laws.

For Duguit, rather, we could see empirically the increasing interdependence between people. Following on the steps of Émile Durkheim, he understood this interdependence as "solidarity" and placed it at the center of the "political community," or the sum of the individuals that compose it (Foster and Bonilla 2011; Mirow 2010). Thus, the end of property should not be the enjoyment of the individual but rather the service to the "political community." How was this accomplished? By means of economic transactions. In other words, for property to fulfill its social function, it had to be productive for the collective wealth of the political community. Implicit in this idea was the notion that the collective wealth of the political community took the shape of the market.

4. Briefly, "land to the tiller," "*la tierra es de quien la trabaja*" in Spanish, refers to the idea that ownership over land should belong to those who work and toil on it. This, of course, raises the question of how value and wealth are produced and who gets to keep the fruits of labor. Within the discussions on agrarian reform, "land to the tiller" refers to a redistributive principle wherein land should be taken away from those who own it but do not work on it (terratenientes, or large landowners), and given to those who work on it but do not own it (landless peasants). This principle has been critiqued by feminist scholars, since there is a tendency to understand labor solely as those activities that create commodities that can circulate through the market, thus rendering domestic and reproductive work invisible. In other words, "land to the tiller" becomes "land to the male peasant worker" (Roquas 2002; Deere and León 2004).

There is a clear resonance between this argument and a very schematic reading of Marx's labor theory of value, where only labor, through its transformation of nature, produces value (for a discussion see Elson 1979; Henderson 2013). Thus, politically, this theory proposes that other classes, such as capitalists and landowners, are parasitic on the value produced by the working classes.

5. Clodomir Santos de Morais was born in 1928 in a rural town in the state of Bahia, Brazil. Due to his political activism, in which he was close to the "Peasant Leagues," then led by Francisco Julião, he was imprisoned for two years after the military coup of 1964; during his imprisonment he shared his cell for a while with Paulo Freire. Eventually, he was able to escape to the Chilean embassy in Rio de Janeiro and from there to Chile. After Chile, he spent time in Panama, Costa Rica, Honduras, Mexico, Portugal, and Nicaragua. In the late 1960s and the 1970s, he worked for the UN as a consultant in Central America on various agrarian reform development programs (Sobrado 2000).

6. This is something neither new nor specific to the Honduran case. As various authors have shown for the post-emancipation period in both the Caribbean islands and the U.S. South, and in the period of disintegration of the hacienda and plantation system in various parts of Latin America, the dream of many former slaves and plantation workers of becoming "free" smallholders quickly turned into processes of dispossession and "reconstitution" into "peasants." That is, they were transformed into an impoverished subject who needed to be brought into the embrace of modernity by the state to become an agent of modernity (Mintz 1979; Woods 1998; Striffler 2001; Yie Garzón 2015; Grossman 1998; Wolf 1966; Edelman 1992).

7. The notion of land recuperation is deeply political in Latin America. In the Honduran context, it is used by peasant organizations—and their sympathizers—to signal that the land that is being occupied was or should be national and thus the patrimony of the Honduran poor peasantry (Posas 1981). This is also part of a broader political and semantic battle in which right-wing actors and mainstream media tend to refer to those same land occupations in terms of "invasions" or "land usurpation." Oversimplifying, we could say that the tension between private property and common good (in terms of the nation) structures this semantic field and the politic struggles around it. It is also a clear example of how the idea of "land to the tiller" continues to animate debates regarding what should be the social function of land.

**CHAPTER 3. THE HIDDEN ABODE OF PRIMITIVE ACCUMULATION**

1. This represents 20,930 hectares sold, out of the original 28,365 hectares distributed (COCOCH 2010, 24).

2. Castro (1994, 109) compares the average income in two palm oil-producing cooperatives with that of a staple crop-producing cooperative. He finds that while the first two reported an income per member of around 300–400 lempiras a month (roughly US$150 to $200), the latter received a maximum monthly income of around 150 lempiras (US$75). Castro also mentions that an informant told him that La Salamá cooperative, the first created in the Aguán, had a collective biweekly income of 70,000 to 80,000 lempiras (p. 108). In general, cooperatives from this period had around fifty associates, which meant that a good estimate of the monthly income of a member of La Salamá was of around 1,400 to 1,600 lempiras (US$700 to $800). Even after subtracting the income used to amortize debts and invest in equipment or production, the story told by this data is that there was a clear economic chasm between those producing palm oil and those producing staple crops.

3. According to De Fonteney (1999, 10), the state "was indebted to the IDB for funding the palm plantations, and to several foreign governments (mainly those of England and the Netherlands) for the cost of three large processing mills, built in 1980. IDB loans had also been used to construct an entire road network for the Aguán and a modern new port for exporting oil and bananas. The State seemed determined to ensure rapid collection of the loans to cooperatives and rapid amortization of the processing plants: regardless of how much palm they delivered, cooperatives were paid 3 lempiras per day per member, which was near or below the going wage for agricultural day-laborers."

Further, it would seem that the state was trying to make a profit out of this process. For example, once the oil palms were planted, the cooperatives were required to pay a fee of 65 lempiras per hectare (around US$33) over a period of twenty years. This was financed through the loans that the country had signed with the IADB and the USAID. Both loans had interest rates of 4 percent; however, the state collected 11 percent from the peasant cooperatives (it was later reduced to 8 percent) (Castro 1994).

4. According to a study on gender inequalities in the Latin American agrarian reforms, in the case of Honduras, only 3.8 percent of the beneficiaries were women, one of the lowest levels in the region (Deere and León 2004, 191).

5. That is, 8.7 percent in the industrial sector and 8.5 percent in the agriculture (Walker 1990, n.p.).

6. For example, between 1980 and 1984 the country's military aid from the United States went from US$4 to $77 million; when adding the total economic aid, the number goes over $200 million, making of Honduras the eighth largest recipient of U.S. foreign aid for this period (Kinzer 2001, 2). This situation was well identified by the World Bank, which in a memorandum of April 1987 argued that "the extraordinary amounts of foreign assistance that have permitted the Government to sustain large external deficits currently mask these structural problems [large inefficient public sector, non-diversified exports, inefficient financial mediation and public deficit], but do not solve them. If the current high level of foreign assistance should decline as a result of shifts in political priorities in donor countries, the underlying imbalances would become unsustainable" (World Bank 1987, iii).

7. For example, the specific physical characteristics of a piece of land could give it a higher level of productivity, which would translate into higher profits (what Marx [1981] calls differential rent I); or, land that has higher levels of investment (i.e., irrigation systems), and thus is also more productive, would probably garner a higher rent and subsequently, price (differential rent II). Nonetheless, productivity understood in these terms is not the only element that can define how land is valued. The monopoly that landowners have over their lands means that they will only sell if they are compelled to, or if they feel that their valuation of the land is being fulfilled (absolute rent). In the case of Honduras, the application of both the LTP and the AML curtailed the ability of the state to expropriate land and consequently, as noted, land prices went up.

8. For example, the president of APROH was the infamous general Gustavo Álvarez Martínez, then supreme leader of the country's armed forces and credited with the creation of Battalion 3-16, which operated as a death squad in the country during the 1980s (Gill 2004). Miguel Facussé was the vice president and Rafael Leonardo Callejas, who signed the country's first SAP in 1990, was the secretary of labor and students' affairs. Other members of the group were Oswaldo Ramos Soto, then-president of the Autonomous University of Honduras (UNAH), José Rafael Ferrari, owner of the only national TV station at the time, and Osmond Maduro, brother of the former president Ricardo Maduro.

9. The exchange rate between lempiras and USD went from 2:1 before the 1990s to 13:1 in 1997.

10. There is not an exact measure of just how much land was alienated. According to a low estimate, more than half of the over fifty-six thousand hectares that were distributed during the agrarian reform period were "legally sold" between 1990 and 1994; the number rises to almost 74 percent in the case of the Aguán (COCOOCH 2010, 24). A different study calculates that in the period between when the first cooperative was sold in the Aguán (Buenos Amigos, July 1991) and 1997, 28,806.7 hectares had been alienated (Macías 2001, 206–8).

11. In the case of Facussé, these claims are based on his Palestinian ancestry, although his family has been living in Honduras for over a century (González 1992, 191). In the case of Morales, he was born in Nicaragua but moved to Honduras 1979 and since then acquired Honduran nationality. His brother Jaime Morales also lived in Honduras between 1979 and 1996 and was Daniel Ortega's vice president in Nicaragua from 2007 to 2012. Finally, Canales's history is harder to track, but he is often identified as being of Salvadoran descent.

12. According to Önder (2018, 73), in a cross-reading of different sources, of the 73 cooperatives (out of the total of 138 existing ones) that sold their land within five years of the implementation of the AML, 28 were oil palm producers, while the remaining ones were dedicated to staple crops.

13. With no lack of irony, President Rafael Leonardo Callejas (1990–94), referring to agrarian reform beneficiaries, asked, "Why are they not going to sell if it has been their lifetime work and effort? . . . I do not agree with those who believe that it is a step back for the Agrarian Reform. On the contrary, it is the culmination of a process. Now, a peasant can receive 500,000 Lempiras for his hard work" (quoted by Suazo 2012, 73).

14. A previous version of this section was published in Spanish. See León Araya (2017).

15. Here, I am paraphrasing Marx's famous quote from volume 1 of Capital: "Let us therefore... leave this noisy sphere where everything takes place in the surface and in full view of everyone, and follow them into the hidden abode of production... Here we shall see, not only how capital produces, but how capital is itself produced. The secret of profit-making must at last be laid bare" (Marx 1992, 279–80).

### CHAPTER 4. DEMOCRACY AS DISASTER CAPITALISM

1. Most of the information and ideas regarding this period in the Aguán, and particularly the role played by the Pastoral Social of the Catholic Church, come from conversations and documents provided by the always generous Peter Marchetti and Jennifer Casolo.

2. For an excellent and detailed discussion on how gender, and particularly the plight of women, was framed in this forum as well as the political reverberation that it had in the aftermath, see Casolo (2009).

3. For example, the per capita foreign aid received by Honduras jumped from US$50 in 1997 to $129 in 1999. Food aid shipments jumped from 21,000 tons in 1997 to 169,000 tons in 1999 (Morris et al. 2002).

4. In fact, a study carried out in the aftermath of Hurricane Mitch in the Central American region shows how the plots of those peasant farmers that used agro-ecological methods, as opposed to slash and burn and traditional agriculture, presented more topsoil, field moisture, and vegetation. Further, "On average, agroecological plots lost 18 percent less arable land to landslides than conventional plots and had a 49 percent lower incidence of landslides" (Holt-Giménez 2002, 10).

5. We find an example of these dynamics in the case of the Garifuna communities in the north coast. The Garifuna are an Indigenous and Afro-descendent group that resulted from the comingling of maroon (African escaped slaves) and Caribbean Indigenous groups (Caribs and Arawakan). They emerged as a differentiated cultural and racial group toward the middle of the seventeenth century on the island of St. Vincent, from which they were expelled by the British at the end of the eighteenth century and relocated to the Central American coast, particularly in what would become Honduras and Nicaragua (González 1988).

Historically, the Garifuna have established their communities along the coast, under a logic of collective control of the land and organized along kinship structures. The fact that at the time the Honduran coast was sparsely populated and with little interconnection with the rest of the country allowed them to maintain their political, economic, and cultural traditions. However, as time went by and the Caribbean was integrated into the rest of the country, the Garifuna lands became the target of various actors, including the state, which saw them as "idle" or "empty" due to the group's self-provisioning economy based on combined agriculture and fishing. In response to the ensuing encroachment on their lands, the Garifuna began to create a set of political organizations that aimed at defending their lands and their way of life. Although their first organizations go back to the 1970s, their first real breakthrough would have to wait two decades. According to Mark

Anderson (2012, 53), "Beginning in the 1980s, the Honduran government came to redefine the nation from an imagined community of mestizos to a multiethnic community and to expand the recognition of collective rights specific to indigenous and Afro-Honduran peoples." As a result, by the mid-1990s, a series of dispersed legal reforms, international conventions, and state programs created a space, however tenuous and unstable, for the negotiations between the state and organizations using the language of ethnic rights. Particularly important in this respect was the ratification in 1994 of the Convention 169 of the ILO on Indigenous and Tribal Rights. Also, in that same year, the first bilingual/intercultural educational program was established, and at the same time, Honduras was officially identified as a multiethnic nation. This transformation had to do more with pressure being applied from outside than with some enlightenment by the Honduras elite's and was part of a general trend in the 1980s and 1990s toward what Charles Hale (2005) has dubbed "neoliberal multiculturalism": the strategy within neoliberal governance to include a limited recognition of cultural rights and endorse the principle of intercultural equality, as a way of curbing or co-opting protest, in the context of the expansion of economic liberalization.

The result of this combination of the adoption of the multicultural framework by the Honduran government and the struggle of the Garifuna communities was a titling process that resulted in more than fifty Garifuna communities receiving collective titles from the state. Although this can be read as a great victory for the Garifuna communities, the overall balance has been contradictory. As Keri Brondo argues, most of the simple titles were circumscribed to the lands in which the communities' hamlets are located, leaving out much of the ancestral lands that the Garifuna claim. Further, "communal land titles were a mechanism to promote private market investment by enhancing land security. That is, communal titles encouraged investment in Garifuna territory by legalizing community limits and opening up property beyond mapped borders for private purchase" (2018, 187). All this is consistent with the imposition of the neoliberal land regime analyzed in the previous chapter.

The aftermath of Mitch came to accelerate and expand this political-economic project. Neoliberal multiculturalism was complemented with sustainable development narratives. As one of the reasons given by the Honduran government to explain the levels of destruction left by the hurricane was the lack of a sustainable use of natural resources (Loperena 2017), the reconstruction process promoted activities such as tourism, understood as an "industry without chimneys" that could reignite the national economy. As a result, various policies were pushed forward, including tax exemptions for the industry, as well as the amendment by the national congress of article 107 of the Honduran constitution, just two days after the catastrophe.

Originally, article 107 prohibited the sale of coastal lands to foreigners, but with the reform, an exception was made for cases where the purpose of the purchase was developing a touristic project. In the case of the Garifuna lands, the combination of the reform with the land titling process mentioned above opened up the way for a process of land grabbing and an ensuing conflict between the Garifuna communities, the touristic developers, and the state, which usually took the side of the latter (Anderson 2012; Brondo 2013; Loperena 2017; Wrathall 2012). One of the results of these policies was the rise of the tourism industry as one of the primary sources of foreign investment in the country.

However, although this shift was supposed to promote a more sustainable development model, it did not foreclose the promotion of the extractive activities of old, such as mining or oil palm plantations.

6. Father Carney was disappeared by the Honduran military while participating in an ill-fated guerrilla incursion from Nicaragua that was quickly crushed by the military soon after it crossed into Honduras. This probably also contributed to the elites' hostilities to the peasant organization taking up his legacy (Martínez 2006; Carney 1985).

### CHAPTER 5. THE FAILED ASSAULT ON STATE POWER

1. Unless explicitly stated, the information regarding the events surrounding the ousting of Zelaya comes from the report of the Truth and Reconciliation Commission (CVR 2011).

2. The elected vice president, Elvin Ernesto Santos Ordóñez, had resigned his post to become the Liberal Party's presidential candidate in the upcoming elections.

3. Due to the low quality of the transcriptions included in the report of the Truth and Reconciliation Commission, as well as the difficulties of presenting a literal transcription that would make any sense in English, these quotes should be understood, rather, as my interpretation.

4. In a note published in 2017 in the Intercept, Jake Johnston documented that the night before the ousting of Zelaya, several Honduran military officials had attended a party thrown by the U.S. embassy's security attaché. It would be expected that various members of the Honduran Congress, as well as the ambassador were also present. Moreover, various Honduras commentators have mentioned that in the run-up to the coup, Hugo Llorens, the then-U.S. ambassador, had attempted to prevent the ousting of Zelaya (Martínez 2010; Meza 2015).

5. As I mentioned before, Barack Obama's first reaction was to denounce the ousting of Zelaya as a bad precedent. However, "After an initially firm reaction to what the U.S. ambassador unequivocally termed a coup—including condemnation and a suspension of non-humanitarian aid—Washington reversed course. Urging Zelaya not to seek reinstatement, then secretary of state Hillary Clinton pushed for speedy elections to normalize the situation" (Chayes 2017, 13).

Apparently, however, this change of heart had to do with the internal dynamics of U.S. foreign policy, wherein the Pentagon and members of Congress close to the military were able to apply pressure and enable the legitimation of the regime. For a report on the role played by the U.S. military in enabling the 2009 coup d'état, see Johnston (2017).

6. Translation of the section's title: "We urgently need Mel, here comes Mel!", as expressed in José Manuel Zelaya's presidential campaign slogan.

7. Over US$23 hundred million for 2006, which meant around a 32 percent increase and represented 26 percent of the gross domestic product for that year.

8. Translation of the section's title: "What is it about Mel that the imperialists can't handle him?" This was a political slogan in support of Zelaya's left turn.

9. Venezuela would sell Honduras forty thousand barrels of Bunker daily for two years, with 60 percent of the bill paid immediately and 40 percent over twenty-five years, with a grace period of two years and an interest rate of 1 percent (CVR 2011, 119)

10. Allegedly, Zelaya managed to secure the votes of his party by assuring Micheletti that he would support him in the party's internal convention and become the presidential candidate. However, Micheletti lost the party's convention and Albin Santos, the vice president, was elected as presidential candidate. This situation drove a wedge between Zelaya and Micheletti.

11. This section's title is yet another pro-Zelaya slogan: "Mel, buddy, the people are with you!"

12. There were also those on the Left who were critical of Zelaya. In an article published a few months before the coup, the Jesuit Ismael Moreno (2009) described the Cuarta Urna as a clear attempt by Zelaya and his associates to cling to power. Further, for Moreno, unless other changes were made within the Honduran political system, calling for a constituent assembly would continue to reproduce the distribution of power between the National and the Liberal Parties, foreclosing the participation of the popular sectors. In his view, a better way of weakening the two-party system's chokehold on Honduran politics was the promotion of independent candidates, like that of Carlos Humberto Reyes, an important labor movement leader, that was being discussed by different sectors of the Left.

However, Moreno continues, in the context of political polarization created by the Cuarta Urna, the candidacy of Reyes was being overshadowed by Zelaya and his dispute with the traditional elites, of which he was also part. Thus, far from solidifying the political criticality and independence of the popular sectors, it weakened it and tied their fate to that of Zelaya.

13. For example, point 1 of the plan demanded the rollback of the water and aqueducts law, which allowed the privatization of the service and the sources; point 3 called for an immediate stop to the evictions of peasant groups, as well as the derogation of the Agrarian Modernization Law and the implementation of a new agrarian reform; point 6 called for the nationalization of fuel imports and the strengthening of the public companies; point 8 called for the derogation of the national mining law and an immediate stop to any further concessions; and point 12 sought to make sure that any policy that could affect the "national" interests was first consulted with the population.

14. For example, his stand regarding the mining law and the drafting of a new one. It is also worth remembering that Decree no. 18-2008 was approved in March, which helped show the government's good will.

**CHAPTER 6. MILITARIZATION, RENT CAPTURE, AND THE STATE-NARCO RELATIONS**

1. This paragraph paraphrases Marx's (2009, 1) *The Eighteenth Brumaire of Louis Napoleon*: "Caussidiere for Danton, Louis Blanc for Robespierre, the 'Mountain' of 1848–51 for the 'Mountain' of 1793–05, the Nephew for the Uncle. The identical caricature marks also the conditions under which the second edition of the Eighteenth Brumaire is issued."

2. In 2006, Zelaya's first year as president, the defense budget represented little under 3 percent (US$63 million and change) of the government's total budget. In 2009, the year of the coup, it had increased to 3.79 percent (US$127 million and change) (Donadio and Tibiletti 2010, 232).

3. As I mentioned in the introduction, the notion of the "narco-state" is not only very vague but also reproduces the image of failure by postcolonial states to uphold the Eurocentric ideals of the state, also present in other monikers, such as "failed state" or "banana republic." Following Allan Gillies's (2018) work, I use here rather the term "state-narco relations" to point toward the creation of a set of relatively stable networks of interchange between agents of the state, including the armed forces, and high-level actors of the drug trade. In this way, we can point to the ways in which licit and illicit practices come together in the daily operation of the state and the production of certain institutional spaces, without thinking about drug trafficking as a "disease" that "invades" an otherwise "healthy" state organism. I use quotation marks to point how problematic this sort of biological metaphors can be when thinking about political practices, as they pathologize what really is a result of human practice and power relations.

4. Juan Ramón Matta Ballesteros was born in Tegucigalpa in 1944. In the 1960s, he migrated to the United States, where he worked as a farmhand in Texas and a supermarket clerk in New York City. He was allegedly deported from the United States on five occasions, and while there is no clarity when he became involved with drug trafficking, his first known charge for this activity was filed in San Diego in 1974.

In Honduras, Matta Ballestero presented himself as a successful businessman with various licit enterprises, ranging from hotels to factories and cattle ranches. He was also known as a philanthropist who constantly helped the poor. His downfall began in 1985, when he was indicted for the kidnap and murder of Enrique Camarena Salazar, a DEA agent working in Mexico. In May of that year, he was arrested and jailed in Colombia, only to escape shortly thereafter after paying a bribe estimated between US$1 and 1.5 million.

He returned to Honduras, were he moved openly around Tegucigalpa, with no fear of being extradited to the United States, as no such treaty existed between both countries. Around this time, he offered to pay Honduras's foreign debt, but, as the legend goes, the then- President José Simón Azcona refused to take him up on it (Dudley 2016).

5. On April 13, 1988, the U.S. Senate Foreign Relations Committee's Subcommittee on Terrorism, Narcotics, and International Operations released a report formally titled Drugs, Law Enforcement, and Foreign Policy but popularly known as the "Kerry Report," since the subcommittee was chaired by Senator John Kerry (D-Mass.). This report explored the phenomenon of drug trafficking and money laundering in Central and South America and the involvement of U.S. law enforcement and intelligence agencies. In relation to this involvement in the case of Honduras the report concluded that "a review of the history of gun running and drug trafficking through Honduras suggests that elements of the Honduran military were involved in the shipment of weapons to the FMLN In El Salvador and in the protection of drug traffickers from 1980 on. These activities were reported to appropriate U.S. government officials throughout the period." More damning was the assertion that "it appears that a compelling factor in United States-Honduran relations was support for American policy in the region, especially support for the Contra war. As long as the Honduran government provided that support, the other issues were of secondary importance" (U.S. Senate Committee of Foreign Relations 1988, 78–79).

6. Translation of this section's title: "Who is afraid behind a palm tree?" This is a com-

mon saying in the Aguán, referring to the cover that palm oil plantations provide for illicit activities.

7. Probably in honor of Florencio Xatruch, a former general and president who fought against the U.S. filibuster force, led by William Walker, that tried to conquer Central America in the 1850s. Tarea Xatruch was also the name given to the troop of 370 soldiers sent by Ricardo Maduro to support the Iraq War in 2003.

8. In said TV show, one of the very few media appearances he made, Facussé claimed that Cesar Ham, the director of the INA and member of the UD Party, was the true guilty party behind the massacre, by making the peasants of the MCA believe that those lands were "theirs." In his own words, "Ham calm down, let's go to court, stop doing politics, you have turned into a murderer, because you sent those poor men to their death. You knew that we were armed and prepared to protect our estates" (Torres Funes 2016).

9. In 2022, after the election of Xiomara Castro, a topic that we will return to in chapter 7, a new peasant group, called Los Mártires de El Tumbador (the El Tumbador martyrs) and composed of more than 150 people, many of them family members of the victims of the 2010 massacre, began working in those same lands.

10. According to Gilberto Ríos (2012), this price was significantly higher than the one presented by an agronomist hired by INA of over US$4,000 per hectare, which was also virtually the price that Facussé had requested initially (he wanted a differentiated rate between cultivated and uncultivated lands). According to Ríos, both prices were unpayable for the peasant organization in any case.

## CHAPTER 7

1. Just as an example, according to the official data of the Honduran National Institute of Statistics (INE), in July 2021 a little less than 74 percent of the country's households were under the poverty line, with remittances representing just under 15 percent of their income, and 22 percent of the gross domestic product (INE 2021). Further, in 2020 the levels of underemployment reached 70 percent, and the country had a crippling public debt of US$15 thousand million, around 57 percent of the gross domestic product.

2. The so-called Engel List, created under a law sponsored by then-U.S. Representative of the Democratic Party Eliot Engel, is a report submitted to Congress by the State Department, listing a group of individuals from El Salvador, Guatemala, Honduras and Nicaragua "who the President has determined have knowingly engaged (1) in actions that undermine democratic processes or institutions; (2) in significant corruption; and (3) in obstruction of investigations into such acts of corruption, including the following: corruption related to government contracts; bribery and extortion; the facilitation or transfer of the proceeds of corruption, including through money laundering; and acts of violence, harassment, or intimidation directed at governmental and nongovernmental corruption investigators." (See https://www.state.gov/reports/section-353-corrupt-and-undemocratic-actors-report-2022/.) The most immediate effect of being included in the Engel List is ineligibility for visas and admission to the United States, for the listed person and other family members.

3. Born in 1958 in Tocoa, Carlos Escaleras was involved in the high school student movement and joined the local human rights committee organized by the Committee for

the Defense of Human Rights in Honduras (CODEH). In the 1980s he worked in the national electricity company (ENEE) and eventually became the president of the company's labor union national board of directors. In the 1990s he was fired as part of the government's attempts to destroy the "red" unions in the public sector, forcing him to start his own family business in Tocoa. He then joined COPA and became very active in various community struggles against the contamination of water sources and other environmental issues. Probably the most important and lethal of these struggles was the fight that he led against the installation of a palm oil extraction plant on the Aguán River's bank by Miguel Facussé. According to a 2014 report by the Interamerican Commission of Human Rights (IACHR 2014), Miguel Facussé tried to bribe Escaleras to stop the protests against the extraction plant. The latter refused and not long after was murdered by paid assassins in October 1997. Although those materially responsible for the murder were eventually captured and sentenced to prison, those who ordered the hit never faced criminal charges. At the time of his death, Escaleras was also the UD's candidate for mayor in Tocoa.

# BIBLIOGRAPHY

Abensour, Miguel. 2011. *Democracy against the State: Marx and the Machiavellian Movement.* Cambridge, U.K.: Polity.
Abrahamsen, Rita. 1997. "The Victory of Popular Forces or Passive Revolution? A Neo-Gramscian Perspective on Democratisation." *Journal of Modern African Studies* 35, no. 11: 129–52.
ACAFREMIN. 2020. "Guapinol resiste: Orígenes del conflicto minero en el Bajo Aguán, Honduras." San Salvador: Alianza Centroamericana Frente a la Minería.
Acuña, Victor Hugo. 2015. "Centroamérica en las globalizaciones (siglo XVI–XXI)." *Anuario de Estudios Centroamericanos* 41: 13–27.
Adorno, Theodor W. 1973. *Negative Dialectics.* Vol. 1. New York: Continuum.
Agüero Starkman, Luisa, and Uriel Naum Ávila. 2014. "Miguel Facussé, el genio de las marcas en Centroamérica." *Forbes México*, November 3, 2014. http://www.forbes.com.mx/miguel-facusse-el-genio-de-las-marcas-en-centroamerica/.
Aguirre Beltrán, Gonzalo. 1967. *Regiones de refugio.* Mexico City: Instituto Indigenista Interamericano.
Allinson, Jamie C., and Alexander Anievas. 2010. "The Uneven and Combined Development of the Meiji Restoration: A Passive Revolutionary Road to Capitalist Modernity." *Capital & Class* 34, no. 3: 469–90.
Alonso-Fradejas, Alberto. 2012. "Land Control-Grabbing in Guatemala: The Political Economy of Contemporary Agrarian Change." *Canadian Journal of Development Studies/Revue Canadienne d'Études du Développement* 33, no. 4: 509–28.
Altiok, Regula. 1998. "Primer foro campesino: Fortalezcamos juntos la reforma agraria." Forum proceedings. Tocoa, Colón.
Amaya Amador, Ramón. 1988. *Destacamento rojo.* Tegucigalpa: Editorial Universitaria, Universidad Nacional Autónoma de Honduras.
Anderson, Mark. 2009. *Black and Indigenous: Garifuna Activism and Consumer Culture in Honduras.* Minneapolis: University of Minnesota Press.
———. 2012. "Garífuna Activism and the Corporatist Honduran State since the 2009 Coup." In *Black Social Movements in Latin America: From Monocultural Mestizaje to Multiculturalism*, edited by Jean Muteba Rahier, 53–73. New York: Palgrave Macmillan.
Anderson, Thomas P. 1983. *The War of the Dispossessed: Honduras and El Salvador.* Lincoln: University of Nebraska Press.
Andreucci, Diego. 2017. "Resources, Regulation and the State: Struggles over Gas Extraction and Passive Revolution in Evo Morales's Bolivia." *Political Geography* 61: 170–80.

Ankersen, Thomas T., and Thomas Ruppert. 2006. "Tierra y Libertad: The Social Function Doctrine and Land Reform in Latin America." *Tulane Environmental Law Journal* 19: 69.

Argueta, Mario. 2008. *Tiburcio Carías: Anatomía de una época*. Tegucigalpa: Guaymuras.

———. 2009. *Ramón Villeda Morales: Luces y sombras de una primavera política*. Tegucigalpa: Guaymuras.

Argueta, Otto, and Knut Walter. 2020a. *La función política de los militares en Centroamérica: El Salvador, Guatemala, Honduras y Nicaragua*. San Salvador: Fundación Heirich Böll.

———. 2020b. "Una institución para todo: La función política de las FF. AA. en Honduras." *Heinrich-Böll-Stiftung* (blog), October 15, 2020. https://sv.boell.org/es/2020/10/15/una-institucion-para-todo-la-funcion-politica-de-las-ff-aa-en-honduras.

Ávila, Jennifer. 2020. "How to Fight for the Environment in Honduras without Becoming a Martyr." Agenda Propia, November 19, 2020. https://www.agendapropia.co/content/how-fight-environment-honduras-without-becoming-martyr.

Ávila, Jennifer, and Danielle Mackey. 2020. "The Hidden Connection between a U.S. Steel Company and the Controversial Los Pinares Mine in Honduras." *Contra Corriente* (blog), November 10, 2020. http://contracorriente.red/en/2020/11/10/the-hidden-connection-between-a-u-s-steel-company-and-the-controversial-los-pinares-mine-in-honduras/.

Bakker, Karen. 2010. "The Limits of 'Neoliberal Natures': Debating Green Neoliberalism." *Progress in Human Geography* 34, no. 6: 715–35.

Ballvé, Teo. 2019. "Narco-Frontiers: A Spatial Framework for Drug-Fuelled Accumulation." *Journal of Agrarian Change* 19, no. 2: 211–24.

———. 2020. *The Frontier Effect: State Formation and Violence in Colombia*. Ithaca, N.Y.: Cornell University Press.

Ballvé, Teo, and Kendra McSweeney. 2020. "The 'Colombianisation' of Central America: Misconceptions, Mischaracterisations and the Military-Agroindustrial Complex." *Journal of Latin American Studies* 52, no. 4: 805–29.

Barahona, Marvin. 1994. *El silencio quedó atrás: Testimonios de la huelga bananera de 1954*. Tegucigalpa: Guaymuras.

———. 2002. *Evolución histórica de la identidad nacional*. Tegucigalpa: Editorial Guaymuras.

———. 2005. *Honduras en el siglo XX: Una síntesis histórica*. Tegucigalpa: Guaymuras.

———. 2018. *Élites, redes de poder y régimen político en Honduras*. Tegucigalpa: Guaymuras.

Baumeister, Eduardo. 2013. "Concentración de tierras y seguridad alimentaria en Centroamérica." Rome: Coalición Internacional para el Acceso a la tierra (ILC) y el fondo de desarrollo noruego. https://simas.org.ni/media/publicaciones/ConcentracionTierrasCentroAmerica.pdf.

Berman-Arévalo, Eloísa, and Diana Ojeda. 2020. "Ordinary Geographies: Care, Violence, and Agrarian Extractivism in 'Post-Conflict' Colombia." *Antipode* 52, no. 6: 1583–602.

Bird, Annie. 2013. "Human Rights Violations Attributed to Military Forces in the Bajo Aguan Valley in Honduras." Washington, D.C.: Rights in Action. https://rightsaction

.org/articles/human-rights-violations-attributed-to-military-forces-in-the
-bajo-aguan-valley-in-honduras.
Bonefeld, Werner. 1995. "The Politics of Debt: Social Discipline and Control." *Common Sense: Journal of the Conference of Socialist Economics* 17: 69–91.
Borras, Saturnino M. Jr., Cristóbal Kay, Sergio Gómez, and John Wilkinson. 2012. "Land Grabbing and Global Capitalist Accumulation: Key Features in Latin America." *Canadian Journal of Development Studies/Revue Canadienne d'Études du Développement* 33 no. 4: 402–16.
Boyer, Jefferson. 1982. "Agrarian Capitalism and Peasant Praxis in Southern Honduras." PhD diss., University of North Carolina at Chapel Hill.
———. 2010. "Food Security, Food Sovereignty, and Local Challenges for Transnational Agrarian Movements: The Honduras Case." *Journal of Peasant Studies* 37, no. 2: 319–51.
Brondo, Keri. 2013. *Land Grab: Green Neoliberalism, Gender, and Garifuna Resistance in Honduras*. Phoenix: University of Arizona Press.
———. 2018. "'A Dot on a Map': Cartographies of Erasure in Garifuna Territory." *PoLAR: Political and Legal Anthropology Review* 41 (2): 185–200.
Brown, Wendy. 2015. Undoing the Demos: Neoliberalism's Stealth Revolution. New York: Zone.
Bucheli, Marcelo. 2003. "United Fruit Company in Latin America." In *Banana Wars: Power, Production, and History in the Americas*, edited by Steve Striffler and Mark Moberg, 80–102. Durham, N.C.: Duke University Press.
———. 2006. "Good Dictator, Bad Dictator: United Fruit Company and Economic Nationalism in Central America in the Twentieth Century." Working paper no. 06-0115, University of Illinois at Urbana-Champaign, College of Business. https://www.researchgate.net/publication/4811811_Good_Dictator_Bad_Dictator_United_Fruit_Company_and_Economic_Nationalism_in_Central_American_in_the_Twentieth_Century.
Bulmer-Thomas, Víctor. 1993. "La crisis de la economía de agroexportación (1930–1945)." In *Historia general de Centroamérica*, edited by Victor Hugo Acuña Ortega, 4:325–98. Madrid: Sociedad Estatal Quinto Centenario.
Cáceres, Miguel, and Sucelinda Zelaya. 2005. "Honduras. Seguridad productiva y crecimiento económico: La función económica del cariato." *Anuario de Estudios Centroamericanos*, 49–91.
———. 2011. "Honduras. Crecimiento económico elitista y violación de derechos sociales. 1990–2009." http://www.militante.org/files/2012/Honduras-Crecimiento-economico-elitista-y-violacion-de-derechos-sociales-1990-2009.pdf.
Canizales, Rolando. 2008. "El fenómeno de los movimientos guerrilleros en Honduras: El caso del Movimiento Popular de Liberación Cinchonero (1980–1990)." *Revista Estudios* 21: 93–112.
Cano, Arturo. 2010. "En Honduras, poderosas fundaciones extranjeras brindan desde comida hasta créditos agrícolas." *La Jornada*, July 9, 2010.
Carney, J. Guadalupe. 1985. *To Be a Revolutionary: An Autobiography*. New York: Harper & Row.

Carney, Judith, and Michael Watts. 1990. "Manufacturing Dissent: Work, Gender and the Politics of Meaning in a Peasant Society." *Africa* 60, no. 2: 207–41.

———. 1991. "Disciplining Women? Rice, Mechanization, and the Evolution of Mandinka Gender Relations in Senegambia." *Signs* 16, no. 4: 651–81.

Casolo, Jennifer. 2004. "'Voz y Voto' in Deed?: Land Rights, Gender and Power in Post-Hurricane Mitch Honduras." M.A. thesis, University of California, Berkeley.

———. 2009. "Gender Levees: Rethinking Women's Land Rights in Northeastern Honduras." *Journal of Agrarian Change* 9, no. 3: 392–420.

Casolo, Jennifer, and Sapana Doshi. 2013. "Domesticated Dispossessions? Toward a Transnational Feminist Geopolitics of Development." *Geopolitics* 18, no. 44: 800–834.

Castree, Noel. 2010. "Neoliberalism and the Biophysical Environment 1: What 'Neoliberalism' Is, and What Difference Nature Makes to It." *Geography Compass* 4, no. 12: 1725–33.

Castro, Angel Augusto. 1994. *Un plan de desarrollo regional: El Bajo Aguán en Honduras.* México: Universidad Iberoamericana.

Chapman, Anne. 1985. *Los hijos del Copal y La Candela: Ritos agrarios y tradición oral de los Lencas de Honduras.* Mexico City: Universidad Autónoma de México.

Chayes, Sarah. 2017. *When Corruption Is the Operating System: The Case of Honduras.* Washington, D.C.: Carnegie Endowment for International Peace.

Chonchol, Jacques. 1962. *La reforma agraria en América Latina.* Rio de Janeiro: Centro de Desenvolvimento Econômico CEPAL/BNDE.

Chouvy, Pierre-Arnaud. 2016. "The Myth of the Narco-State." *Space and Polity* 20, no. 1: 26–38.

Clastres, Pierre. 1989. *Society against the State: Essays in Political Anthropology.* New York: Zone Books.

Clavel, Tristan. 2017. "Cachiros Leader Links Late Honduras Tycoon to Drug Trafficking." InSight Crime, March 22, 2017. http://www.insightcrime.org/news-briefs/cachiros-leader-links-late-honduras-tycoon-drug-trafficking.

COCOCH. 2010. "Reforma agraria, agricultura y medio rural en Honduras: La agenda pendiente del sector campesino." Consejo Coordinador de Organizaciones Campesinas de Honduras. http://www.landcoalition.org/pdf/08_cococh_Reforma_Agraria_en_Honduras.pdf.

COFADEH. 2018. "Violaciones a los derechos humanos en el contexto de las protestas anti fraude en Honduras." Tegucigalpa: Comité de Familiares de Detenidos Desaparecidos en Honduras. http://www.derechos.org/nizkor/honduras/doc/elecciones46.html.

Contracorriente. 2017. "El diputado eterno, un catel narco y un valle inundado de palma africana." Contra Corriente, May 2, 2017. https://contracorriente.red/2017/05/02/el-diputado-eterno-un-cartel-narco-y-un-valle-inundado-de-palma-africana/.

Cooper, Helene, and Marc Lacey. 2009. "In a Coup in Honduras, Ghosts of Past U.S. Policies." New York Times, June 30, 2009. http://www.nytimes.com/2009/06/30/world/americas/30honduras.html.

Cordero, José Antonio. 2009. "Honduras: Desempeño económico reciente." Washington, D.C.: Center for Economics and Policy Research.

Coronil, Fernando. 2019. *The Fernando Coronil Reader: The Struggle for Life Is the Matter*. Edited by Julie Skurski, Gary Wilder, Laurent Dubois, Paul Eiss, Edward Murphy, Mariana Coronil, and David Pedersen. Durham, N.C.: Duke University Press.
Correia, David, and Tyler Wall. 2018. *Police: A Field Guide*. New York: Verso.
Crehan, Kate. 1997. *The Fractured Community: Landscapes of Power and Gender in Rural Zambia*. Berkeley: University of California Press.
———. 2016. *Gramsci's Common Sense: Inequality and Its Narratives*. Durham, N.C.: Duke University Press.
Cruz, José Miguel. 2011. "Criminal Violence and Democratization in Central America: The Survival of the Violent State." *Latin American Politics and Society* 53, no. 4: 1–33.
Cunha Filho, Clayton M., André Luiz Coelho, and Fidel I. Pérez Flores. 2013. "A Right-To-Left Policy Switch? An Analysis of the Honduran Case under Manuel Zelaya." *International Political Science Review* 34, no. 5: 519–42.
CV. 2012. "Informe de la Comisión de Verdad: La voz más autorizada es la de las víctimas." Tegucigalpa: Comisión de Verdad.
CVR. 2011. "Para que los hechos no se repitan: Informe de la comisión de la verdad y la reconciliación." Comisión de la Verdad y Reconciliación.
Dada, Carlos. 2021. "El cacique de Colón ha perdido su fuero." El Faro (blog), December 9, 2021. https://elfaro.net/es/202112/centroamerica/0000025889-el-cacique-de-colon-ha-perdido-su-fuero.
Dahl, Robert Alan. 1973. *Polyarchy: Participation and Opposition*. New Haven: Yale University Press.
Davidson, Neil. 2012. *How Revolutionary Were the Bourgeois Revolutions?* Chicago: Haymarket.
De Angelis, Massimo. 2004. "Separating the Doing and the Deed: Capital and the Continuous Character of Enclosures." *Historical Materialism* 12, no. 2: 57–87.
De Fontenay, Catherine. 1999. "Institutions, Market Power and the Big Push: The Case of Agro-Exports in Northern Honduras." Paper prepared for the University of New South Wales, School of Economics. http://www.researchgate.net/publication/228790814_Institutions_Market_Power_and_the_Big_Push_The_Case_of_Agro-exports_in_Northern_Honduras/file/60b7d521aeb579631e.pdf.
De Smet, Brecht. 2016. *Gramsci on Tahrir, Revolution and Counter Revolution on Egypt*. London: Pluto.
De Soto, Hernando. 2001. *The Mystery of Capital: Why Capitalism Triumphs in the West and Fails Everywhere Else*. Reading, Calif.: Black Swan.
Deere, Carmen Diana, and Magdalena León. 2004. "Revertir la reforma agraria con exclusión de género: Lecciones a partir de América Latina." *El Otro Derecho*, 181–220.
Deutsche Welle. 2021. "Honduras: Xiomara Castro y Salvador Nasralla crean alianza para elecciones." Online, October 14, 2021. https://www.dw.com/es/honduras-xiomara-castro-y-salvador-nasralla-crean-alianza-para-elecciones/a-59498044.
Devine, Jennifer A., Nathan Currit, Yunuen Reygadas, Louise I. Liller, and Gabrielle Allen. 2020. "Drug Trafficking, Cattle Ranching and Land Use and Land Cover Change in Guatemala's Maya Biosphere Reserve." *Land Use Policy* 95: 104578.
Di Iorio, Marco Cáceres. 2010. *The Good Coup: The Overthrow of Manuel Zelaya in Honduras*. Terrace, B.C.: CCB.

Di Lampedusa, Giuseppe Tomasi. 2007. *The Leopard: Revised and with New Material.* New York: Random House.
Diario Colón. 2021. "Alcalde tocoeño Adán Fúnez falsificó documentos para favorecer la minera Los Pinares-Ecotek." *Diario Colón* (blog), February 15, 2021. https://www.diariocolon.com/portada/alcalde-tocoeno-adan-funez-falsifico-documentos-para-favorecer-la-minera-los-pinares-ecotek/.
Donadio, Marcela, and Samantha Kussrow. 2016. *A Comparative Atlas of Defence in Latin America and Caribbean.* Buenos Aires: Red de Seguridad y Defensa de América Latina.
Donadio, Marcela, and María de la Paz Tibiletti. 2010. *A Comparative Atlas of Defence in Latin America and Caribbean.* Buenos Aires: Red de Seguridad y Defensa de América Latina.
Driver, Alice. 2015. *More or Less Dead: Feminicide, Haunting, and the Ethics of Representation in Mexico.* Tucson: University of Arizona Press.
Dudley, Steven. 2016. "Honduras Elites and Organized Crime." InSight Crime, April 9, 2016. https://www.insightcrime.org/investigations/honduras-elites-and-organized-crime-series/.
———. 2019. "How Elites and Narcos Do Business, Politics in Honduras." InSight Crime, October 9, 2019. https://insightcrime.org/news/analysis/how-elites-narcos-do-business-politics-honduras/.
Duménil, Gérard, and Dominique Lévy. 2004. *Capital Resurgent: Roots of the Neoliberal Revolution.* Cambridge: Harvard University Press.
Dunkerley, James. 1993. *The Pacification of Central America: Political Change in the Isthmus, 1987–1993.* London: Institute of Latin American Studies.
ECLAC. 2007. "Honduras: Evolución economica durante 2006 y perspectivas para 2007." Mexico City: Economic Commission for Latin America.
———. 2021. "ECLAC: At Least 4,091 Women Were Victims of Femicide in 2020 in Latin America and the Caribbean, Despite Greater Visibility and Social Condemnation." *Economic Commission for Latin America and the Caribbean* (blog), November 24, 2021. https://www.cepal.org/en/pressreleases/eclac-least-4091-women-were-victims-femicide-2020-latin-america-and-caribbean-despite.
Edelman, Marc. 1992. *The Logic of the Latifundio: The Large Estates of Northwestern Costa Rica since the Late Nineteenth Century.* Stanford: Stanford University Press.
———. 1998. "Transnational Peasant Politics in Central America." *Latin American Research Review* 33 no.3: 49–86.
———. 1999. *Peasants against Globalization: Rural Social Movements in Costa Rica.* Stanford: Stanford University Press.
Edelman, Marc, and Angelique Haugerud. 2005. *The Anthropology of Development and Globalization: From Classical Political Economy to Contemporary Neoliberalism.* Oxford: Blackwell.
EFE. 2021. "Centroamérica tiene casi 30 millones de pobres acechados por el hambre." EFE, April 29, 2021. https://www.efe.com/efe/america/sociedad/centroamerica-tiene-casi-30-millones-de-pobres-acechados-por-el-hambre/20000013-4524664.
Elson, Diane. 1979. "The Value Theory of Labour." In *Value: The Representation of Labour in Capitalism*, edited by Elson, 115–80. London: CSE.

Escobar, Arturo. 2011. *Encountering Development: The Making and Unmaking of the Third World*. Princeton, N.J.: Princeton University Press.
Estrada, Oscar. 2018. "Cómo se quebró CONADI (y quiénes fueron los responsables)." *El Pulso*, July 29, 2018. http://elpulso.hn/como-se-quebro-conadi-y-quienes-fueron-los-responsables/.
Euraque, Darío. 1996. *Reinterpreting the Banana Republic: Region and State in Honduras, 1870–1972*. Chapel Hill: University of North Carolina Press.
———. 2009. "Los árabes de Honduras: Entre la inmigración, la acumulación y la política." In *Contribuciones árabes a las identidades iberoamericanas*, edited by Karim Hauser and Daniel Gil, 233–86. Madrid: Casa Árabe.
———. 2019. "La configuración histórica de las elites de Honduras ante el golpe de estado del 2009." *Anuario de Estudios Centroamericanos* 45: 1–29.
Falla, Ricardo. 1998. "Primeras reflexiones ante la herida del Mitch." *Revista Envío* 201 (December). http://www.envio.org.ni/articulo.php?id=402.
———. 2000. "Land Occupation Opens the Way for Agrarian Reform." *Revista Envío* 230 (September). http://www.envio.org.ni/articulo/1447.
FAO. 2010. "La amenaza hidrometeorológica en Honduras." In *En tierra segura: Desastres naturales y tendencia de la tierra*. http://www.fao.org/docrep/013/i1255b/i1255b00.htm.
Federici, Silvia. 2004. *Caliban and the Witch*. New York: Autonomedia.
Ferguson, James. 1990. *The Anti-Politics Machine: "Development," Depoliticization, and Bureaucratic Power in Lesotho*. Cambridge, U.K.: Cambridge University Press.
FIDH. 2011. "Honduras: Human Rights Violation in Bajo Aguán." International Federation of Human Rights. https://www.fidh.org/IMG/pdf/honduras573ang.pdf.
Figueroa Ibarra, Carlos. 1993. "Centroamérica: Entre la crisis y la esperanza (1978–1990)." In *Historia general de Centroamérica*, edited by Edelberto Torres-Rivas, 35–88. Vol. 6. Madrid: Flacso.
Fontana, Benedetto. 2004. "The Concept of Caesarism in Gramsci." In *Dictatorship in History and Theory: Bonapartism, Caesarism, and Totalitarianism*, edited by Peter Baehr and Melvin Richter, 175–96. Cambridge, U.K.: German Historical Institute and Cambridge University Press.
———. 2012. "The Concept of Nature in Gramsci." In *Gramsci: Space, Nature, Politics*, edited by Michael Ekers, Gillian Hart, Stefan Kipfer, and Alex Loftus, 123–41. Malden, Mass.: Wiley-Blackwell.
Foster, Sheila, and Daniel Bonilla. 2011. "The Social Function of Property: A Comparative Law Perspective." *Fordham Law Review* 80: 101.
Frank, Dana. 2018. *The Long Honduran Night: Resistance, Terror, and the United States in the Aftermath of the Coup*. Chicago: Haymarket.
Fraser, Nancy. 2017. "Behind Marx's Hidden Abode: For an Expanded Conception of Capitalism." In *Critical Theory in Critical Times: Transforming the Global Political and Economic Order*, edited by Penelope Deutscher and Cristina Lafont, 141–59. New Directions in Critical Theory. New York: Columbia University Press.
Fukuyama, Francis. 1989. "The End of History?" *National Interest*, no. 16: 3–18.
Gago, Verónica. 2015. *La razón neoliberal: Economías barrocas y pragmática popular*. Madrid: Traficantes de Sueños.

Gallardo, Helio. 2007. *Democratización y democracia en América Latina*. Quito: Desde Abajo.
Geglia, Beth. 2016. "Honduras: Reinventing the Enclave: Authoritarian Neoliberalism Is Alive and Well as the 'Model Cities' Initiative That Took Hold after Honduras' 2009 Coup Moves Forward." NACLA. *Report on the Americas* 48, no. 4: 353–60.
Gidwani, Vinay. 2008. "Capitalism's Anxious Whole: Fear, Capture and Escape in the Grundrisse." *Antipode* 40, no. 55: 857–78.
Gidwani, Vinay, and Dinesh Paudel. 2012. "Gramsci at the Margins: A Prehistory of the Maoist Movement in Nepal." In *Gramsci: Space, Nature, Politics*, edited by Ekers Michael, Hart Gillian, Kipfer Stefan, and Loftus Alex, 258–78. Malden, Mass.: Wiley-Blackwell.
Gieseking, Jen Jack. 2020. "Mapping Lesbian and Queer Lines of Desire: Constellations of Queer Urban Space." *Environment and Planning D: Society and Space* 38, no. 5: 941–60.
Gill, Lesley. 2004. *The School of the Americas: Military Training and Political Violence in the Americas*. Durham, N.C.: Duke University Press.
Gillies, Allan. 2018. "Theorising State–Narco Relations in Bolivia's Nascent Democracy (1982–1993): Governance, Order and Political Transition." *Third World Quarterly* 39, no. 4: 727–46.
Gilmore, Ruth. 2007. *Golden Gulag: Prisons, Surplus, Crisis, and Opposition in Globalizing California*. Berkeley: University of California Press.
———. 2017. "Abolition Geography and the Problem of Innocence." In *Futures of Black Radicalism*, edited by Gaye Theresa Johnson and Alex Lubin, 225–40. London: Verso.
Girard, William. 2013. "Enacting Pentecostalism: Spirit-Filled Development and the Honduran Coup d'État." PhD diss., University of California, Santa Cruz.
Gleijeses, Piero. 1992. *Shattered Hope: The Guatemalan Revolution and the United States, 1944–1954*. New Jersey, N.J.: Princeton University Press.
Global Witness. 2017. "Honduras: The Deadliest Place to Defend the Planet." Global Witness. https://www.globalwitness.org/en/campaigns/environmental-activists/honduras-deadliest-country-world-environmental-activism/.
González, Nancie L. Solien. 1988. *Sojourners of the Caribbean: Ethnogenesis and Ethnohistory of the Garifuna*. Urbana: University of Illinois Press.
———. 1992. *Dollar, Dove, and Eagle: One Hundred Years of Palestinian Migration to Honduras*. Ann Arbor: University of Michigan Press.
Goodman, David, and Michael Watts. 1994. "Reconfiguring the Rural or Fording the Divide?: Capitalist Restructuring and the Global Agro-Food System." *Journal of Peasant Studies* 22, no. 1: 1–49.
Gordillo, Gastón. 2004. *Landscapes of Devils: Tensions of Place and Memory in the Argentinean Chaco*. Durham, N.C.: Duke University Press.
Gordon, Todd, and Jeffery R. Webber. 2013. "Post-Coup Honduras: Latin America's Corridor of Reaction." *Historical Materialism* 21, no. 3: 16–56.
Graeber, David. 2012. *Debt: The First 5000 Years*. London: Penguin.
———. 2020. *El estado contra la democracia*. Madrid: Errata Naturae.
Graham, Daniel Aaron. 2009. "Ghosts and Warriors: Cultural-Political Dynamics of In-

digenous Resource Struggles in Western Honduras." PhD diss., University of California, Berkeley.

Gramsci, Antonio. 1971. *Selections from the Prison Notebooks of Antonio Gramsci*. Edited by Quintin Hoare and Geoffrey Nowell-Smith. London: Lawrence & Wishart.

Grandia, Liza. 2013. "Road Mapping: Megaprojects and Land Grabs in the Northern Guatemalan Lowlands." *Development and Change* 44, no. 2: 233–59.

Grandin, Greg. 2006. *Empire's Workshop: Latin America, the United States, and the Rise of the New Imperialism*. New York: Henry Holt.

———. 2011. *The Last Colonial Massacre: Latin America in the Cold War*. Chicago: University of Chicago Press.

Grosfoguel, Ramón. 1997. "A TimeSpace Perspective on Development: Recasting Latin American Debates." *Review* (Fernand Braudel Center) 20, nos. 3/4: 465–540.

Grossman, Lawrence S. 1998. *The Political Ecology of Bananas: Contract Farming, Peasants, and Agrarian Change in the Eastern Caribbean*. Chapel Hill: University of North Carolina Press.

Hale, Charles. 2005. "Neoliberal Multiculturalism: The Remaking of Cultural Rights and Racial Dominance in Central America (2005)." *PoLAR: Political and Legal Anthropology Review* 28, no. 1: 10–28.

Hall, Derek, Philip Hirsch, and Tania Murray Li. 2011. *Powers of Exclusion: Land Dilemmas in Southeast Asia*. Honolulu: University of Hawai'i Press.

Hall, Stuart. 1996. "Race, Articulation, and Societies Structured in Dominance." In *Black British Cultural Studies: A Reader*, edited by Houston Baker Jr., Manthia Diawara, and Ruth Lindeborg, 16–60. Chicago: Chicago University Press.

Hall, Stuart, C. Jefferson, and T. Clarke. 1978. *Policing the Crisis: Mugging, the State and Law and Order*. London: Macmillan.

Hall, Tim. 2013. "Geographies of the Illicit: Globalization and Organized Crime." *Progress in Human Geography* 37, no. 3: 366–85.

Handy, Jim. 1994. *Revolution in the Countryside: Rural Conflict and Agrarian Reform in Guatemala, 1944–1954*. Chapel Hill: University of North Carolina Press.

Hart, Gillian. 2002. *Disabling Globalization: Places of Power in Post-Apartheid South Africa*. Berkeley: University of California Press.

———. 2006. "Denaturalizing Dispossession: Critical Ethnography in the Age of Resurgent Imperialism." *Antipode* 38, no. 5: 977–1004.

———. 2008. "The Provocations of Neoliberalism: Contesting the Nation and Liberation after Apartheid." *Antipode* 40, no. 4: 678–705.

———. 2014. *Rethinking the South African Crisis: Nationalism, Populism, Hegemony*. Athens: University of Georgia Press.

———. 2018. "Relational Comparison Revisited: Marxist Postcolonial Geographies in Practice." *Progress in Human Geography* 42, no. 3: 371–94.

Harvey, David. 2007. *A Brief History of Neoliberalism*. New York: Oxford University Press.

Henderson, George. 2013. *Value in Marx: The Persistence of Value in a More-Than-Capitalist World*. Minneapolis: University of Minnesota Press.

Hernández Coto, René Mauricio. 2019. "La organización del Frente Nacional de Resistencia Popular de Honduras." PhD diss., Universidad Nacional de la Plata.

Herrera, Marta. 2002. *Ordenar para controlar: Ordenamiento espacial y control político en las llanuras del Caribe y en los Andes centrales neogranadinos, siglo XVIIII*. Vol. 1. Bogota: Instituto Colombiano de Antropología e Historia, Academia Colombiana de Historia.

Hesketh, Chris. 2017. *Spaces of Capital/Spaces of Resistance: Mexico and the Global Political Economy.* Athens: University of Georgia Press.

Hibou, Béatrice. 2004. *Privatizing the State.* New York: Columbia University Press.

Holden, Robert H. 2004. *Armies without Nations: Public Violence and State Formation in Central America, 1821–1960.* Oxford: Oxford University Press.

Holt-Giménez, Eric. 2002. "Measuring Farmers' Agroecological Resistance After Hurricane Mitch in Nicaragua: A Case Study in Participatory, Sustainable Land Management Impact Monitoring." *Agriculture, Ecosystems & Environment* 93, no. 1: 87–105.

HRW. 2014. "'There Are No Investigations Here': Impunity for Killings and Other Abuses in Bajo Aguán, Honduras." Washington, D.C.: Human Rights Watch. https://www.hrw.org/sites/default/files/reports/honduras0214web.pdf.

Huggins, Christopher David. 2014. "'Control Grabbing' and Small-Scale Agricultural Intensification: Emerging Patterns of State-Facilitated 'Agricultural Investment' in Rwanda." *Journal of Peasant Studies* 41, no. 3: 365–84.

Hunt, Sarah. 2015. "Breaking the Rules, Breaking the Game: External Ideas, Politics and Inclusive Development in Honduras." *Effective States and Inclusive Development Working Paper Series*, no. 52.

Huntington, Samuel P. 1993. *The Third Wave: Democratization in the Late Twentieth Century.* Norman: University of Oklahoma press.

IACHR. 2014. "Carlos Escaleras Mejía and Family vs the Honduran State." Case 12,492 43/14. Honduras: Inter-American Commission on Human Rights. https://www.oas.org/en/iachr/decisions/court/2017/12492FondoEn.pdf.

IHDER. 2018. *84 meses de reforma agraria del gobierno de las fuerzas armadas de Honduras.* 2nd ed. Tegucigalpa: Instituto Hondureño de Desarrollo Rural.

INE. 2021. "LXXII encuesta permanente de hogares de propósitos múltiples." Tegucigalpa: Instituto Nacional de Estadísticas. https://www.ine.gob.hn/V3/imag-doc/2021/11/INE-EPHPM-2021.pdf.

InSight Crime. 2017. "Cachiros." *InSight Crime* (blog), March 27, 2017. https://www.insightcrime.org/honduras-organized-crime-news/cachiros-profile/.

Irías, Gustavo, and Eugenio Sosa. 2009. *La crisis hondureña: Percepciones ciudadanas y perspectivas para la democratización.* Tegucigalpa: Centro de Estudios para la Democracia.

Jacobs, Susie M. 2009. *Gender and Agrarian Reforms. Routledge International Studies of Women and Place.* New York: Routledge.

Jansen, Kees. 1998. *Political Ecology, Mountain Agriculture, and Knowledge in Honduras.* Amsterdam: Thela.

Jansen, Kees, and Esther Roquas. 1998. "Modernizing Insecurity: The Land Titling Project in Honduras." *Development and Change* 29, no. 1: 81–106.

Jeffrey, Paul. 2002. "Looking to Ourselves: The Response to Hurricane Mitch in the Lower Aguán Valley." In *Deciphering Honduras: Four Views of Post-Mitch Political Reality*, edited by Manuel Torres-Calderón, 39–49. Cambridge, Mass.: Hemisphere Initiatives.

Johnston, Jake. 2017. "How Pentagon Officials May Have Encouraged a 2009 Coup in Honduras." *Intercept* (blog), August 29, 2017. https://theintercept.com/2017/08/29/honduras-coup-us-defense-departmetnt-center-hemispheric-defense-studies-chds/.

Johnston, Jake, and Stephan Lefebvre. 2013. "Honduras since the Coup: Economic and Social Outcomes." Washington, D.C.: Center for Economic and Policy Research. http://towardfreedom.org/wp-content/uploads/2014/02/Honduras-2013-11.pdf.

Jones, Jeffrey R. 1985. *Colonization and Environment: Land Settlement Projects in Central America/Colonización y ambiente: Proyectos de asentamientos en Centroamérica*. Turrialba, Costa Rica: CATIE.

Kapuscinski, Ryszard. 1992. *La guerra del fútbol y otros reportajes*. Madrid: Anagrama.

Katz, Cindi. 2008. "Bad Elements: Katrina and the Scoured Landscape of Social Reproduction." *Gender, Place & Culture* 15, no. 1: 15–29.

Kay, Crístobal. 1998. "Latin America's Agrarian Reform: Lights and Shadows." *Land Reform, Land Settlement and Cooperatives* 2: 9–31.

———. 2011. "Andre Gunder Frank: 'Unity in Diversity' from the Development of Underdevelopment to the World System." *New Political Economy* 16, no. 4: 523–38.

Kerssen, Tanya M. 2012. "Hunger Is Political: Food Sovereignty Prize Honors Social Movements." *Food First*, October 15, 2012. https://foodfirst.org/hunger-is-political-food-sovereignty-prize-honors-social-movements/.

———. 2013. *Grabbing Power: The New Struggles for Land, Food and Democracy in Northern Honduras*. Oakland, Calif.: Food First Books.

Kinzer, Stephen. 2001. "Our Man in Honduras." *New York Review of Books*, September 20, 2001. https://www.nybooks.com/articles/2001/09/20/our-man-in-honduras/.

Kipfer, Stefan. 2012. "City, Country, Hegemony: Antonio Gramsci's Spatial Historicism." In *Gramsci: Space, Nature, Politics*, edited by Michael Ekers, Gillian Hart, Stefan Kipfer, and Alex Loftus, 83–103. Malden, Mass.: Wiley-Blackwell.

Klein, Naomi. 2007. *The Shock Doctrine: The Rise of Disaster Capitalism*. New York: Metropolitan.

Kozloff, Nikolas. 2009. "Obama's Real Message to Latin America? The Coup in Honduras." Counterpunch, June 29, 2009. http://www.counterpunch.org/2009/06/29/the-coup-in-honduras/.

La Prensa. 2010. "Célula guerrillera se arma en el Bajo Aguán." *Diario La Prensa*, March 1, 2010. http://www.laprensa.hn/honduras/502250-97/celula-guerrillera-se-arma-en-el-bajo-aguan.

Lahiff, Edward, Saturnino M. Borras Jr., and Cristóbal Kay. 2007. "Market-Led Agrarian Reform: Policies, Performance and Prospects." *Third World Quarterly* 28, no. 88: 1417–36.

Lakhani, Nina. 2020. *Who Killed Berta Caceres?: Dams, Death Squads, and an Indigenous Defender's Battle for the Planet*. New York: Verso.

Lapegna, Pablo. 2017. "The Political Economy of the Agro-Export Boom under the Kirchners: Hegemony and Passive Revolution in Argentina." *Journal of Agrarian Change* 17, no. 2: 313–29.

Lazzarato, Maurizio. 2012. *The Making of the Indebted Man: An Essay on the Neoliberal Condition*. New York: Semiotext.

Lefebvre, Henri. 1991. *The Production of Space*. Malden, Mass.: Blackwell.

———. 2009. *State, Space, World: Selected Essays.* Edited by Neil Brenner and Stuart Elden. Minneapolis: University of Minnesota Press.
LeoGrande, William M. 1998. *Our Own Backyard: The United States in Central America, 1977–1992.* Chapel Hill: University of North Carolina Press.
León Araya, Andrés. 2016. "Democracia desde arriba, democracia desde abajo: Elecciones, poder y conflicto en la Honduras post-golpe de estado." In *Democracias posibles: Crisis y resignificación. Sur de México y Centroamérica,* edited by María del Carmen García Aguilar, Jesús Solís Cruz, and Pablo Uc, 139–66. Tuxtla Gutiérrez: Universidad de Ciencias y Artes de Chiapas.
———. 2017. "Domesticando el despojo: Palma africana, acaparamiento de tierras y género en el Bajo Aguán, Honduras." *Revista Colombiana de Antropología* 53, no. 1: 151–85.
———. 2019a. "Entre la fuga y la captura: Conflicto agrario, desplazamiento y valor en el Bajo Aguán, Honduras." In *Teoría del valor, comunciación y territorio,* edited by Francisco Sierra Caballero. 243–76. Madrid: Siglo XXI de España Editores.
———. 2019b. "The Politics of Dispossession in the Honduran Palm Oil Industry: A Case Study of the Bajo Aguán." *Journal of Rural Studies* 71: 134–43.
León Araya, Andrés, and Sergio Salazar Araya. 2016. "Del cerro al norte: Continuidades y diferencias en la migración campesina hondureña." In *Migraciones en América Central: Políticas, territorios y actores,* edited by Carlos Sandoval, 3–24. San José: Universidad de Costa Rica.
Levy, Jordan Daniel. 2020. "Honduran Political Culture and Ambivalent Experiences during the Outbreak and Immediate Aftermath of the 2009 Coup." *A Contracorriente: Una Revista de Estudios Latinoamericanos* 17, no. 3: 227–54.
Li, Tania Murray. 2007. *The Will to Improve: Governmentality, Development, and the Practice of Politics.* Durham, N.C.: Duke University Press.
———. 2014. *Land's End: Capitalist Relations on an Indigenous Frontier.* Durham, N.C.: Duke University Press.
———. 2018. "After the Land Grab: Infrastructural Violence and the 'Mafia System' in Indonesia's Oil Palm Plantation Zones." *Geoforum* 96: 328–37.
Li, Tania Murray, and Pujo Semedi. 2021. *Plantation Life: Corporate Occupation in Indonesia's Oil Palm Zone.* Durham, N.C.: Duke University Press.
Gutiérrez Rivera, Lirio. 2014. "Assimilation or Cultural Difference? Palestinian Immigrants in Honduras." *Revista de Estudios Sociales* 48: 57–68.
Loperena, Christopher A. 2017. "Honduras Is Open for Business: Extractivist Tourism as Sustainable Development in the Wake of Disaster?" *Journal of Sustainable Tourism* 25, no. 5: 618–33.
Macías, Miguel Alonzo. 2001. *La capital de la contrarreforma agraria: El Bajo-Aguán de Honduras.* Tegucigalpa: Editorial Guaymuras.
Mackey, Danielle, and Chiara Eisner. 2019. "Inside the Plot to Murder Honduran Activist Berta Cáceres." *Intercept* (blog), December 21, 2019. https://theintercept.com/2019/12/21/berta-caceres-murder-plot-honduras/.
Mackintosh, Maureen. 1989. *Gender, Class, and Rural Transition: Agribusiness and the Food Crisis in Senegal.* Atlantic Highlands, N.J.: Zed.
Mahoney, James. 2001. "Path-Dependent Explanations of Regime Change: Central

America in Comparative Perspective." *Studies in Comparative International Development* 36, no. 1: 111–41.
Maldonado, Salvador. 2010. *Los márgenes del estado mexicano: Territorios ilegales, desarrollo y violencia en Michoacán*. Zamora, Mexico: El Colegio de Michoacán.
Malkin, Elisabeth. 2009. "Honduran President Is Ousted in Coup." *New York Times*, June 29, 2009. http://www.nytimes.com/2009/06/29/world/americas/29honduras.html.
Mallick, Ayyaz. 2017. "Beyond 'Domination without Hegemony': Passive Revolution (s) in Pakistan." *Studies in Political Economy* 98, no. 3: 239–62.
Marchetti, Peter. 1998. "Hamlet Sin Principe: An Analysis of the Impact of Agrarian Modernization in the Lower Aguan River Valley." Working paper, Program of Local Development and Social Change, Saint Isidor Parish, Diocese of Trujillo.
Marshall, Jonathan, and Peter D. Scott. 1991. *Cocaine Politics: Drugs, Armies, and the CIA in Central America*. Berkeley: University of California Press.
Martí i Puig, Salvador, and Diego Sánchez-Ancochea. 2014. "La transformación contradictoria: Democracia elitista y mercado excluyente en Centroamérica." *Anuario de Estudios Centroamericanos*, 149–71.
Martín-Baró, Ignacio. 2003. *Poder, ideología y violencia*. Madrid: Trotta.
Martínez, Juan Ramón. 2006. *Oficio de caníbales: Los militares y los guerrilleros en el Patuca*. Tegucigalpa: 18 Conejo.
———. 2010. *Diario del retorno: Lo ocurrido en Honduras, a partir del 28 de junio del 2009*. Tegucigalpa: 18 Conejo.
Marx, Karl. 1981. *Capital*. London: Penguin Classics.
———. 1992. *Capital: A Critique of Political Economy*. Translated by Ben Fowkes. Reprint edition. New York: Penguin.
———. 2009. *The Eighteenth Brumaire of Louis Bonaparte*. Moscow: Dodo.
Massey, Doreen. 1999. "Philosophy and Politics of Spatiality: Some Considerations. The Hettner-Lecture in Human Geography." *Geographische Zeitschrift*, 1–12.
———. 2013. *Space, Place and Gender*. New York: John Wiley.
Mattei, Ugo, and Laura Nader. 2008. *Plunder: When the Rule of Law Is Illegal*. New York: John Wiley.
McCarthy, James, and Scott Prudham. 2004. "Neoliberal Nature and the Nature of Neoliberalism." *Geoforum* 35, no. 3: 275–83.
McKay, Ben, Alberto Alonso-Fradejas, and Arturo Ezquerro-Cañete, eds. 2021. *Agrarian Extractivism in Latin America*. New York: Routledge.
McSweeney, Kendra. 2020. "Cocaine Trafficking and the Transformation of Central American Frontiers." *Journal of Latin American Geography* 19, no. 3: 159–66.
McSweeney, Kendra, and Zoe Pearson. 2013. "Prying Native People from Native Lands: Narco Business in Honduras." *NACLA Report on the Americas* 46, no. 4: 7–12.
McSweeney, Kendra, David J. Wrathall, Erik A. Nielsen, and Zoe Pearson. 2018. "Grounding Traffic: The Cocaine Commodity Chain and Land Grabbing in Eastern Honduras." *Geoforum* 95: 122–32.
Mercado, Julissa. 2014. "Su sangre lleva el azul de su partido." Diario El Heraldo, July 4, 2014. https://www.elheraldo.hn/alfrente/566525-209/su-sangre-lleva-el-azul-de-su-partido.

Meza, Víctor. 2015. *Diario de la conflictividad en Honduras: 2009–2015*. Tegucigalpa: CEDOH.
Meza, Víctor, Ramón Romero, M. Gamero, L. Funes, Leticia Salomón, and Antonio Murga. 2010. *Golpe de estado: Partidos, instituciones y cultura política*. Tegucigalpa: Centro de Documentación de Honduras.
Middeldorp, Nick. 2014. "In Honduras It Is a Sin to Defend Life: An Ethnography of the Discourses, Practices and Dangers of Opposition to Mining in Honduras." M.A. thesis, University of Wagenigen.
Mies, Maria. 1986. *Patriarchy and Accumulation on a World Scale: Women in the International Division of Labour*. Atlantic Highlands, N.J.: Zed.
Mintz, Sidney W. 1979. "Slavery and the Rise of Peasantries." In *Roots and Branches*, edited by Michael Craton, 213–53. New York: Pergamon.
Miranda, Jorge. 2010. *Crónicas del golpe de estado en Honduras*. Tegucigalpa: Editorial Carmina.
Mirow, Matthew C. 2010. "The Social-Obligation Norm of Property: Duguit, Hayem, and Others." Florida International University College of Law ECollections 22: 191.
Mitchell, Don. 1996. *The Lie of the Land: Migrant Workers and the California Landscape*. Minneapolis: University of Minnesota Press.
———. 2003. "Dead Labor and the Political Economy of Landscape—California Living, California Dying." In *Handbook of Cultural Geography*, edited by Kay Anderson, Mona Domosh, Steve Pile, and Nigel Thrift, 233–48. London: Sage.
Modonesi, Massimo. 2016. *El principio antagonista: Marxismo y acción política*. Mexico City: UNAM.
Mollett, Sharlene. 2011. "Racial Narratives: Miskito and Colono Land Struggles in the Honduran Mosquitia." *Cultural Geographies* 18, no. 1: 43–62.
Montoya, Rosario. 2003. "House, Street, Collective: Revolutionary Geographies and Gender Transformation in Nicaragua, 1979–99." *Latin American Research Review* 38, no. 2: 61–93.
Moreno, Ismael. 2009. "Los contenidos de la cuarta urna." *Revista Envío*, May 2009. https://www.envio.org.ni/articulo/3991.
———. 2015. "The Rise and Fall of Los Cachiros Cartel." *Revista Envío*, March 2015. https://www.envio.org.ni/articulo/5005.
Morris, Saul S., Oscar Neidecker-Gonzales, Calogero Carletto, Marcial Munguía, Juan Manuel Medina, and Quentin Wodon. 2002. "Hurricane Mitch and the Livelihoods of the Rural Poor in Honduras." *World Development* 30, no. 1: 49–60.
Morton, Adam David. 2010. "The Continuum of Passive Revolution." *Capital & Class* 34, no. 3: 315–42.
———. 2012. "The War on Drugs in Mexico: A Failed State?" *Third World Quarterly* 33, no. 9: 1631–45.
———. 2013. *Revolution and State in Modern Mexico: The Political Economy of Uneven Development*. Lanham, Md: Rowman & Littlefield.
MUCA. 2010. "Machete de esperanza." Movimiento Campesino Unificado del Aguán.
Neocleous, Mark. 2011. "'A Brighter and Nicer New Life': Security as Pacification." *Social & Legal Studies* 20, no. 2: 191–208.

———. 2013. "The Dream of Pacification: Accumulation, Class War, and the Hunt." *Socialist Studies/Études Socialistes* 9, no. 2: 7–31.
———. 2014. *War Power, Police Power*. Edinburgh: Edinburgh University Press.
———. 2021. *A Critical Theory of Police Power: The Fabrication of the Social Order*. New York: Verso.
Noé Pino, Hugo, Elizabeth Santacreo, and Anna Dunnaway. 2002. "Mesa agrícola hondureña palma africana." Secretaría de Agricultura y Ganadería.
Noé Pino, Hugo, Andy Thorpe, and Rigoberto Sandoval Corea. 1992. *El sector agrícola y la modernización en Honduras*. Tegucigalpa: Centro de Documentación de Honduras.
Nolasco, Arturo. 2013. "$800 millones suman bienes incautados a 'Los Cachiros.'" *La Prensa*, September 25, 2013. https://www.laprensa.hn/sucesos/policiales/390313-98/800-millones-suman-bienes-incautados-a-los-cachiros-bonilla.
OAS. 1964. "Informe oficial de la Misión 105 de asistencia técnica directa a Honduras sobre reforma agraria y desarrollo agrícola (tomo III): Proyecto de colonización del Bajo Aguán." Washington, D.C.: Organization of American States.
O'Donnell, Guillermo, and Philippe C. Schmitter. 2013. *Transitions from Authoritarian Rule: Tentative Conclusions about Uncertain Democracies*. Baltimore: John Hopkins University Press.
O'Donnell, Guillermo, Philippe C. Schmitter, and Laurence Whitehead. 1986. *Transitions from Authoritarian Rule: Comparative Perspectives*. Baltimore: John Hopkins University Press.
Olson, Jared. 2021. "Violent Infiltration: In Honduras Land Battles, Paramilitaries Infiltrate Local Groups—Then Kill Their Leaders." *Intercept* (blog), November 6, 2021. https://theintercept.com/2021/11/06/honduras-paramilitaries-land-rights/.
Olson, Richard Stuart, Ricardo A. Alvarez, Bruce P. Baird, Amelia Estrada, Vincent T. Gauronski, and Juan Pablo Sarmiento Prieto. 2001. *Las tormentas del 98: Huracanes Georges y Mitch; Impacto, respuesta institucional y políticas para desastres en tres países*. Boulder: Natural Hazards Research and Applications Information Center, University of Colorado.
Önder, Umut. 2018. "Construction and Contestation of the Palm-Oil Hegemony in Honduras: The Land Conflict in the Aguán Region and the Aguán CDM Project." PhD diss., University of Sussex.
Ooijens, Johannes Laurentius Petrus, Phreca Bijsterveld, Monique van der Westen, and Jean Jacques Lasseur. 1990. *Alfabetización y mujeres: La experiencia del proyecto Ihder-Anach*. Tegucigalpa: CESO.
OPDHA. 2014. *Informe estadístico de muertes violentas relacionadas al conflicto de tierras en el Bajo Aguán, 2008-2013*. Tocoa, Colón: Observatorio Permanente de Derechos Humanos del Bajo Aguán.
Paley, Dawn. 2014. *Drug War Capitalism*. Chico, Calif.: AK Press.
———. 2018. "Capitalism and Crisis in Central America." In *Sociopolitics of Migrant Death and Repatriation*, edited by Krista E. Latham and Alyson J. O'Daniel, 25–37. Cham, Switzerland: Springer.
Parsons, Kenneth H., Lizette Buchard, and Gustavo Paz. 1976. "La reforma agraria en el sur de Honduras." Tegucigalpa: Instituto Nacional Agrario.

Pastor, Rodolfo. 1985. "El ocaso de los cacicazgos: Historia de la crisis del sistema político hondureño." *Foro Internacional* 26, no. 1: 16–30.
Patel, Raj. 2013. "The Long Green Revolution." *Journal of Peasant Studies* 40, no. 1: 1–63.
Paz, Ernesto. 1984. "Honduras: Crónica de una desilusión anunciada." *Nueva Sociedad* 70: 17–21.
Perelman, Michael. 2000. *The Invention of Capitalism: Classical Political Economy and the Secret History of Primitive Accumulation*. Durham: Duke University Press.
Pérez Brignoli, Héctor. 1989. *A Brief History of Central America*. Berkeley: University of California Press.
Phillips, James. 2015. Honduras in Dangerous Times: Resistance and Resilience. London: Lexington.
Pirker, Kristina, and Omar Núñez. 2010. "Cuatro hipótesis y un corolario en torno al golpe de estado en Honduras." *OSAL* 11, no. 28: 119–43.
Ponce, Riccy. 2020. "A 10 años de la masacre de El Tumbador, las familias de las víctimas y sobrevivientes siguen a la espera de justicia." Defensores en Linea, November 17, 2020. https://www.defensoresenlinea.com/a-10-anos-de-la-masacre-de-el-tumbador-las-familias-de-las-victimas-y-sobrevivientes-siguen-a-la-espera-de-justicia/.
Portillo Villeda, Suyapa. 2021. *Roots of Resistance: A Story of Gender, Race, and Labor on the North Coast of Honduras*. Austin: University of Texas Press.
Posas, Mario. 1981. *El movimiento campesino hondureño: Una perspectiva general*. Vol. 2. Tegucigalpa: Guaymuras.
Posas, Mario, and Rafael del Cid. 1983. "La construccion del sector publico y del estado nacional de Honduras 1876–1979." San José: EDUCA.
Rangel Loera, Nashieli. 2010. "'Encampment Time': An Anthropological Analysis of the Land Occupations in Brazil." *Journal of Peasant Studies* 37, no. 2: 285–318.
Rauda, Nelson, Ximena Villagrán, and Raúl Sánchez. 2017. "Honduras no quiere bosque, quiere aceite de palma." El Faro, April 25, 2017. https://elfaro.net/es/201704/centroamerica/20080/Honduras-no-quiere-bosque-quiere-aceite-de-palma.htm.
Reyes, Carlos. 1980. "El proyecto Bajo Aguan: Situación actual y perspectiva dentro del plan nacional de desarrollo." Tegucigalpa: Universidad Autónoma de Honduras.
Riaño-Alcalá, Pilar. 2008. "Seeing the Past, Visions of the Future. Memory Workshops with Internally Displaced Persons in Colombia." *Oral History and Public Memories*, 269–72.
Ríos, Gilberto. 2012. "MUCA: No es posible hacer reforma agraria con precios de mercado." FIAN Honduras. http://www.fian.hn/v1/index.php?option=com_k2&view=item&id=2056:no-es-posible-hacer-reforma-agraria-comprando-tierras-a-precios-de-mercado.
———. 2014. "Capitalismo, tierra y poder en Honduras." In *Capitalismo: Tierra y poder en América Latina* (1982–2012), edited by Guillermo Almeyra, Luciano Concheiro Bórquez, João Márcio Mendes Pereira, and Carlos Walter, 147–80. Mexico City: CLASCO.
Robinson, William I. 1996. *Promoting Polyarchy: Globalization, US Intervention, and Hegemony*. Cambridge: Cambridge University Press.
———. 2003. *Transnational Conflicts: Central America, Social Change and Globalization*. New York: Verso.

Rocha, José Luis. 2011. "The First Horseman of Neoliberalism: Drug Traffickers." *Revista Envío*, August 2011. https://www.envio.org.ni/articulo/4392.

Roio, Marcos del. 2012. "Translating Passive Revolution in Brazil." *Capital & Class* 36 (2): 215–34.

Roquas, Esther. 2002. *Stacked Law: Land, Property and Conflict in Honduras*. Amsterdam: Rozenberg.

Rose, Nikolas. 1999. *Powers of Freedom: Reframing Political Thought*. Cambridge: Cambridge University Press.

Rosenberg, Mark B. 1988. "Narcos and Politicos: The Politics of Drug Trafficking in Honduras." *Journal of Interamerican Studies and World Affairs* 30, nos. 2/3: 143–65.

Rovira Mas, Jorge. 2002. "Transición a la democracia y su consolidación en Centroamérica: Un enfoque para su análisis." *Anuario de Estudios Centroamericanos*, 9–56.

Rubén, Raúl, and Francisco Funez. 1993. *La compra-venta de tierras de la reforma agraria*. Tegucigalpa: Guaymuras.

Ruhl, J. Mark. 2010. "Trouble in Central America: Honduras Unravels." *Journal of Democracy* 21, no. 2: 93–107.

Salazar Araya, Sergio. 2019. "Las caravanas migrantes como estrategias de movilidad." *Iberoforum: Revista de Ciencias Sociales de La Universidad Iberoamericana* 14, no. 27: 111–44.

Salgado, Ramón. 1994. *El mercado de tierras en Honduras*. Tegucigalpa: Centro de Documentación de Honduras.

Sanyal, Kalyan. 2013. *Rethinking Capitalist Development: Primitive Accumulation, Governmentality and Post-Colonial Capitalism*. New Delhi: Routledge India.

Saravia, César. 2021. "Miriam Miranda: 'El miedo cambió de bando, ahora lo tiene el gobierno.'" *Marcha* (blog), November 28, 2021. https://www.marcha.org.ar/miriam-miranda-el-miedo-cambio-de-bando-ahora-lo-tiene-el-gobierno/.

Schrader, Stuart. 2018. "The Long Counterrevolution: United States-Latin America Security Cooperation." *Social Science Research Council*, https://items.ssrc.org/from-our-fellows/the-long-counterrevolution-united-states-latin-america-security-cooperation/.

———. 2019. *Badges without Borders: How Global Counterinsurgency Transformed American Policing*. Berkeley: University of California Press.

Scott, James C. 1998. *Seeing Like a State: How Certain Schemes to Improve the Human Condition Have Failed*. New Haven: Yale University Press.

———. 2009. *The Art of Not Being Governed: An Anarchist History of Upland Southeast Asia*. New Haven: Yale University Press.

Seigel, Micol. 2018. "Violence Work: Policing and Power." *Race & Class* 59, no. 4: 15–33.

Sesnie, Steven E., Beth Tellman, David Wrathall, Kendra McSweeney, Erik Nielsen, Karina Benessaiah, Ophelia Wang, and Luis Rey. 2017. "A Spatio-Temporal Analysis of Forest Loss Related to Cocaine Trafficking in Central America." *Environmental Research Letters* 12, no. 5: 054015.

Shipley, Tyler. 2013. "The New Canadian Imperialism and the Military Coup in Honduras." *Latin American Perspectives* 40, no. 5: 44–61.

———. 2016. "Genealogy of a Social Movement: The Resistencia in Honduras." *Canadian Journal of Latin American and Caribbean Studies/Revue Canadienne des Études Latino-Américaines et Caraïbes* 41, no. 3: 348–65.

———. 2017. *Ottawa and Empire: Canada and the Military Coup in Honduras*. Toronto: Between the Lines.

Short, Nicola. 2016. *The International Politics of Post-Conflict Reconstruction in Guatemala*. New York: Palgrave MacMillan.

Sieder, Rachel. 1995. "Honduras: The Politics of Exception and Military Reformism (1972–1978)." *Journal of Latin American Studies* 27, no. 1: 99–127.

Silva, Fernando. 2021. "Elites políticas y económicas entre la incertidumbre y esperanza tras la victoria de Xiomara Castro." Contra Corriente (blog), December 6, 2021. https://contracorriente.red/2021/12/06/elites-politicas-y-economicas-entre-la-incertidumbre-y-esperanza-tras-la-victoria-de-xiomara-castro/.

Sioh, Maureen. 2004. "An Ecology of Postcoloniality: Disciplining Nature and Society in Malaya, 1948–1957." *Journal of Historical Geography* 30, no. 4: 729–46.

Smith, Neil. 2000. "What Happened to Class?" *Environment and Planning A* 32, no. 6: 1011–32.

———. 2008. "Comment: Neo-Liberalism: Dominant but Dead." *Focaal* 51: 155–57.

Sobrado, Miguel. 2000. "Clodomir Santos de Morais: The Origins of the Large-Scale Capacitation Theory and Method." In *A Future for the Excluded. Job Creation and Income Generation by the Poor: Clodomir Santos de Morais and the Organization Workshop*, edited by Raff Carmen and Miguel Sobrado, 14–24. New York: Zed.

Soluri, John. 2009. *Banana Cultures: Agriculture, Consumption, and Environmental Change in Honduras and the United States*. Austin: University of Texas Press.

Sosa, Eugenio. 2016. *Democracia y movimientos sociales en Honduras: De la transición política a la ciudadanía indignada*. Tegucigalpa: Guaymuras.

Sosa, Eugenio, and Ana Ortega. 2008. *Ciudadanía emergente: La experiencia del patronato regional de occidente*. Federación Luterana Mundial, Departamento para el Servicio Mundial, Programa Honduras.

Stein, Stanley J., and Barbara H. Stein. 1970. *La herencia colonial de América Latina*. Mexico City: Siglo XXI.

Stolcke, Verena. 1988. *Coffee Planters Workers and Wives: Class Conflict and Gender Relations on Sao Paulo Coffee Plantations (1850–1980)*. London: Macmillan.

Striffler, Steve. 2001. *In the Shadows of State and Capital: The United Fruit Company, Popular Struggle, and Agrarian Restructuring in Ecuador, 1900–1995*. Durham: Duke University Press.

Suazo, Javier. 2012. *Honduras: ¿30 años de politica agraria en democracia?* Tegucigalpa: Asociación Hondureña de Desarrollo e Investigación Económica.

Taylor-Robinson, Michelle M. 2006. "La política hondureña y las elecciones de 2005." *Revista de Ciencia Política* (Santiago) 26, no. 1: 114–24.

Thiesenhusen, William C. 1995. *Broken Promises: Agrarian Reform and the Latin American Campesino*. New York: Westview Press.

Thomas, Peter. 2006. "Modernity as 'Passive Revolution': Gramsci and the Fundamental Concepts of Historical Materialism." *Journal of the Canadian Historical Association/Revue de la Société Historique du Canada* 17, no. 2: 61–78.

———. 2009. *The Gramscian Moment: Philosophy, Hegemony and Marxism*. Amsterdam: BRILL.
Thompson, Edward P. 1967. "Time, Work-Discipline, and Industrial Capitalism." *Past and Present* 38: 56–97.
Tischler, Sergio. 2001. *Guatemala 1944: Crisis y revolución; Ocaso y quiebre de una forma estatal*. Guatemala: D&G.
Torres Funes, Ariel. 2016. "Masacre de 'El Tumbador': Una prisión verde de impunidad." El Pulso, June 27, 2016. https://elpulso.hn/?p=2140.
Torres-Rivas, Edelberto. 1981. *Interpretación del desarrollo social centroamericano: Procesos y estructuras de una sociedad dependiente*. San José: Editorial Universitaria Centroamericana.
———. 2010. "Las Democracias Malas de Centroamérica." *Revista Nueva Sociedad*, 226: 52–66.
Turits, Richard Lee. 2004. *Foundations of Despotism: Peasants, the Trujillo Regime, and Modernity in Dominican History*. Stanford: Stanford University Press.
UNDP. 2006. "Informe sobre desarrollo humano Honduras 2006 hacia la expansión de la ciudadanía." Tegucigalpa: United Nations Development Program.
United States Department of Treasury. 2013. "Treasury Targets 'Los Cachiros' Drug Trafficking Organization in Honduras." September 19, 2013. https://www.treasury.gov/press-center/press-releases/Pages/jl2168.aspx.
U.S. Embassy in Honduras. 2004. "Drug Plane Burned on Prominent Honduran's Property." Wikileaks Public Library of US Diplomacy 04TEGUCIGALPA672_a. Honduras Tegucigalpa. https://wikileaks.org/plusd/cables/04TEGUCIGALPA672_a.html.
———. 2019. "Statement by Secretary Michael Pompeo on Public Designation, Due to Involvement in Significant Corruption, of Honduran Congressman Oscar Ramon Najera." U.S. Embassy in Honduras, December 20, 2019. https://hn.usembassy.gov/statement-by-sec-by-michael-pompeo-on-public-designation-due-to-involvement-in-significant-corruption-of-honduran-congressman-oscar-ramon-najera/.
U.S. Senate Committee of Foreign Relations. 1988. "Drugs, Law Enforcement and Foreign Policy." Washington, D.C.: U.S. Senate Foreign Relations Committee's Subcommittee on Terrorism, Narcotics, and International Operations.
Valencia, Sayak. 2018. *Gore Capitalism*. Cambridge, Mass.: MIT Press.
Velde, Liza ten. 2012. "The Northern Triangle's Drugs-Violence Nexus: The Role of the Drugs Trade in Criminal Violence and Policy Responses in Guatemala, El Salvador and Honduras." Policy briefing. Drugs & Conflict Debate Papers. Transnational Institute. https://www.tni.org/en/briefing/northern-triangles-drugs-violence-nexus.
Vélez Torres, Irene, Sandra Rátiva Gaona, and Daniel Varela Corredor. 2012. "Cartografía social como metodología participativa y colaborativa de investigación en el territorio afrodescendiente de La Cuenca Alta del Río Cauca." *Cuadernos de Geografía-Revista Colombiana de Geografía* 21 (2): 59–73.
Villars, Rina. 2010. Lealtad y rebeldía: *La vida de Juan Pablo Wainwright*. Tegucigalpa: Guaymuras.
Wainwright, Joel. 2012. "On the Nature of Gramsci's 'Conceptions of the World.'" In *Gramsci: Space, Nature, Politics*, edited by Michael Ekers, Gillian Hart, Stefan Kipfer, and Alex Loftus, 161–77. Malden, Mass.: Wiley-Blackwell.

Walker, Ian. 1990. "Deuda y ajuste estructural: El caso de Honduras, 1980–1988." *Revista Centroamericana de Economía* (Honduras). http://www.derechos.org/nizkor/honduras/doc/cedoh11.html.

Wall Street Journal. 2000. "Unilever Agrees to Acquire Cressida for $420.7 Million." March 3, 2000. http://www.wsj.com/articles/SB952007924309020598.

Waxenecker, Harald. 2019. *Redes de poder político-económico en Honduras: Un análisis post-golpe*. San Salvador: Böll.

Webber, Jeffery R. 2016. "Evo Morales and the Political Economy of Passive Revolution in Bolivia, 2006–15." *Third World Quarterly* 37, no. 10: 1855–76.

Wilkinson, Tracy. 2012. "In Honduras, a Controversial Tycoon Responds to Critics." *Los Angeles Times*, December 21, 2012. http://articles.latimes.com/2012/dec/21/world/la-fg-honduras-facusse-20121221.

Williams, Robert Gregory. 1986. *Export Agriculture and the Crisis in Central America*. Chapel Hill: University of North Carolina Press.

Wolf, Eric R. 1966. Peasants. Englewood Cliffs, N.J.: Prentice-Hall.

Woods, Clyde Adrian. 1998. *Development Arrested: The Blues and Plantation Power in the Mississippi Delta*. New York: Verso.

World Bank. 1987. "Honduras Country Economic Memorandum." 6332-HO. http://documents.worldbank.org/curated/en/414451468257338559/pdf/multiopage.pdf.

Wrathall, David J. 2012. "Migration amidst Social-Ecological Regime Shift: The Search for Stability in Garifuna Villages of Northern Honduras." *Human Ecology* 40, no. 4: 583–96.

Wright, Melissa W. 2006. *Disposable Women and Other Myths of Global Capitalism*. New York: Routledge.

Yie Garzón, Soraya Maite. 2015. *Del patrón-estado al estado patrón*. Bogotá: Universidad Nacional de Colombia y Universidad Javeriana.

# INDEX

agrarian conflict(s), 2–4, 38, 45, 58–59, 82, 99, 124, 138, 158, 180, 184.
agrarian frontier, 10, 71.
agrarian reform, 2–10, 14–19, 32, 34, 40–55, 58–59, 63–67, 72–73, 76, 80–83, 88–89, 97–99, 103–5, 114–16, 200n1, 201n4, 201n5, 202n4, 203n10, 203n13.
Agrarian Reform Peasant Training Program (PROCCARA), 51–52, 182.
Agricultural Sector Modernization and Development Law (AML), 82–83, 88–89, 121, 140, 203n7, 203n12; Norton Law, 83.
Agro-Industrial Cooperative of African Palm (COAPALMA), 77–78, 89, 92, 112.
Aguán, the, 18, 72–73, 75–79, 112–18, 157–58. *See also* Aguán Valley, Aguán River, Bajo Aguán.
Aguán River, 2–3, 53, 58, 69, 72, 91, 113–14, 157, 162, 181.
Aguán Valley (Lower Aguán, Bajo Aguán), 2–7, 61–65, 68, 75, 88–90, 96–99, 104–5, 112–14, 122–24, 138–40, 154, 157–66, 174–84, 191.
anti-communism, 28, 34, 36, 59, 107–9, 129, 137, 150–53, 169–74, 187; National Security Doctrine, 8, 109, 128. *See also* counterinsurgency.
anti-imperialism, 31, 59, 135, 137.*See also* imperialism.
Argueta, Mario, 24–29, 32, 34–36, 199n1, 199n2.
armed forces, 17–19, 23–28, 32–39, 42, 87, 103–7, 126, 128, 143, 148–53, 157–69, 185–90, 203n8, 208n3; Honduran,
24–25, 33, 39, 150, 158, 166, 187–88. *See also* military.
Authentic Reclaiming Peasant Movement of the Aguán (MARCA), 164–166, 184. *See also* MUCA.
authoritarianism, 8, 26, 29, 109, 174, 188–89.

Bajo Aguán Project (BAP), 2, 46, 53–60, 64–68, 76–77, 89–90, 96, 180–82. *See also* Mission 105.
banana plantations, 2, 4, 9, 23, 26–33, 42, 53–59, 66, 85–86, 110, 112, 117, 128, 150–51, 179, 200n4, 202n3. *See also* banana strike, United Fruit Company, Truxillo Railroad Co.
banana republic, 1, 11, 20, 28–29, 38, 58–59, 207–8n3.
banana strike, 32–33, 128, 148, 181, 188; Honduras's Paris Commune, 29–32. *See also* banana plantations, United Fruit Company.
Bolivarian Alternative (ALBA), 7, 135, 140; Petrocaribe, 7, 135–37
bourgeoisie, 1, 25–26, 30–31, 37–41, 47–49, 74, 85, 180, 185.

Cachiros, Los, 2, 154–58, 171, 175–76, 178, 180. *See also* Rivera Maradiaga Brothers.
Caesarism, 187–89.
capitalism, 9, 11–13, 27–28, 41–42, 46–48, 52, 58, 62, 64, 70, 73, 74–76, 81–90, 97–99, 103–4, 110–11, 124, 146, 149, 152, 156–57, 170, 181, 186–88, 191, 204n4, 204n15. *See also* disaster capitalism.

Carías, Tiburcio, 16, 25–30, 35, 38, 41, 145, 147, 149, 186, 188, 199n2, 200n6.
Carney, Guadalupe, 117, 205n6; community, 117, 119–20, 166.
Casolo, Jennifer, 18, 54, 75, 84, 113–14, 204n1, 204n2.
Castro, Xiomara, 20, 168–69, 171–73.
cattle ranching, 7, 29, 58, 152, 158.
caudillo, 25–26, 29, 108, 128, 144.
Chávez, Hugo, 1, 6, 135–37, 141, 143, 148–49, 167, 174, 186.
Central America, 1–2, 7–12, 25–26, 32–34, 48, 51, 55, 80, 85–86, 105, 109–10, 113, 151, 153–54, 179, 185–87, 189–93, 204n4, 204n5, 209n7.
Central America and the United States Free Trade Agreement (CAFTA), 130–135, 140.
Central American Common Market (CACM), 34, 37–40.
Civil Guard, 23, 36.
Cold War, 1, 8–9, 11, 25, 30, 36, 59, 107, 109, 128, 150, 153, 173, 187, 190.
communism, 30, 32–34, 36, 48, 52.
Contra, The, 115–16, 152. *See also* Nicaragua.
control grab, 112. *See also* land.
cooperatives, 2, 4, 14–16, 45, 52, 56–60, 63–73, 76–79, 81, 83, 88–92, 97–99, 104, 112, 121–23, 129, 154, 158, 164–66, 179, 181–84, 202n2, 202n3, 203n12. *See also* reformed sector.
Costa Rica, 1, 12, 24, 37, 80, 148–149, 185.
counterinsurgency, 34, 106. *See also* anti-communism.
coup d'état, 12–16, 23–25, 32–37, 40–41, 56, 59, 99, 122, 124, 126–28, 137, 141–45, 148–50, 152, 160, 164, 167–73, 177, 179–80, 186, 188, 193, 204n4, 204n5; military, 133, 162, 1–7, 9.
Cuarta Urna (Fourth Ballot Box), 6, 124–25, 128, 139, 141–44, 149, 175, 207n12.

democracy, 2, 7–9, 17–18, 30–35, 48–49, 103, 106–9, 111, 138, 170–71, 179, 189–93; as pacification, 179; transition to, 7–9, 14, 17–18, 31, 43, 105, 109, 138, 189–93. *See also* transitology.
Democratic Unification Party (UD), 5, 103.
development, 8, 14, 34, 47–51, 53–55, 72, 75, 85–89, 104, 119, 132–33, 146, 157, 180–81, 189–91, 204n5.
dictatorship, 7–9, 14, 17–18, 31, 43, 105, 109, 138, 189–93.
Dinant Corporation, 86–89, 122, 148, 161, 163, 166, 183–84.
disaster capitalism, 103, 110–11, 114, 124, 166, 177.
discipline, 44–46, 51–53, 60, 64, 67–68, 70–72, 79, 97–98, 181–82, 200n1.
dispossession, 4–5, 12–13, 38, 49, 56, 59, 61, 68, 72, 75, 84, 88, 90–93, 105, 111, 124, 181–82, 190, 201n6. *See also* primitive accumulation.
domestication, 64, 73, 75, 99.
drug trafficking, 3–4, 11–12, 18–20, 42, 115, 146–147, 150–62, 165, 170–71, 175, 178, 184–85, 190–91, 207n3, 208n5; narco dollars, 12; narco-state relations, 9, 11–12, 20, 150, 170, 207n3.

El Salvador, 2, 9, 26, 38–40, 50, 54, 56, 59, 81, 106, 115–16, 122, 128, 145, 159, 174, 208n5, 209n2.
El Tumbador massacre, 160–62, 184, 209n9.
elites, 1–2, 6–8, 25, 29, 33, 39, 41–42, 47–49, 57–59, 80, 85, 87, 97, 106–8, 111, 129, 133, 135, 137–38, 142–43, 149–52, 154, 158, 175, 181, 185–86, 188, 193, 206n6, 207n12.
ethnography, 14, 16.

Facussé, Miguel, 4, 6, 86–89, 103–4, 112, 120, 122, 124, 133, 159, 160–64, 176, 184, 203n8, 203n11, 209n8, 209n3.
Falla, Ricardo, 114–15, 117, 120.
El Salvador-Honduras War (Football War, Hundred Hour War), 37, 39.
Frente Nacional de Resistencia Popular (FNRP), 3, 162, 167–68, 175, 177. *See also* LIBRE.

frontier, 2, 4, 162.

Garifuna, 2, 54, 134, 204n5.
gender, 13, 18, 46, 62, 64, 67–68, 72, 74–75, 78–79, 90, 92–94, 96–99, 128, 173, 182, 185, 202n4, 204n2.
Gramsci, Antonio, 13–14, 38, 45–46, 185–87, 193, 200n2.
Guatemala, 9, 14, 26, 32, 59, 116, 209n2.

hacienda system, 47, 201n6.
Hart, Gillian, 6, 13–16, 56, 75; memories of dispossession, 5, 13, 56.
hegemony, 45, 58, 108, 172, 185; hegemonic, 41, 45, 58, 108–9, 172, 185.
Hernández, Juan Orlando (JOH), 16, 127, 145–48, 155, 168–71, 174–75, 188, 190, 199n2.
Honduras, 1–2, 7, 11–13, 17–18, 24–25, 27, 32, 38–42, 49, 79–82, 85–86, 96–98, 104–11, 120, 128–29, 131–35, 144–47, 152–57, 167–75, 179, 188–93.
Honduran Progress Association (APROH), 87, 108, 204n8.
Hurricane Fifí, 44, 56, 60–61, 65, 72, 181.
Hurricane Mitch, 2, 5, 19, 105, 109, 110–15, 119, 124, 127–31, 133, 138, 148–49, 154, 166, 177, 179, 187–88, 204n4, 204n5.

imperialism, 1, 6, 8, 11, 49, 134, 174, 185–87; imperial solidarity, 185–87. *See also* anti-imperialism.
Inter-American Development Bank (IADB), 34, 104.
International Financial Institutions (IFIs), 10, 31, 80, 108, 131.
labor, 4, 10–11, 29–30, 32, 45, 47, 51, 55, 59, 62–68, 72, 77–79, 94–97, 112–14, 120–21, 144, 158–59, 180, 183, 185, 191–92, 201n4; capture, 121; dead, 96–97, 113, 183; living, 96–97. *See also* labor movement, reproductive labor.
labor movement, 10, 25–26, 29–32, 37–42, 48–50, 128–31, 134, 167, 207n12, 207n3; unions, 34, 37, 128, 130, 134, 209n3.
land, 2–5, 8, 10–13, 17–18, 28–30, 32–33, 38, 44–50, 52–64, 66–77, 81–84, 88–99, 103–5, 110–24, 138–40, 150–52, 158–60, 164, 180–82, 191–93, 201n4, 201n7, 203n7, 203n10, 204n5; question, 26, 47, 197; grabbing, 111, 152, 197, 204n5; land occupations, 3, 15, 59, 114–15, 191, 201n7; property, 74, 83–84, 99; landowners, 26, 33, 38, 40, 47–49, 54, 62, 74, 84, 88, 133, 139–40, 154, 161–63, 203n7; landless, 7, 47, 56, 96, 115–17, 180, 185, 201n4. *See also* terratenientes.
landscapes, 7, 18, 45–46, 52, 54, 65, 68, 72, 77–79, 96–99, 111–13, 179, 183–84, 193, 200n1.
Lefebvre, Henri, 16, 83, 193; regressive-progressive method, 16, 83, 193.
Lenca, 59, 134, 147.
liberalization, 9–10, 25, 81, 86, 111, 135, 145, 151, 157, 191, 200n3.
Liberal Party (Partido Liberal, PL), 23–26, 30, 33–37, 126, 132–37, 148, 156, 167, 171–77.
liberal thought, 14, 104, 138.
Libertad y Refundación Party (LIBRE), 168–178.
Lobo, Porfirio (Pepe), 15, 127, 130–32, 143, 145, 154, 155, 163, 175, 192.
López Arellano, Oswaldo, 24, 36–42, 50, 86, 148–49, 186–88.

maquila, 10, 132–33, 150.
maras, 12, 188, 190.
Marchetti, Peter, 104, 112, 120, 204n1.
Marx, Karl, 75–76, 84, 90, 96–98, 138, 147–48, 201n4, 203n7, 204n15, 207n1; Marxism, 9, 16.
Massey, Doreen, 6, 8, 14, 49.
Melgar Castro, Juan Alberto, 42, 51, 152–53.
mestizo, 204n5.
Micheletti, Roberto, 125–27, 145, 162, 207n10.
migration; internal, 46, 57, 60, 68, 70–71, 93, 181, 193; emigration, 38, 85; to the United States, 10–12, 120, 132, 151, 154, 165, 171–73, 185, 190.
military, 1–4, 7–9, 15, 23–43, 45, 49–50, 56–59, 74, 77, 84–87, 106–10, 115–17,

128, 135, 138, 145–50, 152–60, 162, 164–66, 177, 185–91, 203n6, 206n4, 206n5, 208n5. *See also* armed forces.
milpa, 61–63, 67, 91, 94–96, 120, 184.
Mission 105, 53–56. *See also* Bajo Aguán Project.
modernization, 10, 13–14, 17, 25, 27, 31–35, 43, 47–52, 74, 82, 103–4, 150, 154, 180–82, 185; capitalist, 17, 25.
monetization, 46, 64, 69, 73, 98–99, 182.
monocrops, 10–11, 57, 73, 91, 111–14, 120, 123, 151, 183–84.
Moskitia, 151, 157.

Nájera, Óscar, 58, 153–58, 174–78, 184.
National Agrarian Institute (INA), 34, 44, 55–58, 60, 64–70, 76, 83, 89, 103–5, 112, 116, 119, 121, 139, 154, 181, 209n8, 209n10.
National Association of Honduran Peasants (ANACH), 40, 59–61.
National Coordination of Popular Resistance (CNRP), 130–31, 140–44, 177.
National Federation of Farmers and Cattlemen (FENAGH), 82, 84, 139–40.
National Front of Popular Resistance (FNRP), 3, 162, 167–68, 175–77.
National Investments Corporation (CONADI), 86–87.
National Party (PN), 25–26, 33–42, 127, 132, 145, 148–49, 154, 169, 171–75.
National Peasant Federation of Honduras (FENACH), 59.
nature, 44, 49, 54, 62–63, 182, 185–86, 201n4; production of, 63.
need economies, 76, 88, 90, 112, 114, 184.
neoliberal project, 13, 18, 21, 74–75, 82–87, 103, 131, 144, 151–52; organized abandonment, 10.
Nicaragua, 10, 12, 26, 30, 48, 80, 105–6, 115–16, 128, 135, 152, 174, 203n11, 204n5, 206n6, 209n2.*See also* Contras, Sandinistas.
north coast (Honduras), 2, 19, 23, 25, 27–31, 37–38, 58, 61, 105, 110, 115, 133–34, 200n6, 204n5.

Obama, Barack, 1, 148, 157, 206n5.
oil palm, 4, 7, 21, 44, 55, 57, 62, 65–78, 88, 90–98, 111–14, 120–23, 152, 156, 158, 160–65, 181–84, 192, 202n3, 203n12; industry, 4, 6–7, 11, 45–46, 66, 69, 73, 76–78, 86–91, 97–99, 112, 114, 150, 154–55, 158–59, 161–62, 166, 178–79, 182–84, 187, 191, 194, 202n2, 208n6.
Olancho, 2–5, 54, 115, 129, 132, 154, 157.
Organization of American States (OAS), 38, 53–60, 65–66, 167, 170, 180.
organized crime, 11–12, 146, 150, 158–61, 166.
Osorto, Henry, 118–20, 139.

pacification, 108, 179, 191–93.
Panama disease, 2, 54, 66.
passive revolution, 13–14, 17–18, 45, 49, 74, 110, 178, 185; revolution from above, 13.
Pastoral Social (PS), 103–4, 204n1.
Paz García, Policarpio, 42, 152.
Peasant Movement of the Aguán (MCA), 114–22, 139, 160–61, 166, 184, 209n8.
peasants, 5–7, 28–29, 38, 40, 46–47, 49–50, 52, 56–57, 59–60, 68, 71–72, 84, 88, 96, 113–22, 129, 140, 161, 163, 180–82, 193, 200n1, 201n4, 201n6, 209n8; movement, 2, 4–5, 25, 32–33, 37–42, 48, 59, 83–84, 103, 105, 112–17, 123–24, 128, 138–42, 149, 159, 163–64, 184; organization, 2, 6–7, 14–15, 20, 26, 40, 52, 59–61, 114, 124, 138–39, 159, 163, 181, 201n7, 206n6, 209n10.
Permanent Observatory of Human Rights of the Aguán (OPDHA), 15.
plantation, 2, 4, 10–11, 14, 18–20, 27, 31–32, 38, 46, 54, 58, 66, 73, 75, 80, 89–92, 95–99, 113–14, 120, 122, 129, 152–66, 182–85, 191, 194, 201n6, 208n6.
police, 15, 35–36, 107, 118–20, 128, 143–46, 160, 163–64, 169, 177, 189, 191, 199n2.
Popular Organizations Network of the Aguán (COPA), 129–30, 176–77, 209n3.
primitive accumulation, 4, 74–75, 90, 96–97, 105. *See also* dispossession.

racialization, 13, 85, 88, 93, 108.
reform sector, 75–77, 88–89.
reformist military regime, 41–43, 59, 84.
Regional Military Training Center (CREM), 115–19, 160–61.
rent, 27, 45, 84, 186–88, 202n7; capture, 77–79, 89, 148–51, 165.
Rivera Maradiaga Brothers, 3, 154–58, 161–62, 174, 176. *See also* Cachiros, Los.
Rodas Alvarado, Modesto, 24, 35, 37, 133, 136, 148.
Rodas Baca, Patricia, 136, 137, 148.

Sandinistas, 12, 106, 153, 186.
San Pedro Sula, 27, 30–31, 35, 37–38, 85, 143, 145, 152, 200n6.
Santos de Morais, Clodomir, 51–52, 72, 201n5.
School of the Americas, 42, 152.
social function doctrine, 47–48, 56, 74, 84, 98, 200n3, 203n7.
social reproduction, 45–46, 72, 84, 99, 151; reproductive labor, 69, 84.
Special Development and Employment Zones (ZEDES), 146, 170–73.
Standard Fruit Company (UFCO), 66, 88. *See also* banana plantation.
state, 2, 4–5, 7, 9–16, 24–29, 36, 39–42, 44, 46–49, 54–60, 60–71, 74–79, 81–83, 85, 87–88, 97–98, 106–11, 113, 120, 125–29, 134–36, 138, 140–44, 148, 150–53, 157–59, 163, 170, 177, 179–88, 190–93, 200n1, 200n3, 202n3, 204n5, 207n3; capture, 2, 188; failed state, 11, 170, 207n3; against democracy, 193.
structural adjustment, 10, 79–82, 84, 86, 88–89, 103, 124, 166.
subaltern, 5, 7, 10, 13–14, 25, 28, 37, 40, 42, 106, 109, 124, 127–31, 133–40, 142, 145, 148–49, 159, 177, 181, 185–88, 193.
subject formation, 7, 18, 46, 62, 70, 72, 97, 111, 179, 182–83, 191, 200n1, 201n6.

Tegucigalpa, 23, 27, 30, 36, 39, 118, 123–25, 129–30, 138–39, 142, 152–53, 156, 162, 166–67, 208n4.

terratenientes, 6, 57, 118, 122–23, 194, 201n4. *See also* land.
Tocoa, 3–6, 57–58, 69–70, 78, 95, 103, 120, 122, 155–57, 168, 175–76, 184, 209n3.
transitology, 8–9, 109, 189.
Trujillo, 2, 116, 122, 139, 161.
Truxillo Railroad Co. 2, 54, 116. *See also* banana plantations.
Turcos, los, 85, 108.

Unified Peasant Movement of the Aguán (MUCA), 4–7, 114, 121–24, 130, 159, 162–63, 184.
United Fruit Company (UFCO), 2, 24, 26–27, 30–32, 42, 74, 147–48. *See also* banana plantations.
United Nations Economic Commission for Latin America and the Caribbean (ECLAC), 41.
United States of America, 10, 12, 23, 30, 32–33, 45, 47, 105–9, 115–16, 120, 126, 130–31, 147, 152–55, 158–59, 164–65, 171, 175–76, 179, 185–89, 200n2, 202n6, 208n5, 209n2.
United States Agency for International Development (USAID), 82, 85, 114, 202n3.

value, 77–78, 98–99, 151, 184, 193, 201n4.
Vásquez Velásquez, Romeo, 148–49, 190.
Venezuela, 1, 6–7, 126, 135, 137, 140–43, 149, 161, 167, 174, 206n9.
Villeda Morales, Ramón, 23–25, 33–37, 41, 45, 50, 59, 148–49, 188, 193, 199n1.

war on drugs, 12, 153, 187, 190.

Zelaya, Manuel "Mel," 1–2, 4–7, 12, 14, 19–20, 25, 28, 119, 123–28, 132–45, 148–49, 154, 156, 162–63, 166–70, 173–75, 179, 186, 188, 190, 193, 206n5, 207n10, 207n11, 207n12, 207n2.

# GEOGRAPHIES OF JUSTICE AND SOCIAL TRANSFORMATION

1. Social Justice and the City, rev. ed.
   BY DAVID HARVEY

2. Begging as a Path to Progress: Indigenous Women and Children and the Struggle for Ecuador's Urban Spaces
   BY KATE SWANSON

3. Making the San Fernando Valley: Rural Landscapes, Urban Development, and White Privilege
   BY LAURA R. BARRACLOUGH

4. Company Towns in the Americas: Landscape, Power, and Working-Class Communities
   EDITED BY OLIVER J. DINIUS AND ANGELA VERGARA

5. Tremé: Race and Place in a New Orleans Neighborhood
   BY MICHAEL E. CRUTCHER JR.

6. Bloomberg's New York: Class and Governance in the Luxury City
   BY JULIAN BRASH

7. Roppongi Crossing: The Demise of a Tokyo Nightclub District and the Reshaping of a Global City
   BY ROMAN ADRIAN CYBRIWSKY

8. Fitzgerald: Geography of a Revolution
   BY WILLIAM BUNGE

9. Accumulating Insecurity: Violence and Dispossession in the Making of Everyday Life
   EDITED BY SHELLEY FELDMAN, CHARLES GEISLER, AND GAYATRI A. MENON

10. They Saved the Crops: Labor, Landscape, and the Struggle over Industrial Farming in Bracero-Era California
    BY DON MITCHELL

11. Faith Based: Religious Neoliberalism and the Politics of Welfare in the United States
    BY JASON HACKWORTH

12. Fields and Streams: Stream Restoration, Neoliberalism, and the Future of Environmental Science
    BY REBECCA LAVE

13. Black, White, and Green: Farmers Markets, Race, and the Green Economy
    BY ALISON HOPE ALKON

14. Beyond Walls and Cages: Prisons, Borders, and Global Crisis
    EDITED BY JENNA M. LOYD, MATT MITCHELSON, AND ANDREW BURRIDGE

15. Silent Violence: Food, Famine, and Peasantry in Northern Nigeria
    BY MICHAEL J. WATTS

16. Development, Security, and Aid: Geopolitics and Geoeconomics at the U.S. Agency for International Development
    BY JAMEY ESSEX

17. Properties of Violence: Law and Land-Grant Struggle in Northern New Mexico
    BY DAVID CORREIA

18. Geographical Diversions: Tibetan Trade, Global Transactions
    BY TINA HARRIS

19. The Politics of the Encounter: Urban Theory and Protest under Planetary Urbanization
    BY ANDY MERRIFIELD

20. Rethinking the South African Crisis: Nationalism, Populism, Hegemony
    BY GILLIAN HART

21. The Empires' Edge: Militarization, Resistance, and Transcending Hegemony in the Pacific
    BY SASHA DAVIS

22. Pain, Pride, and Politics: Social Movement Activism and the Sri Lankan Tamil Diaspora in Canada
    BY AMARNATH AMARASINGAM

23. Selling the Serengeti: The Cultural Politics of Safari Tourism
    BY BENJAMIN GARDNER

24. Territories of Poverty: Rethinking North and South
    EDITED BY ANANYA ROY AND EMMA SHAW CRANE

25. Precarious Worlds: Contested Geographies of Social Reproduction
    EDITED BY KATIE MEEHAN AND KENDRA STRAUSS

26. Spaces of Danger: Culture and Power in the Everyday
    EDITED BY HEATHER MERRILL AND LISA M. HOFFMAN

27. Shadows of a Sunbelt City: The Environment, Racism, and the Knowledge Economy in Austin
    BY ELIOT M. TRETTER

28. Beyond the Kale: Urban Agriculture and Social Justice Activism in New York City
    BY KRISTIN REYNOLDS AND NEVIN COHEN

29. Calculating Property Relations: Chicago's Wartime Industrial Mobilization, 1940–1950
    BY ROBERT LEWIS

30. In the Public's Interest: Evictions, Citizenship, and Inequality in Contemporary Delhi
    BY GAUTAM BHAN

31. The Carpetbaggers of Kabul and Other American-Afghan Entanglements: Intimate Development, Geopolitics, and the Currency of Gender and Grief
    BY JENNIFER L. FLURI AND RACHEL LEHR

32. Masculinities and Markets: Raced and Gendered Urban Politics in Milwaukee
    BY BRENDA PARKER

33. We Want Land to Live: Making Political Space for Food Sovereignty
    BY AMY TRAUGER

34. The Long War: CENTCOM, Grand Strategy, and Global Security
    BY JOHN MORRISSEY

35. Development Drowned and Reborn: The Blues and Bourbon Restorations in Post-Katrina New Orleans
    BY CLYDE WOODS
    EDITED BY JORDAN T. CAMP AND LAURA PULIDO

36. The Priority of Injustice: Locating Democracy in Critical Theory
    BY CLIVE BARNETT

37. Spaces of Capital / Spaces of Resistance: Mexico and the Global Political Economy
    BY CHRIS HESKETH

38. Revolting New York: How 400 Years of Riot, Rebellion, Uprising, and Revolution Shaped a City
    GENERAL EDITORS: NEIL SMITH AND DON MITCHELL
    EDITORS: ERIN SIODMAK, JENJOY ROYBAL, MARNIE BRADY, AND BRENDAN O'MALLEY

39. Relational Poverty Politics: Forms, Struggles, and Possibilities
    EDITED BY VICTORIA LAWSON AND SARAH ELWOOD

40. Rights in Transit: Public Transportation and the Right to the City in California's East Bay
    BY KAFUI ABLODE ATTOH

41. Open Borders: In Defense of Free Movement
    EDITED BY REECE JONES

42. Subaltern Geographies
    EDITED BY TARIQ JAZEEL AND STEPHEN LEGG

43. Detain and Deport: The Chaotic U.S. Immigration Enforcement Regime
    BY NANCY HIEMSTRA

44. Global City Futures: Desire and Development in Singapore
    BY NATALIE OSWIN

45. Public Los Angeles: A Private City's Activist Futures
    BY DON PARSON
    EDITED BY ROGER KEIL AND JUDY BRANFMAN

46. America's Johannesburg: Industrialization and Racial Transformation in Birmingham
    BY BOBBY M. WILSON

47. Mean Streets: Homelessness, Public Space, and the Limits of Capital
    BY DON MITCHELL

48. Islands and Oceans: Reimagining Sovereignty and Social Change
    BY SASHA DAVIS

49. Social Reproduction and the City: Welfare Reform, Child Care, and Resistance in Neoliberal New York
BY SIMON BLACK

50. Freedom Is a Place: The Struggle for Sovereignty in Palestine
BY RON J. SMITH

51. Loisaida as Urban Laboratory: Puerto Rico Community Activism in New York
BY TIMO SCHRADER

52. Transecting Securityscapes: Dispatches from Cambodia, Iraq, and Mozambique
BY TILL F. PAASCHE AND JAMES D. SIDAWAY

53. Non-Performing Loans, Non-Performing People: Life and Struggle with Mortgage Debt in Spain
BY MELISSA GARCÍA-LAMARCA

54. Disturbing Development in the Jim Crow South
BY MONA DOMOSH

55. Famine in Cambodia: Geopolitics, Biopolitics, Necropolitics
BY JAMES A. TYNER

56. Well-Intentioned Whiteness: Green Urban Development and Black Resistance in Kansas City
BY CHHAYA KOLAVALLI

57. Urban Climate Justice: Theory, Praxis, Resistance
EDITED BY JENNIFER L. RICE, JOSHUA LONG, AND ANTHONY LEVENDA

58. Abolishing Poverty: Towards Pluriverse Futures and Politics
BY VICTORIA LAWSON, SARAH ELWOOD, MICHELLE DAIGLE, YOLANDA GONZÁLEZ MENDOZA, ANA GUTIÉRREZ GARZA, JUAN HERRERA, ELLEN KOHL, JOVAN LEWIS, AARON MALLORY, PRISCILLA MCCUTCHEON, MARGARET MARIETTA RAMÍREZ, AND CHANDAN REDDY

59. Outlaw Capital: Everyday Illegalities and the Making of Uneven Development
BY JENNIFER LEE TUCKER

60. High Stakes, High Hopes: Urban Theorizing in Partnership
BY SOPHIE OLDFIELD

61. The Coup and the Palm Trees: Agrarian Conflict and Political Power in Honduras
BY ANDRÉS LEÓN ARAYA

www.ingramcontent.com/pod-product-compliance
Lightning Source LLC
Chambersburg PA
CBHW031737230426
43669CB00007B/373